## NORTHEAST CONFERENCE ON THE TEACHING OF FOREIGN LANGUAGES

# VOICES FROM THE FIELD:

## *Experiences and Beliefs of Our Constituents*

**TRISHA DVORAK, Editor**
**REBECCA R. KLINE, Chair**
**1995**

National Textbook Company
Lincolnwood, Illinois USA

# 1995 Board of Directors

Published by National Textbook Company, a division of NTC Publishing Group
© 1995 by NTC Publishing Group, 4255 West Touhy Avenue,
Lincolnwood (Chicago), Illinois 60646-1975 U.S.A.

5 6 7 8 9 0 VP 9 8 7 6 5 4 3 2 1

This volume is affectionately and respectfully dedicated to Theodore (Tug) Andersson, who died before we could arrange the interview we had planned with him.

# Theodore (Tug) Andersson
## 1903–1994

Professor of French and Spanish at Yale University and of Spanish and Bilingual Education at the University of Texas.

Inspiration to the many foreign language students who came under his personal influence. Motivator of important changes in philosophy and methods in foreign language teaching. Responsible for the beginning and promotion of Foreign Language in the Elementary School. Founding Father of the Northeast Conference.

He was charming, caring, patient, always willing to go out of his way to counsel or support teachers or administrators. Most of all, he was singularly devoted to the cause of foreign language learning and teaching everywhere. He never lost an opportunity to further their advance. He was my good friend and I only regret that he did not live long enough to enjoy this tribute.

Mary P. Thompson

# Acknowledgments

The Northeast Conference on the Teaching of Foreign Languages expresses its sincere gratitude to the following individuals and institutions, without whose support the project reported in these pages might not have reached its present form:

Richard Donato
The University of Pittsburgh

J. David Edwards
Joint National Committee for Languages

Richard D. Lambert
National Foreign Language Center

Kurt E. Müller
Kurt Müller Associates; Polyglot Press

C. Edward Scebold
American Council on the Teaching of Foreign Languages

Clara Yu
Middlebury College

Exchange: Japan

Prentice Hall

Yale University Press

# Contents

# Voices from the Field: An Introduction

Rebecca R. Kline

The Pennsylvania State University

Lee Kohler[1] is on the school board in Fillmore, a town of about 15,000 in the Susquehanna Valley. During the course of our interview, he has mentioned both positive and negative personal experiences in foreign language classes. He claims his own children are "getting more conversation" in their Spanish class than he did, a change he calls an improvement. Mr. Kohler comments that "a lot of people find languages somewhat difficult, and they think they'll never need it, so that gives them a mental block." I ask whether there are some people who "definitely should" study languages or, on the contrary, whether certain groups "definitely should not." He pauses, stroking his chin, then leans forward: "Well, I look at foreign language as an arts-type field, and the vo-tech students don't appreciate the finer things or go to museums, so languages probably wouldn't interest them."

As I reread the interview transcript or listen again to the tape, Lee Kohler's comment raises a number of questions in my mind. What shapes and maintains such a belief? What impact might it have on this individual's decisions? Should something be done to change it, and if so, what? How might we, as foreign language educators, react to Mr. Kohler's statement?

Perhaps different questions arise in the minds of my readers, however: What prompted this person to speak so frankly with his interviewer, whom he knew to be a foreign language teacher? Did he assume she would agree with him? Was he hoping to provoke her? How did she respond? Would other school board members, in Fillmore and else-where, share Kohler's belief?

There are no simple answers to any of these questions. People's be-liefs, values, and behaviors are immensely complex and evolving con-structs. It is unlikely that any amount of research on "beliefs about foreign language study" would allow us to predict Lee Kohler's actions as a school board member, since those actions could be influenced by an unwieldy number of factors, some of which emerged during our interview:

- Kohler's own experiences as a foreign language learner,
- his children's experiences,
- his work-related contact with speakers of other languages,
- his impressions of local foreign language teachers,
- the beliefs of other school board members,
- media presentation of then-current events in Cuba,
- the presence of ethnic communities in his town,
- the priority he accords CAI, and, as of last summer,
- his expectations about and impressions of me and our conversation.

When issues of concern to foreign language professionals surface, and we cannot reliably predict what important constituent groups—such as school board members—will do, feelings of desperation or resignation or cynicism may result. Indeed, it was in response to just such a set of emotions, conveyed time and again by colleagues at all levels of instruc-tion, that the project on which this volume is based was created.

In the following pages, I describe briefly the purpose and genesis of the project, offer a rationale for the choice of a qualitative approach, present the study design, and introduce the chapters that constitute this book. Those who are familiar with recent volumes of the Northeast Conference Re-ports may be surprised by the break with tradition reflected here, espe-cially given the quality and success of those volumes. My hope is that the surprise will be a pleasant one, that the "other" voices echoing in these pages will complement, challenge, and interlace with our own.

# Purpose of the Voices from the Field Project

The cat has curled up on the floor in my attic office against a mountain of papers—creamy letterhead stationery, ephemeral faxes, fedex re-ceipts, neon-colored post-its, legal pad sheets covered with scribble, and enough computer paper to repopulate a small forest. Still photographs, tapes, videocassettes, and a transcriber lurk nearby. The cardboard label announcing "Northeast Conference Reports Project—Do NOT Move!" has long since disappeared.

I sift through these documents, alternately bemused and astonished. A xeroxed telephone bill reveals that Trisha Dvorak and I began work on this project some eighteen months ago. A page of notes from one of our phone conversations records its genesis: halfway down the page, I read, "we, langs., lang. requirement, lang. students feel marginalized . . . how to move in from the margins?" and then, "points of view of interest groups on value, purpose, place of lang. study." A list follows:

1. Talking to individuals about language study
2.   "   " administrators about where language fits in ➤ rhetoric vs. reality
3. Talking to other teachers (math, history, etc.)

It was at once simple and overwhelming. If we wanted to know why our place in the educational landscape often seemed precarious or why our role in students' lives could appear insignificant, we just had to talk to people: to ask, and then to listen.

In subsequent months, a team of author-investigators was assembled, groups to be interviewed were identified, and a set of questions was developed and piloted. Using qualitative methods of investigation, the project would constitute the basis for the 1995 Northeast Conference Reports. Its primary objective was to better understand the impact of foreign language study in the lives and experiences of individuals in a number of different categories, each defined as part of our constituency. A second objective involved discovering where these individuals would locate language study in their overall view of education. The underlying agenda, however, was to provide members of the profession with fresh— and perhaps systematically overlooked—perspectives on ourselves and our work, through a series of in-depth interviews.

What might we learn through these interviews? First, even if we did discover foreign language study to be a negligible ingredient in many lives, we might at least have a clearer idea why that was the case. (If our own defeatist attitudes were marginalizing us, for example, we might see new solutions to the problem.) Second, however, we might find that we had influenced some people in unsuspected ways and that our impact was not as minimal as we had supposed. With hope thus restored (cf.

Bourg et al., 1994), we could redirect and refine efforts to improve the current situation.

The Conference theme and title of this volume is **Voices from the Field**. Only through voices, perhaps, can we appreciate the authenticity of interviewee language and the uniqueness of interviewee perspective, which no statistic can convey. With these 1995 Reports, we thus highlight another dimension of the project's agenda: demonstrating the potential of qualitative approaches to research in our field. These investigative methods uncover the meaning people attach to what they do, rather than imposing meaning from the outside. They offer a richly detailed portrayal of individuals, contexts, problems and actions. The goal of the qualitative researcher is not to locate what is predictable in human behavior—in Lee Kohler's behavior—but instead to convey its complexity and to understand Kohler's perspective on it.

The questions addressed by this project are thus:

1 What is the perceived impact and significance of foreign language study in the lives of interviewees from a variety of constituent groups?
2 What is the perspective of these interviewees on the place and value of foreign language study in American education today?

An implicit third question is: Can this project demonstrate the potential of a qualitative approach to readers of the Reports?

In the next section, I comment briefly on prior studies involving perception and perspective (often labeled "attitude") in order to argue for the appropriateness of in-depth interviewing as a research method for the investigation.

# A Rationale for Qualitative Research Techniques

## A Sampling of Prior Studies

The Voices from the Field project, embracing the broad spectrum of groups and topics that it does, cannot easily be placed under any general rubric. Javorsky, Sparks, & Ganschow's (1992) work on the perceptions that learning disabled students have about foreign language courses is germane, but so is Fixman's (1990) study of the perceived foreign language needs of American businesses. The literature includes Gardner (1985) and Gardner & Lambert's (1972) ground-breaking work on the impact of attitude and motivation in language learning. It encompasses attitude surveys (Davis et al., 1992; Glisan, 1987; Horwitz, 1988; Morello, 1988; Papalia, 1978) and survey investigations of outcomes (Carlson et al., 1990; Herman, 1991). And recommendations for improving our image are made variously by members of our own profession (Conroy, 1992; Lide, 1993; Patrikis, 1988), our administrators (Allan, 1993; Baranick & Markham, 1986), our government leaders (Simon, 1991), and our fellow teachers (Crosby, 1987). What does such a disparate list suggest in terms of future direction?

An answer to that question might be found in some of the contradictions that emerge as one reads these authors. Let me concentrate on two examples. In a number of cases, "vocationalist" arguments are made for the value and potential impact of foreign language study. Herman (1991), for example, cites and subscribes to alumni claims that the study of French increased their "marketability" (pp. 54, 55). The American Council on Education Commission on International Education concurs in its policy statement, citing the National Governor's Association: "Knowledge of other languages is essential for business and trade with economic competitors" (American Council on Education Commission on International Education, 1989, p. 2). Yet Fixman (1990), after interviewing 32 business representatives concludes that, "while cross-cultural understanding was frequently viewed as important for doing business in a global economy, foreign language skills rarely were considered an essential part of this" (p. 25). Lambert (1990) agrees, noting that the "English-language-bound culture" of corporations (p. 59) is likely responsible for the perception among international business program graduates that foreign language skills are of limited value.

As foreign language educators, we ourselves reflect this inconsistency. The aforementioned Bourg et al. (1994) statement encourages the study of French in part because it "will offer wide opportunities for international business concerns" (p. 12). But Patrikis warns against "efforts to restructure foreign language education so that it responds more precisely to future professional demands" (p. 18). Can we, then, in all good conscience, create and support the perception that foreign language study increases the chances of professional success? Can we claim that foreign language study will play that sort of role in our students' futures? How will students react to leaving our classrooms with that sort of expectation, only to find that it is not fulfilled in many cases?

A second issue raised by the literature is the concern of almost any group surveyed with the role language instructors should play in teaching about culture. Roberts (1992) puts it succinctly in reporting the findings of her survey of freshman attitudes towards language: "the data from this study highlight the strength of students' belief that a greater under-standing of culture is a primary reason for foreign language study, not just a by-product" (p. 281). Likewise, Allan (1993), a liberal arts college dean, labels the teaching of culture "more serious work" than instruction in language (p. 11). Surveys of public school administrators (Koppel, 1982) and elementary school principals (Baranick & Markham, 1986) both found that, although support for foreign language study was luke-warm, its greatest attraction lay in its ability to "increase cross-cultural awareness and understanding" (Koppel, 1982, p. 438). Yet a perusal of any of our professional journals or of the table of contents of any text-book will reveal that we have not been centrally concerned with the teaching of culture. Our field of inquiry is usually called "second lan-guage acquisition," and our programs are articulated around the devel-opment of linguistic skills. Most work on cross-cultural awareness is done in other disciplinary domains.

This apparent incongruity raises more questions, primarily focused on whether we are missing golden opportunities to have a greater influ-ence as professionals and as citizens by failing to accept what we hear from constituent groups about the potential impact of teaching culture.

To conclude this brief overview, I speculate that part of our feeling of marginalization—our "visibility" problem, to paraphrase Lide (1993)—may be due precisely to a tendency we have to talk to each other, rather than to "others." We are missing messages from students, busi-ness leaders, parents, deans. "Our profession's inclination toward insu-larity," writes Patrikis, "is not a source of intellectual or administrative strength" (1988, p. 16). Conroy (1992) worries that "we elect to remain 'foreign' in the worst sense. . . . We do not talk to colleagues in other disciplines. . . . We pride ourselves on not speaking the administration's language" (p. 14).

What is the impact of that attitude on those around us? Horwitz (1989) points to the ironic risk of speaking our own special language: "we think of our classrooms as 'communication-centered' or 'grammar-focused,' . . . while our students are more likely to think of their courses as 'hard' or 'easy'" (p. 61). Brod (1988) elaborates, suggesting that we need to "help a poorly informed public clear away the cobwebs of folklore and fuzzy thinking about language" (p. 13), an aim we have not achieved and cannot achieve through speaking mostly to each other. Glenn A. Crosby, a chemist who addressed the Washington and Oregon Associations of Foreign Language Teachers at their conference in 1985, writes, "for all the anguish that is exhibited publicly about the demise of the liberal arts, foreign languages in particular, I do not hear these concerns articulated to those of us in the sciences" (p. 183). As an individual who learned German not because it was necessary to his professional activities, but instead because "foreign language acquisition is necessary to be an educated, sentient person with empathy for foreign peoples and cultures and a capacity to experience the world through other eyes, other words, and from other orientations" (1985, p. 183), Crosby deserves our attention.

## Qualitative Research Methods

The contradictions, opinions, prescriptions, findings, and insights presented in the preceding several pages stimulate our curiosity. By what means can we develop a clearer understanding of the complex role foreign languages play, or could play, in shaping people's beliefs? How can we get a sharper picture of our own place in people's view of education? Given the significant number of survey investigations reported here, such an approach might seem to recommend itself. Yet as Erickson (1991) remarks, survey research involves unchallenged "self-report" (p. 348), and even with the best of intentions (which no researcher can guarantee), people may provide flawed data because they either do not understand the question, are unsure of the answer, or are reluctant to give an entirely honest response. These difficulties can also beset in-depth interviews, but the interviewer has at least some means of overcoming them (such as rephrasing a misunderstood question). Erickson points to another challenge to the validity of survey data, which is the potential of questions to "predetermine the information they seek from research subjects and collect relatively little information on each individual subject" (1991, p. 348). This problem is exacerbated by the difficulty of ensuring a high rate of return on questionnaires.

A more fundamental issue, however, than the logistics of using an investigative technique effectively, is the match among the study's questions, its design and the research methods employed. Generally, there is little disagreement that broad questions targeting complex phenomena lend themselves to a qualitative approach. Qualitative methodology is also suggested "for research that is exploratory or descriptive and that stresses the importance of context, setting, and subjects' frame of reference" (Marshall & Rossman, 1989, p. 46). It is often advised when researchers feel perplexed that theory, policy, or "folk wisdom" do not seem to explain their experiences or predictions (Marshall & Rossman, 1989, pp. 22, 46). Erickson (1991) emphasizes that "one is not so much interested in cause per se as one is interested in explanation in terms of meanings and understandings held by those who one has studied" (p. 339). Our problem in this project is a broad one: to understand better our marginalization in the overall scheme of American education. Our questions are oriented toward the "subjects' frame of reference" (Marshall & Rossman, 1989, p. 46), and they will likely involve description of complex phenomena. Finally, other research methods, while not without value, have thus far failed to fully address the problem we identify.

The research design we adopted will make more sense if viewed within the larger frame of a qualitative orientation. As Taylor & Bogdan (1984) explain,

> The term methodology refers to the way in which we approach problems and seek answers. . . . Our assumptions, interests, and purposes shape which methodology we choose. When stripped to their essentials, debates over methodology are debates over assumptions and purposes, over theory and perspective. (p. 1)

The debates in question contrast qualitative and quantitative approaches, which derive from, respectively, positivist and phenomenological theoretical perspectives. Taylor & Bogdan (1984) summarize the primary difference, stating that the "positivist seeks the facts or causes of social phenomena apart from the subjective states of individuals," whereas the "phenomenologist is committed to understanding social phenomena from the actor's own perspective" (pp. 1, 2). Marshall & Rossman (1989) add that qualitative research "views inquiry as an interactive process between the researcher and the participants," and "relies on people's words as the primary data" (p. 11). Qualitative researchers are thus concerned with the impact of their study on participants; they tend also to make their own role and identity clear to their readers so that the "interactive process" can be judged for its potential effects. To minimize any negative impact, the researcher "suspends, or sets aside, his or her own beliefs, perspectives, and predispositions" (Taylor & Bogdan, 1984, p. 6).

Glesne & Peshkin include the following table of the "predispositions" of the two methodologies in their book on qualitative research. While not all researchers would agree with all characterizations, this table summarizes the advantages and disadvantages of each methodology fairly well. For the purposes of the Voices from the Field project, it is perhaps most important to note that "interpretation" and "understanding" are the goals, rather than "generalization" and "prediction." A great deal more could be said about qualitative research and about particular methods of data collection and analysis. I encourage readers to explore some of the cited handbooks.

| Comparison of Characteristics of Quantitative and Qualitative Research[a] | | |
|---|---|---|
| | *Quantitative Mode* | *Qualitative Mode* |
| Assumptions | Social facts have an objective reality<br>Primacy of method<br>Variables can be identified and relationships measured<br>Etic (outsider's point of view) | Reality is socially constructed<br>Primacy of subject matter<br>Variables are complex, interwoven, and difficult to measure<br>Emic (insider's point of view) |
| Purpose | Generalizability<br>Prediction<br>Causal explanations | Contextualization<br>Interpretation<br>Understanding actors' perspectives |
| Approach | Begins with hypotheses and theories<br>Manipulation and control<br>Uses formal instruments<br>Experimental<br>Deductive<br>Component analysis<br>Seeks consensus, the norm<br>Reduces data to numerical indices<br>Abstract language in write-up | Ends with hypotheses and grounded theory<br>Emergence and portrayal<br>Researcher as instrument<br>Naturalistic<br>Inductive<br>Searches for patterns<br>Seeks pluralism, complexity<br>Makes minor use of numerical indices<br>Descriptive write-up |
| Researcher Role | Detachment and impartiality<br>Objective portrayal | Personal involvement and partiality<br>Empathetic understanding |
| [a]Adapted from Glesne & Peshkin, 1992, p. 7. | | |

Within an overall qualitative theoretical framework, we chose in-depth interviews as our primary research instrument. The next section is devoted to outlining the study design.

## Study Design and Procedures

The Voices from the Field project was a multi-site, team study based on data gathered through in-depth, semi-structured interviews. Several conditions conducive to the use of such interviews were present: we were operating under significant time constraints, we wanted to interview a "broad range of people," and our primary concern was "subjective human experience" (Taylor & Bogdan, 1984, pp. 80–81). Most importantly, perhaps, we believed that the stories told by interviewees would be compelling, unexpected, edifying, useful, and trustworthy. We believed also that a number of our colleagues could bring their training and sensitivity to the task of interviewing with positive results.

The interview questions, or protocol, appear in Appendix A of this volume. In a structured interview study, all respondents would be asked exactly the same questions. Our protocol was semi-structured to allow interviewers some leeway, in consideration of the great diversity of people to whom they would be speaking. Simply put, one cannot ask a nine-year-old in a FLES program and a college president the same questions.

In addition to the protocol, author-investigators received "informed consent" documents to be signed by each interviewee or interviewee guardian (see Appendix B). They were also provided with a set of guidelines, dealing with issues ranging from co-researchers to audiotaping to tips for successful interviewing (for the latter, we cited Seidman, 1991).

Six different "constituent groups" were identified, each assigned to a specific author or pair of authors. For each group, authors were provided with an enumeration of the categories of individuals they should try not to overlook. Based on "purposeful sampling" principles or "theoretical sampling" (Glaser & Strauss, 1967), this enumeration did not aim for representation but rather for inclusion. We wanted to be sure, for example, that both rural and urban classroom learners were interviewed for the classroom language learners group. We were concerned about the need to hear the voices of an approximately equal number of males and females in each group. We also hoped that a variety of races, ethnicities, social classes, levels of performance in language, ages, educational backgrounds, and so on, could be included. We requested that our author-investigators seek to speak with individuals who were studying or had studied a number of different languages. And finally, we established a minimum number of interviews to be conducted for each chapter, ranging from 10 to 30.

The researchers made their own contacts and arrangements, locating interviewees primarily on an opportunistic basis, but always taking into account the deliberate sampling principles we had conveyed. Researchers were located throughout the United States, which may have enhanced the positive effects of this opportunistic approach in that it provided inadvertently for geographical diversity among our interviewees. When chosen, potential interviewees received a letter briefly describing the purpose of the study (see Appendix C). The average interview length was one hour, and most interviews were tape-recorded in a location comfortable and convenient for the interviewee.

As is typically the case with qualitative studies, initial data helped each author to refine his or her interview protocol. Thus, the processes of data collection and data analysis occurred concurrently. Authors searched their interview transcripts for common threads or emerging themes or patterns in people's words, experiences, and ideas. Some found links with theoretical frameworks or with other studies, while others related several categories or themes without reference to outside work.

Presentation of the results of a qualitative study is not bound by strict conventions, and the variety in our chapters reflects some of the range of possible choices. The concluding section of this chapter aims to prepare readers for the discoveries that lie ahead.

# Listening to the Voices:
# An Overview of the 1995 Reports

The perspectives of people from six different groups were solicited and explored during the course of this project. Their experiences with and views about foreign language study constitute the bulk of the data analyzed by the authors. They knew they had the profession's ear and were encouraged to speak frankly. Only one group included foreign language teachers, so the voices that echo through these pages may be unfamiliar, but they are also, by and large, engaging.

In their chapter, Joan Kelly Hall and Jackie Davis present the results
of conversations with classroom learners. Their team spoke with foreign
language education majors, elementary school children, older students,
doctoral candidates, and so forth. They identified three common themes,
discussion of which led them to focus on five issues. The third of these
issues, to cite only one example, is learner expectations. Hall and Davis
report that the majority of those interviewed undertook language study
thinking that learning a language would be easy and would take very
little time, only to be quickly disillusioned: "It doesn't take one day and
just say something and you're all done with Spanish," explained one
sadder but wiser fourth grader! What is significant about this chapter is
its presentation of the voices of those we see daily in our schools.

Gwendolyn Barnes-Karol investigated the experiences of 20 language
learners in "non-traditional environments," ranging from language
camps to dual-language schools to FLAC (foreign languages across the
curriculum) programs, and representing 14 different languages. Her
chapter reports four common threads, focusing on what she calls the
"interpersonal dimension of language learning." To convey clearly the
differences among her interviewees, within her four-category framework, Barnes-Karol reproduces many of the stories they told, lending
her chapter a distinctive flavor and providing a new perspective on issues
raised in the others.

No single informant in any chapter affected me quite as much as Tom,
who was interviewed by María Teresa Garretón for her chapter on native
speakers as language learners. I will not soon forget the image of Tom
as a teenager, worriedly tape-recording himself in his native Polish to
determine whether he had acquired an American accent. Garretón
weaves research on motivation into discussion of her findings, focusing
as well on the role played by culture in the lives of her 15 interviewees.
For teachers whose classrooms seem homogeneous, this chapter will
open eyes.

In his chapter, Frank B. Brooks explores the perceptions of teachers
in subject areas other than foreign language. Despite their generally
negative memories of language study ("It was very stressful, it wasn't
pleasant"), most of these teachers encouraged their students to treat
foreign languages seriously and stated that languages should be "a part
of the North American educational scene." One teacher reported that
foreign language study had helped her to be more tolerant of children
from different linguistic backgrounds in her elementary school. Readers

may struggle with the contradictions implicit in this chapter's stories.

Susan Terrio and Mark Knowles have co-authored a chapter that examines the opinions on language learning held by individuals outside academia, reflecting perspectives from the worlds of business, government, the arts, and journalism. Aware that "attitudes related to second language study differentiate professionals in a large metropolitan center from those is a smaller regional one," Terrio conducted her interviews with individuals in the nation's capital, while Knowles interviewed others in the nation's heartand. Their chapter approaches the research through overt conceptual and theoretical framing. Terrio analyzes her data in light of findings on elites. Like several other authors, she acknowledges some of the challenges she faced in conducting her research:

> In Washington . . . the art of representation is highly elaborated and demands exhibiting multiple selves and identities in specific, located situations for particular ends. Sorting out personal views from political agendas on certain issues can be difficult.

One reads "Voices outside Academia: The View from the Center," inferring how this process occurred during interviews with Susan Stamberg, Jeffrey Munks, Congressman James Oberstar, or Deputy Secretary of Education Madeleine Kunin! And one reflects on the agreement among Terrio's interviewees that foreign languages should be learned for utilitarian purposes. Knowles's informants adopt a similar attitude, but their regional orientation appears to discourage their subscribing to the idea of a national foreign language requirement. For his part, Knowles decries the failure of most second language acquisition research to account sufficiently for social forces such as "community attitudes," as he has been able to do in this chapter.

The final chapter in this volume differentiates itself from the other five, in that Dolly Young's and Mary Kimball's interviewees are distinguished foreign language educators, *our* teachers, in fact. Most, however, are now retired (if only nominally!). And in many cases, their impression was that their years of experience and accumulated wisdom were being ignored by younger colleagues. These "venerable voices" ring loud and clear in the pages of this chapter, their insights helping to establish the themes common to interviewee perspectives in each of the other five groups.

Editor Trisha Dvorak identifies and analyzes these themes in the final chapter of the volume, reflecting as well on the significance of this research project and on avenues for further investigation.

In concluding this chapter and appreciating the variety and richness present in each author's work, I add my own call for more qualitative studies in our field to others' (e.g., Johnson, 1993; Watson-Gegeo, 1988). A major component of the effort to achieve this goal will be the establishment of a research methods curriculum that enjoys the support of professionals at all levels and in all parts of the country, and that prepares a cadre of investigators for future studies. I hope that the project reported in this volume will generate enthusiasm for such an undertaking.

The essence of qualitative approaches is the search for meaning—the meaning people attach to what they do and to what happens to them. Interviewing allows people to use their own words, to write their own stories, and to interact with the researcher. This volume will serve to provide an idea of what we may learn when we stop talking to ourselves. Or of what we can hear when we listen.

# Note

[1]A pseudonym, as are names of people and places in this chapter that might reveal an anonymous interviewee's identity.

# References

Allan, G. (1993). View from the top: What a liberal arts dean expects from a language department. In S. L. Slick & R. B. Klein (Eds.), *Managing the foreign language department: A chairperson's primer* (pp. 9–17). Valdosta, GA: Southern Conference on Language Teaching.

American Council on Education Commission on International Education. (1989). *What we can't say can hurt us: A call for foreign language competence by the year 2000.* Washington DC: ACE.

Baranick, W. A., & Markham, P. L. (1986). Attitudes of elementary school principals toward foreign language instruction. *Foreign Language Annals, 19,* 481–489.

Bourg, M., Masson, D., Thomas, R., Sandmel, B., Mueller, R., Barnicle, R., Gray-LeCoz, A., Hart, B., Kitts-Eisert, K., Langsam, H., Lyons, L., Roy-Morgan, Y., & Pearson, M. E. (1994). Restore hope. *American Association of Teachers of French National Bulletin, 19*(3), 12.

Carlson, J., Burns, B. B., Unseem, J., and Yachimowicz, D. (1990). Study abroad: The experience of American undergraduates. *Contributions to the Study of American Education.* New York: Greenwood Press.

Crosby, G. A. (1987). Does a scientist need foreign languages? *Foreign Language Annals, 20,* 181–183.

Davis, J. N., Gorell, L. C., Kline, R. R., & Hsieh, G. (1992). Readers and foreign languages: A survey of undergraduate attitudes toward the study of literature. *The Modern Language Journal, 76,* 320–332.

Fixman, C. S. (1990). The foreign language needs of U.S.-based corporations. *The Annals* of the American Academy of Political and Social Science, 511, 25–46.

Gardner, R. C. (1985). *Social psychology and second language learning: The role of attitudes and motivation.* London: Edward Arnold.

——, & Lambert, W. E. (1972). *Attitude and motivation in second language learning.* Rowley, MA: Newbury House.

Glaser, B. G., & Strauss, A. (1967). *The discovery of grounded theory: Strategies for qualitative research.* Chicago: Aldine.

Glesne, C., & Peshkin, A. (1992). *Becoming qualitative researchers: An introduction.* New York: Longman.

Glisan, E. W. (1987). Beginning Spanish students: A survey of attitudes at the University of Pittsburgh. *Hispania, 70,* 381–394.

Herman, G. (1991). Majoring in French: An alumni perspective. *ADFL Bulletin, 22,* 54–57.

Horwitz, E. K. (1988). The beliefs about language learning of beginning university students. *Modern Language Journal, 72,* 283–294.

Javorsky, J., Sparks, R., & Ganschow, L. (1992). Perceptions of college students with and without learning disabilities about foreign language courses. *Learning Disabilities: Research and Practice, 7,* 31–44.

Johnson, D. M. (1993). Classroom-oriented research in second-language learning. In A. O. Hadley (Ed.), *Research in language learning: Principles, processes, and prospects* (pp. 1–23). Lincolnwood, IL: National Textbook Company.

Koppel, I. E. (1982). The perceived contribution of foreign language to high priority educational goals. *Foreign Language Annals, 15,* 435–439.

Lambert, R. D. (1990). Foreign language use among international business graduates. *The Annals of the American Academy of Political and Social Science, 511,* 47–59.

Lide, F. (1993). The dynamics and visibility of the postsecondary foreign language enterprise: A five-year survey of the *Chronicle of Higher Education.* In D. P. Benseler (Ed.), *The dynamics of language program direction* (pp. 65–89). Boston: Heinle & Heinle Publishers.

Marshall, C., & Rossman, G. B. (1989). *Designing qualitative research.* Newbury Park CA: Sage Publications, Inc.

Morello, J. (1988). Attitudes of students of French toward required study. *Foreign Language Annals, 21,* 435–442.

Papalia, A. (1978). Students' beliefs on the importance of foreign languages in the school curriculum. *Foreign Language Annals, 11,* 21–23.

Patrikis, P. C. (1988). Reports and reforms: Where are the foreign languages? *ADFL Bulletin, 11,* 14–19.

Robert, L. P. (1992). Attitudes of entering university freshmen toward foreign language study: A descriptive analysis. *The Modern Language Journal, 76,* 275–283.

Seidman, I. E. (1991). *Interviewing as qualitative research: A guide for researchers in education and the social sciences.* New York: Teachers College Press.

Simon, P. (1991). A decade of change to a decade of challenge. *Foreign Language Annals, 24,* 13–18.

Taylor, S. J., & Bogdan, R. (1984). *Introduction to qualitative research methods: The search for meanings* (2nd ed.). New York: John Wiley & Sons.

Watson-Gegeo, K. A. (1988). Ethnography in ESL: Defining the essentials. *TESOL Quarterly, 22,* 575–592.

# Voices from the Traditional Classroom: Learner Reflections

Joan Kelly Hall

and Jackie Davis

*University of Georgia*

## Introduction

While there has been much research conducted over the years concerned with various aspects of foreign language pedagogy, there is still very little we know of the impact that language learning has had on our students *from the perspective of the students.* That is to say, except for the personal anecdotes occasionally shared by a few of our students in the course of our everyday teaching and which we sometimes share with our colleagues, there has been little systematic attention given to their stories. More specifically, we have taken little notice of the significance that our students report foreign language learning has had in their lives. This chapter is one attempt to direct some of our investigatory attention along this particular path.

Our specific focus in the study reported upon here was to talk with and listen closely to the voices of thirty students currently studying a foreign language. In doing so, we hoped to ascertain, among other things, the kinds and degree of influence that foreign language learning has had for them, and their perceptions of what factors have played a significant role in their learning. What we have found through this experience is that our learners, when given the opportunity to reflect upon and share their opinions, are quite perceptive about their practices as learners, about our own practices as teachers, and about the import, both positive and negative, that these practices have had for them.

And, while these students' experiences with language learning varied according to a number of factors—for example, the ages at which they were learning a language, the languages they were learning, the number of years they had been studying, and whether they had traveled to the target country—there were several issues and concerns woven into the stories that were shared by all or almost all of the participants. These common experiences and reflections form the primary focus of the chapter. Before reporting on these, however, we first provide a brief overview of how the data were collected and analyzed, and then present a general description of the participants. After presenting our findings, we provide a short discussion on their relevance to the field of foreign language pedagogy, and conclude with suggestions for future studies.

# Methodology

## Data Collection and Analysis[1]

The primary data set is comprised of thirty semi-structured interviews. Four graduate students in Foreign Language Education at a southeastern university were the interviewers. The format and process for each interview followed the general procedures outlined in the Introduction to this volume (p. xviii). We analyzed the data using the qualitative techniques of inductive, thematic analyses (Erickson, 1986; Spradley, 1979). An initial framework for the data was first constructed by three of the four interviewers and the principal investigator after the interviews were completed. At this time, a consensus was reached on what the recurring themes and categories of responses seemed to be. These categories and themes were then corroborated and/or modified, and specific responses and comments identified, by a thorough analysis of the transcribed data by each of the two authors of this paper. We then shared our analyses with each other, and subsequently modified and blended them, the final results of which are presented here.

## Participants

Thirty learners of foreign languages were interviewed, ranging from seven to fifty years of age; an equal number (N= 15) of females and males were interviewed; 40% (N= 12) were students of grades K–12, 50% (N= 15) were at the university level, and 10% (N= 3) were older, nontraditional-aged students who had returned to school to study a foreign language. One had returned to study Greek and Latin and another was studying for a PhD in Classics. The third interviewee was studying Spanish in order to be able to communicate with the family of his fiancée, who was a native Spanish speaker.

At the undergraduate level, three of the participants were language education majors, another three were language majors, and four were taking a language course in order to fulfill the language requirement for their program of study. Of the four students at the graduate level, two participants were pursuing a Masters in Foreign Language Education, one a PhD in the same program, and the last was undertaking studies in Chinese while pursuing a Masters in the Teaching of English to Speakers of Other Languages.

In addition, we interviewed one student in the first grade who had just begun learning a foreign language, one in fourth grade who was in her second year of language study, and one in fifth grade who had had some kind of classroom language instruction since the first grade. Four were middle school students. At the high school level, two students were in their first year of study, one in his second, and two were third-year students.

All but two respondents were native speakers of English. Of these two, one reported speaking Spanish at home, having learned English in the early years of schooling, and was currently a student of French. The other student was a native of Japan for whom English was a second language. She reported that Spanish was her current and third language of study, taken at the university level as part of her program of study in international business. Three of the respondents were African American, one a Hispanic American, one a citizen of Japan and the rest were Americans of European descent. All were students in educational institutions located in the eastern part of the United States.

We ought to note here that although this was not intended to be a representative sample of all learners of foreign languages nor of all foreign languages, we tried to include as wide a variety of learners and languages as possible.

| Characteristics of Interview Participants | | | | | |
|---|---|---|---|---|---|
| | *K–8* | *9–12* | *Undergrad* | *Graduate* | *Non-trad* |
| Female<br>N = 15 | 1 F<br>1 J<br>1 L<br>1 S | 2 F<br>1 S | 1 G<br>1 J<br>1 L<br>2 S | 1 J<br>1 S | 1 L |
| Male<br>N = 15 | 1 J<br>2 S | 2 S | 1 F<br>1 G<br>2 J<br>2 S | 1 C<br>1 G | 1 L&Gr<br>1 S |
| Total Participants | 7 | 5 | 11 | 4 | 3 |

Note. The letters represent the following languages:
C = Chinese; F = French; G = German; Gr = Greek; J = Japanese;
L = Latin; S = Spanish.

The table indicates the language that the interviewees said they were studying at the time of the interview. Spanish was the most common language (12 learners) while Japanese was studied by six students, French and Latin by four each. One of the Latin students reported that he was taking Greek at the same time. Three learners were students of German and one studied Chinese. We should note that many of the participants reported having studied other languages at other times, in addition to that which they were currently studying. All three of the Japanese learners at the university level, for example, stated that they had taken other languages in high school but decided to study Japanese when they became university students. As one stated, "And when I came to school here [a university], for some reason Japanese just seemed to take hold of me and I became very interested and just began studying it and went from there" (I:15)[2]. Another student had studied Spanish in high school but took up Japanese upon entering the university because, he stated:

> I got the chance to go visit him [his brother] when he was over there [Japan] with my parents for about ten days and that was the first time I got to have a [taste of] Japanese culture and language. . . . And I just decided with the Japanese business being prevalent now and more job opportunities probably available with Japanese, that I would go ahead and study Japanese. (I:14)

# Common Themes

This section is organized around three themes that best draw together the threads of talk that were common to all or almost all of the interviewees. The first deals with the reasons they undertook the study of another language. The second is concerned specifically with classroom learning, i.e., those factors they thought influenced, either positively or negatively, their learning. The last topic addresses more generally the benefits they thought that their language study has had for them.

## Why Study a Foreign Language?

The most basic reason cited for beginning formal language study by all but two of the participants was simply because they had been required to, either because it was part of the school curriculum and there was no choice about whether to take a language, or because it was a university entrance requirement. One of the two for whom it was not a high school requirement did not start language study until he reached the university, explaining that because he had lived in a very rural area, there had been no opportunity for formal study until then. The other respondent, because he had not been required to take a foreign language at any time in his studies, did not begin formal Spanish instruction until about five years after he had graduated from college at which time he decided to enroll in a Spanish course being taught at a local community college.

Nineteen respondents reported beginning language study in grade school, most of whom began in FLES programs in the early grades. Most of the others reported that they began either in a FLEX program or regular language study in middle school. Two participants, having parents whose work required living in another country for a short period of time, reported beginning language study while living in the country of that language, and nine participants reported beginning language study in high school.

It is interesting to note here that eight of the respondents reported having had informal contact with other languages before beginning formal language training. Several participants, for example, remembered hearing their grandparents speak languages other than English in the home. One undergraduate French education major, for example, recalled hearing his grandmother speak Hungarian. "My grandmother was Hungarian," he said, "and all I heard was screaming in Hungarian . . . it's just one of those memories you hold very dear, and I love her to death, is how she spoke Hungarian" (I: 17). Three others, having mothers for whom English is not the native language, reported that they remembered hearing their moms speak in their native tongues to friends or other family members. A student of Japanese, for example, reported that, "my mother's Japanese so she speaks or spoke Japanese with her Japanese friends either on the phone or when they came to visit" (I: 12). A few other participants reported that they grew up in ethnic neighborhoods where French and Spanish were considered community languages. Yet another participant, an elementary school student, reported that he began informal training in Hebrew at home with his father before he began studying a foreign language in school. And, finally, one of the participants remembered having a teenage babysitter studying Spanish in high school who would speak to her: "Of course, Spanish meant nothing to me then. But I was so fascinated that she could actually say stuff, and I couldn't understand her and it sounded like gibberish, and I tried to mimic her and everything. I'm five, and she's probably fifteen or something. So she was my idol" (I: 23).

There are two final points that were made that relate to the issue of a language requirement. First, although almost all the participants were initially required to study a foreign language, no learner reported feeling that the requirement negatively influenced or was in any way detrimental to his or her studies. In fact, most were glad that they were made to take something they might not otherwise have had exposure to and almost all felt that everyone *should* be required to study another language. As one participant whose future aspirations include obtaining a PhD in Japanese literature stated, "If they hadn't had the requirement I probably wouldn't have taken foreign language. I know I wouldn't have" (I: 16). The learner who had come back to school specifically to study Spanish stated, "I think everybody should study foreign languages. I don't think it's emphasized enough in America. I was able to go all the way through college and was never required to take a foreign language. I wish I had, but it's never too late" (I: 26).

Second, there was almost unanimous agreement that language study should begin as early as possible. A student of Latin pointed to children of other countries who studied languages in their regular school programs as something that ought to be given consideration in the schools of the United States. She noted:

> We don't start young enough. We try to teach them when they're in high

school. At that point they either don't care or have other things that are more important to them . . . and these other countries, if you look at them, they start at age five and by the time they're in high school they're already fluent. I think if we would do things like that, we wouldn't have such a problem. You wouldn't have to force kids to do it. (I: 27)

An undergraduate student of Spanish education was passionate in her concern that foreign language study begin at an early age. She stated,

But, as we all know, it needs to start early, early, early . . . it should definitely start from kindergarten. We could be turning out students at the school level at almost bilingual status. And they would be more ready to accept the world and to go places and experience new things. (I: 29)

A graduate student of Spanish language education, expressing similar sentiments, summed up most respondents' feelings about beginning language study as early as possible when she stated, "I think that everyone should study foreign languages from day one, from kindergarten" (I: 23).

In addition to its status as an academic requirement, foreign language study was undertaken for two additional reasons: to enhance one's employment possibilities in the job market, and to acquire a tool for learning about different cultures.

Several participants at the high school and university levels recognized the importance of knowing another language for the purpose of securing good jobs. One high school junior, for example, noted that:

When you get into the job market or whatever, a lot of businesses will look on that favorably knowing that if you need to, that you can communicate overseas. Or you can communicate with another firm that you're working with in Mexico, or a firm that you're working with in Spain, just knowing that you have the ability to negotiate or do business with Spanish speakers. . . . Some businesses are going to need people who can communicate with them. (I: 7)

Another high school junior, when talking about her goal of becoming a translator, explained, "we need a lot of communication for trade and there are a lot of people here who are from different nationalities and I think now it's needed a lot more with DC and New York, like, for jobs. I mean, you can get jobs if you know two or three languages" (I: 5). And an undergraduate noted that she thought that the fact that she spoke two languages, Japanese and English, and was studying a third, Spanish, would enhance her marketability in international business.

A last reason given for studying a foreign language was to be able to learn about and get to know people from different cultures. A student of German stated, "I really like other cultures and think it helps people to understand other people from around the world" (I: 28). Another interviewee noted, "I just see language as a powerful tool in connecting with people in completely different cultures" (I: 13). For yet another participant, studying to become a teacher of Spanish, "it's an exciting prospect to be able to communicate with someone outside your own culture" (I: 29). Their aspirations for using the language included being able to interact with native speakers both here in the United States and in their travels to other countries as well as to be able to read some of the great works of that culture. One interviewee was especially excited about this opportunity:

> That is the ultimate to have the knowledge of the world at your fingertips in the original language it was written in. . . . My ultimate goal is to be able to read literature and to be able to read those most profound and beautiful works and to really connect with them in the original language that they were written because the stories and ideas are so incredible. (I: 13)

Several of the older students also mentioned the self-knowledge that comes about through the learning of another language and its culture(s). One of the nontraditional-aged students explained, "If you've never studied another culture and come to grips with understanding that other culture you never quite understand your own because you've never been aware of the differences" (I: 22).

At the lower elementary grades, the students did not articulate their reasons for studying other languages outside of the fact that such study was part of their school day. One fourth grader in her second year of studying Spanish explained, "It wasn't my choice. See, just this Spanish teacher started coming in last year and it wasn't really my decision, she just came in" (I: 11). A first grader, when asked why his class was studying Japanese, stated, "I don't know. I guess they just want to talk that language a little bit" (I: 10). However, when asked why anyone would want to learn another language, a few of them made similar connections to the outside world. The fourth grader, for example, when asked why she thought people studied foreign languages, responded, "because if somebody, like they get a job and their boss is foreign and maybe speaks Spanish or something, they would understand them . . . or, like, if they went on a trip to Spain, they would know Spanish" (I: 11).

In sum, there were three primary reasons given for studying another language: (a) it was required, (b) it opened doors to better jobs, and (c) it afforded an opportunity to learn about and interact with people from different cultures. And, while "having to take it" was cited most frequently, no one expressed regret about having done so. Indeed, there was overall satisfaction with their language study, past and current, and a strongly expressed feeling that the study of other languages should be engaged in by everyone, beginning as early as possible.

## Key Issues in Classroom Learning

A second major theme addressed by these participants concerned the context or environment of classroom learning. The interviewees most frequently dealt with three specific issues: (a) the important role that the teacher has played in creating or hindering one's excitement and ability to learn, (b) the impact that classroom activities and resources have had on their developing and maintaining an interest in the language, and (c) how challenging, yet rewarding, the process of language learning is. We take up each of these in turn.

All participants reported that the language teacher played a highly significant role in their learning. It was for many, in fact, one of the primary influences that they cited in explaining whether they liked their language classes, and upon which they based their decisions to continue studying a particular language or to continue language study beyond the required number of years. One woman, explaining why she decided to return to school to study Latin, credited her first teacher of Latin, taken in eighth grade, for instilling in her a love of that language. She kept in contact with this woman over the years and recounted a moving story about their relationship:

> My own favorite Latin teacher died at the age of 96 and I was her pall-bearer and the day after her burial, I was offered all of her Latin and Greek books. The next year I crept into her classroom, my old learning environment, and I really felt, and have felt, her patronage almost all my life. (I: 25)

The students majoring in language education in particular mentioned the significant influence that their own language teachers had had on them. A student teacher of Spanish, for example, spoke passionately of her own high school Spanish teacher. She commented, "The teacher, of course, I mean, she's my saving grace. She is the one who turned my life around. [teacher's name], if it wasn't for her and her enthusiasm and her love for the language and the culture, I wouldn't be here today" (I: 29).

There were learners who did not feel the same bond with their teachers, and talked about persisting with language study *in spite of* the teacher and what they considered to be poor learning conditions. A ninth grader complained about the lack of control exercised by the teacher and its consequences:

> She [the Spanish teacher] really doesn't have the class under control because everyone is passing notes and everything goes out of control and you can start doing your math homework in the middle of Spanish and she doesn't care. . . . No one takes them [the language classes] seriously. . . . People will switch seats in the middle. Maybe people do things in the middle of it. And, personally I don't study it as much. (I: 1)

An undergraduate student of Latin education discussed how her own learning had been affected by the teachers she had had, particularly at the university level. She recounted, "I've found some of the professors frustrating in a way that they're very old school and it's very hard. I mean you have to put on your face and go in there knowing you're going to be badgered when you get in there . . . and to me, I don't think that's the way it should be taught" (I: 27). One unfortunate incident between a teacher and another student left a particularly vivid memory:

> The professor . . . the way he comes across is very bad. And he would make you feel like you were so stupid to the point that you're almost ready to leave his class. And one day a girl left in tears because he made her read something and she has a problem with stuttering when she gets nervous. And he made her finish ten lines of something that he should have let her stop on one line after he saw what was happening and he didn't and he didn't care . . . and she's hung in there which is surprising to me because if it had been me I probably would've dropped the class after being treated like that. (I: 27)

A few other interviewees expressed similar concern about the teachers they had had, noting how the teachers' lack of interest in or ability to teach the students created a less than stimulating environment. No interviewee, however, reported stopping language study due to the negative impact they perceived the teacher to have. Instead, they reported that they often learned how to work around the teacher, using their classmates or friends who spoke the language they were learning to get what they did not feel they were getting from the classes. In some cases, they spoke of biding their time until the following year when they were able to choose a different teacher.

The interviewees generally expressed ambivalent feelings about other aspects of the learning environments they experienced in the beginning years of language study, i.e., their classmates, the resources used and the activities engaged in. For some students, their classmates were a significant part of the classroom environment, making the class itself better or worse. One undergraduate student of Japanese was quite articulate about how he perceived the effect of his peers on the classroom ambiance:

> The classmates . . . some of them I like being with and some of them I
> don't. . . . A lot of people don't pay attention and don't study a lot. So a
> few of them will just stare off into space during class or do something
> else. And it's such a small class that you can't help but notice. In other
> classes, in big lecture classes, people can read the newspaper and the
> teacher won't even know that it's going on. But in a small class if people
> don't pay attention or if people are smart alecky or something, then it's
> very obvious. . . . But some students show genuine interest and are keep-
> ing up with the class. And even some of the students who are having a
> difficult time with it, like, there is this one lady who I think is 30 years
> old, and . . . she seems to have sort of a difficult time with it [language
> study] but she works very hard and I respect that a lot. (I: 14)

Another student, a high school freshman, seemed resigned about her
learning environment when she described her classmates as "well,
they're very hyper and everyone acts up and my teacher can't control
anyone because no one takes it seriously. The teacher is very nice and
she really tries, but the class is so out of hand, no one can do anything"
(I: 1). For these and some of the other learners, having to deal with
classmates whose lack of interest in the language class was evident in
their classroom behavior was a source of not a little resentment and
frustration.

In discussions of the classroom lessons themselves, "boring" was a
term used by most participants to describe the first couple of years of
language study, both at the high school and university levels. A university student majoring in Spanish explained why he perceived the first
and second-year sequences of courses at the university to be "hideous .
. . awful":

> They spend 45 minutes discussing, you know, two phrases and you have
> people talk about it for two minutes and then you go the next day and no
> one remembers any of it. It's just a nightmare . . . she would speak in
> Spanish for about ten minutes out of the whole class . . . I mean, pretty
> much if you're, if you have a pulse, you're not going to be challenged in
> those [classes]. (I: 18)

A high school freshman in her second year of Spanish expressed similar
concerns about the relatively simple and unstimulating nature of the
material that was taught in her class. She explained, "But, I mean, with
Spanish it's like conjugating verbs . . . you do the exact same endings
and there're just some basic words you have to know and then you can
put together sentences and that's all you need to know . . . once you get
through the conjugations and . . . like table is *la mesa* and chair is *la
silla* . . . there's not much more to it than that" (I: 1).

Many of those who felt less positive about their formal learning conditions expressed frustration with the book they used in class, often claiming that they felt that the teacher relied too heavily on it. One high school student pointed out, "It's good having the book as a reference but I really don't like living out of the book" (I: 6). This same student offered suggestions for the kinds of activities she thought would make a difference in the classroom:

> I think we need more fun activities, things that involve us more with French . . . like when she tells us to speak French we really don't consider that a fun activity. . . . When she's like "have a conversation in the foreign language," no one has a conversation in French in the class. I mean everyone's talking in English and she knows it and we all know it. But I think there needs to be more, I guess what they would consider enrichment activities. (I: 6)

A few of the participants expressed concern about what they perceived to be the irrelevance of the material being learned. A student of Spanish at the university level, for example, thought that the material presented in the book was not the kind of language he and his peers would actually need:

> They never teach you any of the slang expressions, they never teach you how to actually express yourself. College students don't want to be talking about—What was it about? Do you remember those chapters on picnicking in a park?—They . . . need to have a chapter on . . . how do you say, what are the different words for saying, you know, guy, chick, person. Things like that that make people want to talk about it. But when you ask people to talk about the park and the sidewalk, and the traffic light, then you turn people off too much. (I: 18)

There were a few exceptions to this general feeling of tediousness regarding beginning language study. A high school student in his second year of Spanish spoke very highly of both the teacher and his classmates in contributing to a positive learning environment. Of his teacher he noted, "[she] does a real good job with wanting us to learn how to speak Spanish so that we could be understood in a Spanish country, not just be able to write down Spanish but being able to communicate in Spanish in what she calls street Spanish" (I: 7). Of his classmates, he pointed out how well they all worked together to help each other in the learning process:

> We all get along real well. We're not in a lot of classes together but I think that everybody kinda helps each other out . . . there is one girl whose parents teach Spanish on the college level and so she kinda helps everybody else out, you know, it kinda helps when you can get help from another student . . . they can put it in a perspective where you can under-

stand it more easily. There's one who lived in Miami and had lots of friends who were Spanish speakers and she has a really good accent, and we can all model our accent after hers. And the classmates are all really nice people. I think we work well together. (I: 7)

In addition to this student, the elementary school students reported that they enjoyed their language classes. Trying different foods, singing songs and playing games were cited by all as the activities they most enjoyed. In fact, one little girl, during the interview, took the opportunity to sing one of the songs she had learned in Japanese to the interviewer.

Many of the students for whom beginning language study was uninspiring reported that as they moved from the lower to the more advanced levels, language learning became more interesting. There were two primary reasons they thought this was so. First, they felt that in the upper level language courses, because they were involved in more reading and writing activities, they felt more challenged by the material. And second, because the language classes were generally smaller, they were able to get to know their classmates better, and thus develop more lasting relationships with them and their teachers. This, in turn, they reported, stimulated their interest in using the language to interact with their classmates even outside of class. One learner explained the specific factors that helped sustain his interest in studying at a more advanced level: "It's a small pool . . . so you get to make pretty good friends within that department. You're in a lot of classes with them and you get to know the professors pretty well, too" (I: 18). The student of Chinese spoke of why he liked his upper level Chinese classes: "it was the small family atmosphere [which made it] very easy to do those extracurricular things . . . we really got to know each other well" (I: 13). Others also spoke of how they felt less intimidated, and more closely connected to their peers in the smaller, upper division classes, which they felt created a more stimulating and caring environment within which to learn the language.

Although the participants' feelings about their learning environments differed, there was one point most of them did agree on: the process of becoming a competent user of the foreign language was far more difficult than they had imagined it to be. Except for two of the three students in the elementary grades, all of the interviewees stated that they had entered language study with the expectation that it would be fairly easy to master and were subsequently quite surprised at how long it was taking them to be able to use the language with any ease. The ninth grader studying Spanish, for example, when asked if learning Spanish was what she had expected it would be, responded:

> No, because if you try to speak fluently, like speak a serious message, you're gonna speak like this . . . before you say a verb you have to conjugate it in your head and then you have to go through "well what does that word mean" and you say like a word a minute . . . and a five word sentence takes you five minutes. (I: 1)

Even the fourth-grade student of Spanish noted how difficult she thought the process was:

> It is harder to learn 'cause in spelling she [the teacher] can just say "okay" and say how to do it and read the directions and then you do it. But Spanish is not that easy. It doesn't take one day and just say something and you're all done with Spanish. It takes a long time to learn Spanish. (I: 11)

Yet another learner, a university student, pointed out his frustration at not being able to express himself in writing in the foreign language as easily as he could in English: "It makes a big difference between being able to express yourself as you can after speaking it [English] for 21 years and being able to express yourself with the few things you've learned in class" (I: 18). In fact, during one language course, his frustration at his limited writing ability was so great, that he "gave a copy of one of my history papers [in English] to [Spanish teacher's name] to show him 'look I'm not an idiot in terms of writing.' And he got a kick out of that, and it gave him hope at that time that I could learn to write better." Many of the respondents reported that they had initially been unaware of the long-term investment of time and energy that foreign language study required. No respondent, however, felt that the commitment needed was not worth it. The thoughts of one of the non-traditional aged students seem to express well the feelings of most of the respondents:

> [foreign language study] demands more self-discipline . . . and I think for foreign language study the early investment is so, so big for the returns which come later . . . it's a kind of investment in an unknown future . . . . it's delayed gratification . . . it really requires a huge investment and a belief that somewhere down the road it's really gonna all make sense and be worthwhile. (I: 25)

For some participants, the learning process was an intensely personal one in which they oftentimes felt fragile. When relating her experiences of living in Japan for a time, a participant defined the process of trying to communicate with her family as an "up and down process . . . not only is it up and down, it goes backwards. It takes a long time and it shatters your ego a lot" [1: 16]. A learner of German, for whom language learning was a "deeply personal . . . intimate" experience, talked of how exhausting trying to speak the language was. He told of his visit to Germany where, "I was forced for the first time in my life to speak German, and . . . I went through a period of culture shock after the first week or so. I was just so tired of trying to concentrate and frustrated with not being able to really express myself" (I: 24).

Many of the respondents expressed the disappointment they initially felt upon realizing that the notion of "total fluency" is, in reality, an unachievable state. Language learning was instead, they discovered, a life-long process. One student who had studied Japanese as well as lived in Japan for a number of years, stated, "the biggest disappointment is the fact that no matter how long I study language, I will never be fluent. Or as fluent as I want to be . . . there's never an end to it. . . . I can't really see the light at the end of the tunnel" (I: 12). Another student of Japanese shared her frustration at not becoming "fluent" during the year and a half she spent in Japan. She explained:

> I expected to be fluent by the time that I came back and people are always like so "Are you fluent?" and I'm like "No." And they're like "Why not?" and they look at you like you have some deficiency or something. . . . People don't know but it's very aggravating because it's kind of like they look at you like you have a problem because you can't go to a foreign country and come back and be able to speak it fluently. (I: 16)

For a university student of Spanish, however, the fact that there really was no end to language learning was perceived more positively: "I don't think you can learn language and say 'I've already finished learning' when that's done because it's never finished . . . language changes . . . every time there are new words coming up, so I think positive about it" (I: 20).

There was one disappointment with the process of learning a language that a few participants reported experiencing. According to these students, it was the realization that what they had learned in class was not always what was most practical, i.e., what was used in everyday conversation. One learner explained, "I think my biggest disappointment was when I finally went to Japan and I realized that what I had been spending two years learning was not what Japanese people typically spoke" (I: 5). And, for one student of Spanish, both this same lack of connection between classroom talk and "authentic" talk, and the lack of frequency with which they practiced with native speakers were disappointing:

> [we] don't have the ability to practice a lot with native speakers, especially in the classroom setting, you don't get very much speaking done. And the

things you do talk about are certainly not conversational. You know,
you'll be talking about some literary term or . . . something like that . . .
so you don't get to learn what you need to actually converse in a language.
So that's always disappointing when, you know, you can study for 4 or 5
years and meet natives and not be able to carry on a conversation. (I: 18)

A last disappointment, although expressed by only one participant,
is worthy of note. An elementary-grade student who was studying two
languages, Spanish in school and Hebrew at home, expressed great concern with the language program in his school, which was a special,
enrichment program. He recounted how, because the teachers in the
program changed from year to year, the students were made to relearn
the same content. For him, this was a major disappointment. He stated,
"I guess I expected to learn something . . . but you don't get to learn
anything new, ever" (I: 4). Apparently, for this young learner, the lack
of curriculum planning from year to year in his school, produced a static,
unstimulating, and thus disappointing foreign language classroom.

An important point to make here is that however frustrated the participants stated they often felt in the process of language learning, these
same learners reported feeling stimulated by and appreciative of the
personal challenge afforded by language study. The biggest challenge
for most of the interviewees was in attempting to focus more on language
use than on usage when communicating, that is, to subdue their desire
to have their language be grammatically correct, and instead, to focus
on getting the message across, on communicating with another. One
learner of Chinese, for example, noted how challenged he felt in trying
to use the language to communicate. In his words:

Really the biggest challenge was just to be able to let go in order to
communicate. Use it instead of just study it, not regurgitate it but actually
use the language as a means to expression. . . . To me, to be able to let
go is to be able to say to myself "It is okay to make mistakes. It is okay
not to say everything right." (I: 13)

Another student compared the learning of a foreign language to the
excitement of being a child again. For him, the challenge was in redis-
covering the intricate beauty of even the most seemingly mundane uses
of language:

I was basically illiterate all over again. . . . It was fun, like going to
kindergarten or something . . . because, I mean I couldn't say for the first
year or so . . . "where's the bathroom?" things like "I'm hungry." Just
very simple things. . . . So you have to push yourself like a child would.
(I: 15)

Another learner, a graduate student of Spanish education, noted how challenging she found the learning of Spanish to be:

> [it was like] wow! This is so much fun. It was like I was putting pieces of a puzzle together . . . it's like an everyday challenge. Whatever we're discussing in class, if I can follow along, and when the professor calls on me to say something back, I'm like a little kid, you know, anxious to answer. (I: 23)

A final noteworthy comment on the challenge of learning another language was made by a perceptive high school sophomore, who spoke of how, through her own struggles in learning French, she reached a deeper understanding of the process itself. She explained:

> I mean I understand the frustrations of learning a new language but maybe you'll understand why some people have such a hard time. It's incredibly difficult. And you don't really think about it in English because you started it for such a long time. You kinda been building it for so many years that . . . we're learning different tenses in French and we don't even think about the tenses in English. And, in French we have to think about it. So, maybe it makes you think about it. Maybe it makes you think a little more. (I: 6)

In sum, the interviewees reported that there were specific factors in their formal language training that in some way affected their learning. A most significant factor was the language teacher, who was perceived to be either a positive influence in helping to develop an interest in the language, or somewhat of an obstacle to have to work around. They also reported that their being able to maintain an interest in their studies was affected by the materials and activities used in the classrooms, and the relationships they were able to form with their peers. A final point that was significant to them in their learning was the realization of how difficult yet challenging the process of learning another language could be.

# Long-Term Benefits of Language Study

In this section we report on the long-term benefits that the participants perceived the learning of foreign languages has had or will have for them. Three broad themes best capture their reported experiences and thoughts: (a) an expanded interest in learning additional languages, (b) the growing ability to establish and maintain interpersonal relationships with a wide variety of people, and (c) the development of a more expanded perspective of the self, of others and of the world. We discuss each of these below.

For many participants, the learning of one foreign language engendered the desire to learn other, additional languages. The following story, told by an undergraduate student of French education, exemplifies the developing interest in languages of which many of the participants spoke. In the interview he recounted the dramatic influence learning French had on him:

> I have grown fond of languages that I never was [fond of] before . . . I had no ambition at all to learn an oriental language and now I can't wait. I don't care if I'm in school for the next 15 years of my life. One way or another I'm going to learn as many languages as I can. (I: 17)

This same student told how, having grown up in an area in which many Spanish speakers lived, he had no desire to learn another language, particularly Spanish. In fact, he reported that he resented the fact that Spanish was spoken at all. It was only because of the language requirement in high school that he began studying French. His interest in the language grew as he studied, however, so much so that he decided to become a French teacher. And, as this interest in language developed, he was able to look back and reflect on his earlier childhood disinterest in Spanish and reframe his memories in a more positive light:

> I did what I thought was right at that time and that was denial, denying what was happening around me . . . but, needless to say, I did move out of there, I did change my way of thinking. I'm more fascinated with languages than ever before. I'm fascinated with the world as far as speakers go. I just wish that I could understand everybody. (I:17)

Another learner expressed similar sentiments about the influence of language study. For him, learning one foreign language created an interest in wanting to learn more. He stated, "I think that I saw Chinese as a way to really make contact with the Chinese culture, with Chinese people, and subsequently, I am interested in studying other languages. I would like to study Spanish or . . . a European language now that I have studied a language that is so completely distant from English" (I: 13).

For most of the interviewees, a tangential benefit of language study proved to be the development of self-confidence and self-esteem produced in part by their exposure to, and growing potential to develop relationships with, a variety of different people. Especially significant to these learners were the feelings of success and competence they experienced in their interactions with native speakers. One student reported how good it made him feel to speak with others in German and to be praised for his ability to communicate. Another student in high school had had the opportunity to travel to France with her family, an opportunity which turned out to be a wonderful experience. She talked about being able to connect with the French people with whom she spoke, and how good communicating with them made her feel. It was this experience, she stated, that helped rekindle her interest in the formal study of French. She explained, "I told my mom I didn't want to take foreign language anymore and she said, 'remember how you felt in France, how you were really excited about your speaking French.' And it's kinda, it's what keeps me going, the thought of being able to speak it and how good it feels to understand" (I: 6). An undergraduate student of Japanese spoke of how learning to speak helped her overcome her shyness. Indeed, she reported, it helped her develop interpersonal skills that she has found useful in all of her dealings with others:

> I feel that it really helped me in everything I do. My dealings with people, just everything really with people. I work in a restaurant right now and I used to be very shy, but one thing . . . if you are learning a language you have to talk, you can't be shy or you're never going to learn it. That helped me as far as my shyness went. (I: 16)

Others also spoke of the perception of increased self-confidence and self-respect engendered by their growing abilities to use the foreign language with native speakers. A learner of Chinese expressed how good speaking to others made him feel: "It [speaking Chinese] makes me feel more confident. I had one Chinese person tell me that my Chinese is better than theirs because I spoke more of the standard accent than they did. It is just a real good feeling to be able to speak Chinese and have others understand me" (I: 13).

Many of these learners reported that they were interacting and developing relationships not only with native speakers of the languages they were studying, but with other learners of those languages as well. In addition, they were also developing an interest in interacting with, and subsequently coming to know, a wide variety of international students. An undergraduate student of Japanese who was dating a Japanese woman he had met at his school, for example, stated that in addition to the many Japanese friends he had made, he enjoyed getting to know others who spoke different languages. A graduate student of German reported similar feelings. He stated that, "learning another language has enhanced my life experiences in general . . . my experiences with friends have been enhanced, and . . . my self-respect is much higher" (I: 24). This same student reported, "I've got plenty of them [friends who speak other languages]. . . . We've got about 1500 foreign people at this university . . . being in that social scene I've known an awful lot of people who speak more than three languages, even."

Another learner of Japanese told of the relationships she was developing with other learners of Japanese and of the positive influence they were on her. She described how she felt more attuned to, more compatible with, learners of Japanese who also had the opportunity to live and study abroad. After spending time in Japan, she recognized that she and her Japanese-speaking friends enjoyed a very special kinship:

> The people I met in Japan that speak Japanese, I feel that I have more in common with them and they understand me because they know what I've been through. It's kind of like your childhood friends who have grown up with you and they know what you're about . . . it seems like, I don't know why, but, the people that speak Japanese are on the same wavelength as me. (I: 16)

Other participants also shared this feeling of having developed friendships and a degree of mutual understanding with their peers who were also learning the language.

A final example of the kinds of interactions and relationships the development of which were thought to be influenced by language study was provided by a student of Latin and Greek. In his interview, he reported having similar, positive interactions with others, but with an interesting twist that we think is worth noting here. According to him, becoming proficient enough in Latin and Greek to be able to use it to interact with others was not a primary goal. Rather, he stated that becoming a competent reader of the great works written in Latin and Greek was what he hoped to achieve and *interacting with other readers* about these works what he found most stimulating. He recounted one memorable experience he had in one of his language classes:

> We had like ten adult learners . . . and we had people in there that could read Greek, a housewife, someone who had been an engineer and not taken any humanities . . . an undergrad, people from all walks of life, and it was shared between a professor that was a Greek professor and a professor that was English . . . and between the ping pong of that we went through a lot of shared inquiry. I found the shared inquiry fascinating because how the housewife saw the *Odyssey* was completely different from how I as a bachelor, someone who's always been in academics looked at it . . . and it was just beautiful to see how different people's minds were . . . and it made me realize that Homer is all things to all people. (I: 22)

Clearly, for this student, language study was important in that it provided the opportunity to read some of the classics of Western thought. This, in turn, and more significantly for him, afforded the chance to exchange ideas with, and learn from, other readers.

The third theme shared by most of the respondents addressed the impact that language study had on the development of a more expanded world view. Many of the participants spoke of how their awareness and understanding of other cultures and viewpoints grew alongside their developing language abilities. One undergraduate student of French noted, "As a consequence of learning this language . . . I do want to go to Eastern Europe and I do want to go to a French-speaking country, say West Africa. I would never—I'll be honest with you—I would never have chosen to go to an African country . . . but then after you study what's going on and you read articles . . . [you] understand it" (I: 17). He went on to say that by studying French, "I've broken down a lot of walls, not just about the French . . . but just about everybody. I just started looking around, going, 'this is a small world, this is a small world'." A student of Japanese reflected on the influence that studying the language had had on him, particularly in making him more aware of international events:

> As a person I don't think I'd understand as much about the world and current events . . . understanding the language, you come to understand the culture. So, when you see something on the news about Japan American relations, or the NAFTA treaty with Mexico and that sort of thing, if you know the language and a little bit of the culture, then you understand the effects of the things a little bit better. (I: 14)

Another individual, a student of German, felt similarly. He noted how his understanding of the German culture increased as his language abilities grew. "You see the world in a new light," he commented. "Rather than just saying 'look at those crazy Germans' you have an idea of what the people are like, what motivates them, what goes on" (I: 28).

Others spoke of how they developed a deeper awareness of their own cultural identities through language study, specifically the understanding of the fundamental role that culture plays in their own ways of thinking and living. The learner of Chinese shared his thoughts on how learning the language had changed him:

> I expected . . . just to fulfill my requirement. But it really opened the door to Chinese culture. It opened the door to Eastern philosophy. I think in a lot of ways it opened the whole world to me . . . it just made me realize how different so many different places in the world are. And how the Western or American way of thinking is by no means the only way . . . you take it for granted, that there are certain ways to do things. I learned so much about my own culture, about myself through studying Chinese. (I: 13)

An undergraduate learner of Japanese spoke of how her trip to Japan made her more aware of her own culture:

> I think you take your own culture for granted a lot, or at least, I did. . . . I was thinking about that yesterday as a matter of fact because I was in the bookstore and there was this book on gestures around the world . . . and it had one for the U.S. and there were some things that I never even

realized that we do that would be considered, I don't know, gestures like
that someone coming here would have to know. (I: 16)

A last, and particularly moving, story about the impact of language
learning on one's perspective on life was shared by a high school French
student. When asked to relate experiences she had had with another
language outside the classroom, she recounted how, when she was
younger, her grandfather would tell stories about growing up in France:
"I'll say he was really old, like 98, and his mind would wander, and he
would talk about how his father crossed the mountain from France to
Italy with cattle and would go back and forth" (I: 5). She noted that at
that time, she had little understanding of or interest in these stories.
Learning the French language and about French culture in the classroom,
however, helped her to better appreciate her grandfather. "I can understand my grandfather a little bit more," she explained. "I wasn't very
close to him but I can understand some of the things that he did, like
raising children and why he did certain things."

In sum, there were three general benefits that the learners reported their
language studies to have. According to them, studying a foreign language
fostered (a) a more general interest in languages and language learning; (b)
an interest in getting to know and interact with not only native speakers of
the language they were studying, but with individuals from many different
cultures; and (c) an interest in international events as well as a perspective
on life that made clear how intertwined language and culture are.

We ought to note that the three young elementary students had little
to report on what they thought the broader interpersonal and intercultural
consequences of language learning have been for them. One learner, for
example, reported that he thought that learning other languages had no
effect on his life, "because I don't usually have to use them at all" (I:
4). This perception, shared by the other youngsters, is perhaps related
to the fact that outside of their classmates, all three students reported
knowing few other language learners. In addition, they each lived in
communities which included few nonnative speakers of English. It is
quite likely then that, except for their language classes, they had little
potential for contact with learners or speakers of other languages, either
as schoolmates or as community members. Lacking such potential contact, which proved so powerful to the learners in middle and higher
grades, it is possible that the younger learners therefore could not perceive any broader consequences of such study outside of the confines of
their classes.

# Discussion of Findings

While it is impossible to generalize about the impact that foreign language learning has on those who experience it from this set of thirty interviews, five broad issues have emerged here which we feel are significant to our field, and therefore worthy of discussion and further investigation.

## Experience

The first, and most apparent, has to do with the positive relationship between experience and attitude. Namely, the more experienced language learners had more to say about language learning and their perceptions of its impact on their lives. More specifically, the more experience they reported having with formal language learning, including study abroad, the more the participants' thoughts reflected a deeper, and more positive consciousness of language, of language learning, of the role of culture, and of themselves as linguistic-cultural beings. Even those who had had some initial, and somewhat negative, contact with speakers of other languages prior to beginning study reported that the experience of learning a foreign language had made a positive difference in their lives. This seems significant in light of the fact that many of these learners didn't experience formal foreign language training until they had reached high school, a time by which sociocultural attitudes and beliefs are already rather well-formed (Tajfel, 1981, 1982; Tajfel & Turner, 1986).

That these learners seemed able to more fully develop and/or change their perceptions of themselves and culturally different others in positive ways, is an indication of the profound consequences of language learning. Specifically, it makes apparent that foreign language learning can and does stimulate in significantly positive ways the development of self- and other-knowledge, as well as beliefs and attitudes about language and culture, and that this new awareness may differ from the beliefs into which individuals were socialized as children. That is to say, for example, that formal language learning may have helped these individuals reflect on and modify in beneficial ways, the beliefs and attitudes toward themselves and culturally different others which they had been raised by their family, peer and/or community groups to hold.

If this is so, then it seems reasonable to suggest that language learning might have an even greater impact if begun at an earlier age, a point made by many of the respondents in their interviews. The reflections of the three participants who had had early formal language instruction made clear the positive impact that this early foreign language training had had on them. Two learners began English language instruction in the beginning years of schooling and took up a third language later on; at the time of the interviews, the high school learner, a native Spanish speaker, reported that she was studying French and the university learner, a native Japanese speaker, reported that she was studying Spanish. One learner reported having learned Italian as a child during the short time that his father was on sabbatical in Italy. In addition, he studied French in high school and was returning to school to study Latin. All three learners affirmed the importance of their earlier experiences with language learning.

Unfortunately, although early language study seems to have made an impact on these three learners, we have too little data here upon which to base any claims about how long-term experiences for those who began language study in their early years differed in any meaningful way from those who reported beginning language study either in or after high school. An investigation of the impact of language study, begun at different ages and studied for different lengths of time, on the learners' socioculturally constructed attitudes, beliefs and behaviors would certainly be valuable. It would be interesting to know, for example, how the processes of conscious reflection on the linguistic and cultural practices, beliefs, and world views of others, so integral to the process of foreign language learning, aid in their ability to reflect on and modify their own linguistic and cultural practices, beliefs, and world views.

As more FLES and immersion programs are implemented and maintained in the United States, we will eventually have a substantial pool of learners for whom language training is an integral part of their K–12 schooling, and who can provide us with insight into the impact that such long-term study has. Tapping into the available pool of ESL learners may also provide insight into the variety of long-term socio-attitudinal effects that learning additional languages at an early age may have. Additionally, exploring these issues with those who have been participants of immersion programs in Canada and elsewhere would provide some interesting comparison data.

## Significance of Learning Environment

A second issue has to do with the significance that formal learning conditions have for language learners. According to many of the participants in this study, the beginning years of language training at the high school and university levels were perceived to be "boring" and something to be endured. The teacher was cited as a possible contributor to such an environment by acting in such ways that were uninspiring, for adhering too closely to the book, for allowing too wide a range of classroom social behaviors, and for making the acquisition of the basics tedious. Obviously, these factors did not stop these students from pursuing further language study; nevertheless, many of those who continued spoke of their doing so *in spite of* what they considered to be poor learning conditions. Surely, it would be worthwhile to look more deeply into this area. We propose here three sets of questions to help frame such investigations, the answers to which would provide critical insight to formal language learning.

*Motivation to Persevere*

What motivated these learners to persevere in studying what they considered to be "boring" subject matter, and to move to advanced language courses taken in addition to those required for their programs of study? Did contact with native speakers of the target language play a part in motivating them, and thus help to override the poor learning conditions? If this is so, we must then ask, what kind of contact is significant? Reports from one of the learners, a high school French student, may provide a clue. She pointed out how her flagging interest in French, due to what she thought were boring classes and a less than inspiring teacher, was rekindled through *successful interaction* with native speakers of French. Certainly, it would be both interesting and helpful to know what the situational and/or behavioral factors are by which those interactions, and others, are considered successful. There is some research, done primarily in the fields of intercultural communication (e.g., Gudykunst, 1994; Gudykunst & Kim, 1992), and pedagogy, specifically that which is concerned with cooperative learning (e.g., Slavin, 1990), that suggests that there are, in fact, behaviors which make a difference in how successful an intercultural interaction is for all participants, and what the short- and long-term consequences might be. We suggest that it would be worthwhile to the field of foreign language learning to make use of some of this research, as we look more deeply into the kinds of contact with native speakers that foreign language learners report are significant to their feeling successful, and thus motivated to continue their study. It would also be worthwhile to look more deeply into other factors outside the classroom that learners report provide the motivation to continue formal foreign language study despite what they consider to be poor learning conditions.

*Learners Who Do Not Persevere*

A second set of questions concerns those learners who choose not to continue their language study after completing the required course of study. We did not interview any learners here who had stopped taking language, although we did interview a few who would have stopped upon reaching the university had there been no language requirement to fulfill. Of this latter group, none reported that they felt negatively disposed toward the language because of the requirement. In fact, most of these learners reported that they were glad that they had been obligated to study it. Many even moved on to the more advanced levels, which they reported finding more interesting, relevant, and challenging.

Nevertheless, it would be useful to interview learners who had begun and then discontinued language study once the requirement was fulfilled, as well as those who report having had negative experiences with such study. Our own experiences as teachers and students tell us that there are, in fact, quite a few such people. One interviewer for this study, for example, noted that an elementary student refused to be interviewed because he said that he intensely disliked having to take Spanish. In our informal interactions with such students, both young and old, they have shared stories of unhappy classroom experiences, that is, of having felt anxious, ignorant and even at times humiliated when made to speak the foreign language. Others have spoken of their negative feelings toward the speakers and/or cultures of the language they were being made to learn. These experiences and feelings have had consequences for these learners in that they stop, or do poorly enough that they must stop, language study, and thus, they are of obvious significance to the field. These issues, we feel, extend beyond those dealing with individual intelligence, aptitude or motivation, and are more appropriately viewed from a sociocultural perspective, in which learners' moves are interpreted within the larger backdrop of their classroom communities, and more broadly, their social communities. There are connections, for example, between how well a learner does or does not do and the classroom environment in which she participates, and between the learner's attitudes and beliefs regarding those whose language is being learned, and the sociocultural community within which she lives. Unfortunately, very little research in the field of foreign language pedagogy has dealt in any way with these issues (but see Brooks, 1992, for an initial attempt). We propose that such a move be made; that, specifically, we begin exploring, on the one hand, the connections between classroom experiences and poorly performed or abandoned language study, and on the other the connections between these learners' perceived social identities of self and culturally different others, and their experiences with language study.

### Classroom Learning Communities

A final set of questions deals with the formal learning situation itself. Although these interviews have provided us with some idea of what happens in some language classrooms, especially in the beginning levels, there is very little research that has examined classroom life in any meaningful way. We have only glimpses, for example, of the kinds of communities that are formed in classrooms, of the variety of activities that are used and the sociocognitive consequences brought about by participation within them. We are relatively ignorant of the roles that teachers do and do not play in providing adequate linguistic, cultural and social environments, and of the ways in which students respond to and help create the various kinds of classroom settings. We can only guess at how language instruction varies across levels. It is safe to say that foreign language teachers and their students participate in a social world about which we know very little. Clearly, we need to engage in long-term ethnographic research that would help us sort out the answers to some of the questions raised here, and which would, over time, help us to create learning communities within which teachers and students can develop in mutually supportive ways.

## Expectations

A third issue we think worth raising here deals with the kinds of expectations that these learners reported having prior to entering into language study. Almost all of the participants, with the exception of the learners in the early elementary grades, reported thinking that language study, particularly learning to speak the language, would be easy. They were, they reported, quite unaware of the kind of long-term investment that learning to function in another language required until they began their own language studies. All acknowledged the strong feelings of inadequacy and self-doubt, and the personal struggles they encountered as they became aware of their identities as cultural beings, particularly as they tried to express their own ideas, either in writing or speaking. They expressed how important it was to feel acknowledged as significant and intelligent by the other, either the target language speaker on the street, their peers in the language course, or the professor reading their written compositions. Being treated with respect despite their halting use of the language, seemed most important to their developing and maintaining a level of self-esteem and confidence about their language abilities, indeed about themselves as individuals. And, they reported, that it was only after considerable time and practice that any of these learners felt able to knowledgeably express themselves in the other language.

That these learners' initial expectations varied greatly from their experiences is interesting for two reasons. First, it makes apparent the American cultural myth that learning other languages is easy and quick. This myth is ubiquitous, reinforced by movies in which we see the protagonist becoming instantly bilingual after a short stay in the other culture, and by companies selling video and audio tapes purporting to make one fluent almost overnight. We further sustain this belief by expecting study abroad programs to produce near instant mastery. The Japanese learner we mentioned earlier, who, upon her return, complained of being constantly harried by questions which exhibited the expectation that she be fluent in Japanese, exemplifies the misperception of the ease with which languages are learned. The pedagogical consequences of the differences between our perceptions of what we as Americans think language learning is supposed to be, and our actual experiences, are worthy of further investigation.

The stories these learners have told of the difficulty of learning another language are important for another reason. They corroborate, in part, both the stories told by nonnative learners of English of the struggles they undergo in their schooling, and the research that has shown how complicated, and academically consequential learning in another language can be. There are many poignant stories, for example, of how ESL students who were academically successful in their first language have been placed into special-education programs, or forced into vocational tracks solely because of their limited English abilities, moves which quite often result in individual failure and increased drop out rates. And, although the academic consequences have not been as severe for the foreign language learners interviewed here, their language learning experiences seem quite similar to those of many ESL students.

This similarity was obvious to one interviewee. This learner reported that his early memories of having to "sink or swim" in a school in a foreign country made him far more aware of the dilemmas that foreign students face and he stated that he makes a special effort to reach out to the foreign students in his classes. We do not think, however, that most other foreign language learners, if those interviewed here are typical of the larger group, are conscious of the similarity between their experiences and the experiences of those who are in our ESL and bilingual education programs. We suggest that it would be beneficial to both fields, ESL and foreign language learning, to make that link. We might do this by creating opportunities for both groups of learners to come together, perhaps for example, as peer tutors, which would help them form positive social and academic alliances. We also should continue developing the dialogue between professionals in both the ESL and foreign language fields so that we can share concerns, and provide mutual support for establishing and maintaining public recognition and aid to continue our programs. Joining the various choirs of voices can only serve to enhance the goals of both programs and the experiences of both groups of learners.

## Self- and Other-Reflection

A fourth issue that emerged from these interviews has to do with the reflections on one's self and others as both linguistic and cultural beings that these learners reported experiencing via their language studies. They found themselves, for example, better able to look at the behavior of others and judge it within the value system set up by that culture. They were able to recognize the cultural influences embedded in their own linguistic and nonlinguistic behaviors. In addition, they reported becoming more interested in international affairs, and in making friends with people from different cultures. These comments lend support to the claim that through standing apart from our own language practices and engaging in the reflective examination of the practices of others, we learn not just about those whose language we are learning, but we also begin to develop a self-consciousness about ourselves and our sociocultural worlds (Hall, 1993). It would be worthwhile to further investigate how via our pedagogical practices we can continue to facilitate such self- and other-reflection and understanding.

## Knowing the Learner

A final point that we think is most significant is not concerned with what the participants reported here about foreign language learning. Rather, it deals with the impact that the interviewers reported this project has had on them. In our debriefing meetings held after all interviews were completed, the four interviewers commented on how personally enriching they found the process of interviewing language learners to be. They stated that interviewing others gave them a chance to consciously reflect on their own reasons for language study, which, in turn, reaffirmed their own feelings about the significance that language study has had for them.

One interviewer suggested that this particular research activity, interviewing learners of foreign languages, could be a most worthwhile activity for language education majors to engage in as part of their training in pedagogy. It might be, for example, that they could be asked as part of a methods course to interview a variety of learners in different levels, different programs and different institutions. The teacher candidates could then pool their data, analyze and interpret the findings, and develop ideas about how they think they can make a positive contribution to the learning experiences of their future students. Engaging in this and other similar research projects may help future teachers to develop an awareness of the consequences that their own teaching practices can have.

# Conclusions

Based on the findings from this study of thirty language learners, we think it is safe to assert that learning other languages has made a significant contribution to the lives of most of these learners. While starting language study because they were required to do so, most of those interviewed here reported that they were glad they had, especially since they thought it enhanced their job marketability and allowed them to learn about different cultures.

They reported their formal learning experiences were significant, the beginning years negatively so for the most part, because they perceived these experiences to be more of an obstacle to surmount to get to the more advanced, and, to them, more interesting levels. They also reported that they found that the teacher and the classroom resources and activities used had the potential to inspire or hinder their interest in further language study. We also discovered that these learners' initial expectations about language learning were different from their actual experiences. Most of the learners found that language learning was a difficult and time-consuming process, requiring a substantial investment of energy, and one that was intimately tied—positively or negatively—to the development of their personal sense of self-worth and confidence. And, while those in the early elementary grades also reported finding language learning difficult, unlike many of the older students, the younger students found their language classes to be fun and nonthreatening.

Finally, although many of these learners thought that the experience of learning one language had encouraged them to study others, they also reported some distinctly non-linguistic and even non-academic benefits resulting from their language training. They reported having developed an expanded interest in establishing and maintaining interpersonal relationships with a wide variety of people, as well as a heightened self- and world-perspective.

To conclude, the interviews we have reported upon here provide us, the professionals of foreign language pedagogy, with fresh perspectives on language learning. They inform us about the critical roles that foreign language teachers and the classroom environments we create play in helping our students to develop linguistically and culturally rich life-mosaics. We further suggest that it would behoove us as professionals to begin using these stories as initial points of departure for further reflection upon and refinement of our own beliefs and practices about teaching and learning.

We began this study with a set of questions that asked learners to articulate the place that foreign language learning has had in their lives. We end this chapter by offering a new set of questions, engendered by our reflections on the conversations we had with these learners. We hope that these and other questions will help to frame future conversations. They include:

1 What would the ideal foreign language learning experiences look like?
2 What *are* the formal classroom conditions of language learning as they currently exist, particularly those of the beginning years, and what can be done to improve them and maximize the students' learning potential?
3 How can we bring together learners of foreign languages and nonnative learners of English in ways that enrich the academic experiences of both groups?
4 How do the experiences of language learning vary, perceptually or otherwise, according to the ethnicity, social class, regional origin, and gender of the learners?
5 How does building teachers' awareness of their own pedagogical be-

liefs and practices affect the development of their classroom communities of learners?

Our students are active participants in the process of learning. Providing them with opportunities to speak and actively listening to their voices, as this project has done, are crucial steps in our continued development as professionals in the field of foreign language pedagogy.

# Notes

[1]We are very grateful to the following people who helped us complete this project: to P.A. McGee, Dale Buff and Demetria Kendrick who helped conduct the interviews, and to Katie Hall and Kelly Hall, the primary transcribers of the tapes, and their able assistants, Joyce Gianato, Becky Hendren, Gina Nozza, and Dianne Fields. Finally, we thank the many people who agreed to be interviewed for sharing with us their time and thoughts.

[2]In order to keep the identity of the participants as anonymous as possible, each was given a number from 1 to 30. A notation like I:15, then, identities the participant as Interviewee (I) Number 15.

# References

Brooks, F. B. (1992). Communicative competence and the conversation course: A social interaction perspective. *Linguistics and Education, 4,* 219–246.

Erickson, E. (1986). Qualitative methods in research on teaching. In M. Wittrock (Ed.), *Handbook of research on teaching* (pp. 119–161). New York: MacMillan.

Gudykunst, W. B. (1994). *Bridging differences: Effective intergroup communication.* Thousand Oaks, CA: Sage Publications.

———, & Kim, Y.Y. (1992). *Communicating with strangers: An approach to intercultural communication.* New York: McGraw-Hill.

Hall, J. K. (1993). The role of oral practices in the accomplishment of our everyday lives: The sociocultural dimension of interaction with implications for the learning of another language. *Applied Linguistics, 14*(2), 145–166.

Slavin, R. (1990). *Cooperative learning: Theory, research, and practice.* Englewood Cliffs, NJ: Prentice Hall.

Spradley, J. (1979). *The ethnographic interview.* New York: Holt, Reinhart, Winston.

Tajfel, H. (1981). *Human groups and social categories: Studies in social psychology.* Cambridge: Cambridge University Press.

——— (Ed.). (1982). *Social identity and intergroup relations.* Cambridge: Cambridge University Press.

———, & Turner, J. (1986). The social identity theory of intergroup behavior. In S. Worchel & W. Austin (Eds.), *Psychology of intergroup relations* (pp. 56–82). Chicago: Nelson-Hall.

# Voices from beyond the Classroom: Foreign Language Learners in Non-Traditional Environments

Gwendolyn Barnes-Karol

*St. Olaf College*

## Introduction

. . . language is much more than *books,* because language is *experiences.*[1]
—Barbara, former participant in Spanish-language LAC[2] and study abroad programs

The one goal that perhaps all foreign language instructors agree on, regardless of their philosophy of teaching or their methodological preferences, is that we want to prepare our students to be able to use their language beyond the confines of the classroom, beyond the book—communicating real things to real people in the real world. For most of us, the true test of one's ability to use another language is one's ability to survive (and, hopefully, flourish) in a country where that language is the native language. Furthermore, the majority of us most likely see life in the target culture as the most exhilarating and inspiring arena in which to use one's language and the culminating experience to which, in an ideal world, all language learners would aspire. Yet, our own anecdotal experience demonstrates that vast numbers of foreign language learners never use their language in a significant way outside of the language classroom.

At the same time, the opportunities to begin or to continue learning a language in what we refer to here as "non-traditional" environments are multiplying in number and becoming increasingly diverse. School children in some areas of the country can now begin their language learning as kindergartners, in special foreign language in the elementary school (FLES) programs, immersion programs, or dual-language schools[3] (see Curtain & Pesola, 1994; Rosenbusch, 1991; Salomone, 1991). They, and their older brothers and sisters, can keep their language skills alive at summer language camps, where activities from canoeing to crafts are done in the target language. Advanced high school and college students find that study abroad programs no longer cater only to the future foreign language teacher or the humanities major. Now, experiences ranging from au pair programs to study/service opportunities to field research programs abroad in the natural and social sciences to overseas internships in business and technical fields complement the full array of more conventional liberal arts-oriented semester- or year-abroad programs (for examples of diverse programs, see Hernández & Terry, 1994; *Peterson's Study Abroad,* 1994; Steen, 1994). On some campuses, qualified students can use their foreign language expertise to study a subject or field outside the foreign language department through "(foreign) language(s) across the curriculum" offerings. They may find options ranging from a Scandinavian history course with a partial reading list and an optional weekly discussion session in Norwegian or Swedish; to an interdisciplinary course taught in German on the city of Berlin incorporating the perspectives of bilingual faculty from departments as diverse as geography, engineering, and speech communications; or full or partial on-campus "immersion" semesters, in which they take a block of courses offered by different departments, but taught in French or Spanish (see Grandin, Einbeck, & von Reinhart, 1992; Krueger & Ryan, 1993; Straight, 1994). Finally, adults of all ages and walks of life, interested in refreshing or beginning a foreign language, discover exciting possibilities at intensive, summer residential immersion programs at selected colleges and universities.

Why do some language learners choose to go beyond the "books" of the conventional foreign language classroom to the "experiences" offered by this myriad of non-traditional language learning environments? What are their motivations? How do they integrate both classroom-based and non-classroom-based types of learning? What do these other language learning experiences contribute to their knowledge of language and culture, their ability to use the foreign language, their ability to relate to native speakers of the language? What impact do these experiences have on them as people and on their lives outside the academic world? I explored these and related questions in interviews with twenty volunteers who had studied one or more foreign languages in one or more of the above non-traditional environments (dual-language schools, language camps, study abroad programs, LAC courses, or summer residential immersion programs) conducted during the months of May, June, and July 1994, in one New England and two Midwestern states.[4]

## Description of Research Methods and Profile of Interviewees

All twenty interviewees participating in this study were volunteers who had been identified by a current or former foreign language instructor as having participated in at least one of these types of non-traditional language learning experiences and who were perceived to be eager to talk about their experiences, whether positive or negative. Guided by the general procedures outlined in the Introduction to this volume (p. xviii), I interviewed all volunteers individually, face to face, for approximately one hour each, following a semi-structured interview format. All interviews were conducted in English, except for one conducted in Spanish with a native speaker of Dutch. Interviews were tape-recorded and transcribed afterward to insure the accuracy of the data collected. All names used in this article are pseudonyms, to protect the identity of those interviewed for the study. In addition, any references to the institutions where they currently study or have studied have been changed to generic descriptions (i.e., my high school) for the same reason.

Table 1 presents an overview of the demographic characteristics of the interviewees. As the table illustrates, the volunteers for the study came from a variety of age groups and included full-time students, individuals making the transition between various levels of education or between school and careers, and people employed full time. The individuals employed at the time of the interviews or who were about to begin new positions soon afterward worked in the fields of accounting

(1 individual), advertising/marketing (1), clerical services (1), and foreign language/ESL education (4 individuals). Nineteen were U.S. residents (from the states of California, Colorado, Illinois, Minnesota, New York, and South Carolina), and one was a resident of the Canadian province of Ontario. Nineteen interviewees were native speakers of English; one was a native speaker of Dutch. The twenty interviewees included fourteen females and six males. Attempts to arrive at a more balanced gender ratio among volunteers failed, but this ratio probably reflects the reality of gender imbalances in foreign language study, both in classroom and non-traditional environments, more closely than an artificially imposed balance would have.

| Table 1. Demographic Profile of Interviewees | | | | | | | | | |
|---|---|---|---|---|---|---|---|---|---|
| | *Gender* | | *Vocation*[a] | | | *Education attained*[b] | | | |
| *Age* | *M* | *F* | *Student* | *Employee* | *Other* | *4–8* | *9–12* | *13–16* | *17+* |
| 10–15 | 1 | 3 | 4 | 0 | 0 | 2 | 2 | 0 | 0 |
| 16–20 | 3 | 0 | 1 | 0 | 2 | 0 | 2 | 1 | 0 |
| 21–25 | 1 | 7 | 4 | 1 | 3 | 0 | 0 | 7 | 1 |
| 26–30 | 0 | 3 | 1 | 1 | 1 | 0 | 0 | 0 | 3 |
| 31+ | 1 | 1 | 0 | 2 | 0 | 0 | 0 | 0 | 2 |
| Total | 6 | 14 | 10 | 4 | 6 | 2 | 4 | 8 | 6 |

Note. The values in each column represent the number of interviewees in each category. Each interviewee is tabulated once in each of the three categories of gender, vocation, and education attained.
[a]The "Student" and "Employee" sub-categories represent individuals engaged full time in the indicated activities. The "Other" sub-category represents individuals in transition between high school and college, college and employment, or jobs.
[b]Education attained is the last grade in which the interviewees had enrolled at the time of the interview.

The most salient characteristic of the interviewees as individuals and as a group was their willingness to seek out multiple language learning experiences, either studying more than one foreign language, or studying one or more languages in multiple non-traditional settings. Table 2 highlights the numbers of languages studied by interviewees as a function of age. The majority (15 of 20) studied more than one foreign language, and as the age of the interviewees increased, so did the likelihood of their studying two or more foreign languages.

| Table 2. Number of Foreign Languages Studied by Interviewees | | | | | |
|---|---|---|---|---|---|
| *Age* | *Number of Foreign Languages* | | | | |
| | *1* | *2* | *3* | *4* | *5* |
| 10–15 | 2 | 2 | 0 | 0 | 0 |
| 16–20 | 1 | 2 | 0 | 0 | 0 |
| 21–25 | 2 | 5 | 0 | 0 | 1 |
| 26–30 | 0 | 1 | 1 | 1 | 0 |
| 31+ | 0 | 0 | 1 | 0 | 1 |
| Total | 5 | 10 | 2 | 1 | 2 |
| Note. The values in each column represent the number of interviewees. | | | | | |

While Spanish and French were the most frequently studied foreign languages, as a group, the interviewees had studied fourteen different foreign languages. Table 3 illustrates the numbers of individuals, by age group, who have studied each of these languages. Of those who had studied more than one foreign language, many concentrated on the frequently seen combinations of French and Spanish, French and Italian, Portuguese and Spanish, or Chinese and Japanese. However, other interviewees studied what might be perceived as unusual combinations of languages: Japanese and Norwegian, French and Chinese, Armenian and French, for instance. Several interviewees expressed the desire to learn additional languages in the future.

The variety of the interviewees' non-traditional language learning experiences was as rich as the diversity of the languages they had studied. Table 4 summarizes the numbers and types of experiences in which the twenty participants have taken part.

| Language | Age | | | | | |
|---|---|---|---|---|---|---|
| | *10–15* | *16–20* | *21–25* | *26–30* | *31+* | *Total* |
| Arabic | 0 | 0 | 0 | 0 | 1 | 1 |
| Armenian | 0 | 0 | 1 | 0 | 0 | 1 |
| Chinese | 0 | 0 | 2 | 1 | 1 | 4 |
| EFL[a] | 0 | 0 | 0 | 0 | 1 | 1 |
| French | 0 | 0 | 6 | 2 | 2 | 10 |
| German | 1 | 1 | 2 | 1 | 0 | 5 |
| Italian | 0 | 0 | 0 | 2 | 0 | 2 |
| Japanese | 1 | 0 | 1 | 0 | 0 | 2 |
| Latin | 0 | 0 | 0 | 1 | 0 | 1 |
| Malay | 0 | 0 | 0 | 0 | 1 | 1 |
| Norwegian | 1 | 0 | 0 | 0 | 0 | 1 |
| Portuguese | 0 | 1 | 1 | 0 | 0 | 2 |
| Spanish | 3 | 3 | 3 | 2 | 2 | 13 |
| Russian | 0 | 0 | 1 | 0 | 0 | 1 |

Table 3. Foreign Languages Studied by Interviewees

Note. The values represent the number of interviewees in each age group who have studied the indicated languages. Row totals can be calculated from the table for each language, but since most interviewees studied more than one language, column totals will exceed the total number of subjects (20).

[a]English as a Foreign Language

| | | Language Learning Experiences[a] | | | | |
|---|---|---|---|---|---|---|
| *Age* | *N* | *Dual Language Programs*[b] | *Summer Language Camps* | *Study Abroad Programs* | *LAC Courses*[c] | *Summer Residential Programs* |
| 10–15 | 4 | 13 | 11 | 0 | 0 | 0 |
| 16–20 | 3 | 0 | 1 | 4 | 1 | 0 |
| 21–25 | 8 | 13 | 14 | 14 | 14 | 1 |
| 26–30 | 3 | 0 | 0 | 5 | 0 | 10 |
| 31+ | 2 | 8 | 0 | 3 | 0 | 7 |

Table 4. Participation in Non-Traditional Language Learning Experiences

[a]The values represent the number of experiences in each category for the indicated number of interviewees in each age group.
[b]Each year of enrollment in a dual-language school is counted as one experience.
[c]Language(s) across the curriculum courses. In the case of multi-course LAC immersion programs, each individual LAC course is counted as one experience.

Four of the twenty interviewees had studied in dual-language elementary and/or secondary schools. Two are currently enrolled in English/Spanish dual-language schools (K–8 level) in a major metropolitan area; one had attended an Armenian/English dual-language school from kindergarten through twelfth grade; and Valerie, the native speaker of Dutch included in this study, had attended an English/Spanish dual-language school in Peru. A total of four interviewees had attended summer language camps to learn Chinese, French, German, Japanese, Norwegian, and Spanish, and all but one had attended more than one camp. One former camper had attended a combination of nine French and Chinese camps and had been a Chinese camp counselor for five summers. Of the six people who had taken LAC courses, two took courses taught in English with supplementary readings and a weekly discussion session in the foreign language, and five took individual courses or blocks of courses (the latter referred to as partial or full on-campus "immersion" semesters) in other disciplines taught entirely in the foreign language by bilingual instructors from those disciplines. At the time they were interviewed, six people were enrolled in residential summer immersion programs studying Spanish (2 individuals), Arabic, German, French, and Italian; of these six, five had attended summer residential immersion programs in the same or another language previously.

It is worthy of note that the types of language learning experiences in which interviewees participated seem to correlate with age. The younger participants in the study were most likely to have attended summer language camps, probably because of the rapid growth of such opportunities in recent years. Few interviewees studied abroad before their last two years of high school, and participation in study abroad programs was most frequent during college years. In many ways, interviewees between the ages of 21 and 25 have been at the right place at the right time in terms of their being able to take advantage of the widest variety of types of experiences. In addition to access to a variety of summer camps and study abroad opportunities, they have been in college during the current development of LAC courses. Adults over the age of 25, many of whom had previous experience studying abroad, now find that summer residential immersion programs allow them to integrate intensive foreign language study into the multiple demands of pursuing a career and maintaining a home or raising a family and provide an appropriate intellectual environment for the mature learner.

The most frequently shared experience among participants in the study was some type of study abroad experience. However, the actual types of experiences varied greatly from person to person. They ran the gamut from the short-term student exchanges (usually month-long or summer-long school trips with a family stay); to the quarter-, semester-, or year-long program usually involving formal course work abroad, residence with native speakers in a family or dormitory situation, and, sometimes, a service or field work component; to the do-it-yourself experience. Fifteen of twenty interviewees had studied abroad in some form in the past. Eight had had only one type of foreign study experience; four had had two; two interviewees had had three previous foreign study experiences; and one participant had had four experiences abroad. The countries in which they had studied and resided, thirteen in number, cover the globe: France (7 interviewees had studied there), Spain (3 interviewees), China (2), as well as Bolivia, Costa Rica, Ecuador, Germany, Italy, Mexico, the province of Quebec in Canada, Russia, and Venezuela (all countries where one person had studied). Ten interviewees were definitely planning a first or additional foreign experience at the time they were interviewed (in Brazil, Costa Rica, France, Germany [2 interviewees], Italy, Lebanon, Russia, Spain, and another yet-to-be-confirmed Spanish-speaking country). Indeed, by the time this article appears, the three participants preparing to go to Brazil and Germany will already be back home. Even those interviewees currently too young to go abroad had already begun thinking about future foreign study.

Beyond their genuine interest in multiple and diverse language learning opportunities, common threads that ran throughout the interviewees' narratives focused on: (a) their motivations, both initial and current, for language study; (b) the complex, and often problematic, relationships between conventional classroom foreign language study and their "nontraditional" learning experiences; (c) the importance of the interpersonal dimension of language learning in non-traditional environments; and (d) their perception of the value of knowing a foreign language, as evidenced by their personal use of their foreign language(s) in non-academic endeavors as well as their philosophical support for language study. While there were undercurrents pervasive throughout the views of the twenty interviewees, they also diverged on several points, as will be demonstrated in the pages ahead. Regardless, it needs to be emphasized that their views should not be understood as conclusions applicable to current or former participants in non-traditional language learning experiences across the United States, but rather, as an accurate portrayal of the observations of a limited group within the specific context of this study.

# Interview Themes

## Motivations for Language Study

> . . . in my opinion, it maybe takes some *spark* or something, like the Ecuador trip, to . . . push [a] person to want to learn. . . . The difference would be [having] the ambition to want to learn more.
> —Owen, former participant in a high-school level LAC social studies course and study abroad course in Ecuador

Before conducting the interviews for this study, I erroneously hypothesized that the individuals comprising this particular target population under study would have been those who fell in love with their first foreign language class (or teacher!), found foreign language study easy,

were model students, and, inspired—or, sparked, to use the language of
the epigraph above—by teacher-mentors whose enthusiasm for the language and culture never waned, moved steadily, course by course, toward
that ultimate goal of study abroad. With perhaps three exceptions, this
was not the case among the participants in this study.

Their initial reasons for enrolling in a foreign language, whether in
a conventional classroom setting or a non-traditional environment, varied widely. In the case of the four participants who are currently enrolled
in or had studied previously in dual-language schools, they had no choice
in the matter; their parents made the decision to introduce their children
to a foreign language at the kindergarten level. At times, this parental
decision had unpleasant consequences, in the child's eyes. Both Valerie,
the native speaker of Dutch who attended English-Spanish schools in
Peru for eight years, and Kathryn, who attended an Armenian-English
school in the U.S. throughout elementary and secondary school, recalled
vividly, as kindergartners, the terror of attending school and not understanding anything. Kathryn described her experiences in these words:

> . . . the first half of kindergarten, I believe, I went to public school. And
> second half of kindergarten, that's when I started [attending the Arme-
> nian-English school]. I didn't know anything, and the thing with pre-kin-
> dergarten and kindergarten, everything's in Armenian to get them [the
> students] started. . . . I didn't know what anybody was saying, and my
> mom said that I was crying when I came home from school, [because]
> everything was in Armenian and I couldn't understand it.

Her dislike of being compelled to study Armenian throughout school
lasted for years, until she found a personal motivation to use it.

> [The] school I went to was basically kindergarten throughout high school,
> so we learned Armenian throughout the whole thing. They [the teachers]
> were very pushy; they really wanted you to speak Armenian during the
> classes . . . and also outside, but, you know, no one ever does. And, it's
> weird, because . . . until I graduated, I hated it. It was hard for me 'cause
> I spoke it with my father, but my father doesn't read or write [Armenian],
> so he couldn't help me with my homework. My mom's American, so she
> couldn't help. So, I was struggling . . . especially when we got to higher
> levels, with compositions and poetry and writing . . . it was a horror. I
> could not handle it. But, then, while I was going to the university . . .
> there were Armenians from overseas . . . so I started hanging out with
> [them]. And, I spoke Armenian with them. And my Armenian improved
> so much. [In high school] . . . I would always be searching for words. . . .
> I was scared, I didn't want to talk. But, now, it just comes so easily. I
> mean, if there's an Armenian person, I'll just automatically speak Arme-
> nian. . . . I don't know what happened, it just—whew!

What moved Kathryn to embrace the language she resented throughout school was when she, on her own, found a meaningful use for it: making new friends at college. That experience was a turning point for her, one that changed her perception of Armenian and made her willing to use it and continue to learn it forever.

Most of the participants, however, began their language study in a conventional classroom and received no particular parental guidance or input. Moreover, their initial motivations for language study were often rather commonplace. One had always had foreign friends and been intrigued by their languages, some just wanted to try something "different" in school, others dreamed of going to a foreign country some day, and yet others wanted to learn the language of their immigrant ancestors. Many enrolled in a language because it was simply required or because it seemed like good preparation for college. For a few, enrollment in a language was almost accidental. Julie, soon to be a veteran of seven summers of Norwegian camp, took Norwegian because, seven years ago, her grade school got a Norwegian teacher instead of an art teacher. Barbara, who recently graduated from college with a Spanish major, originally wanted to study German. She explained:

> I'd met someone as . . . a child . . . who had been to Germany, and she taught me to count to 20 in German. . . . I was very interested in other languages, and I checked out a book repeatedly from our public library on German, for kids, that had pictures of fruits and vegetables and different things, and then it had the German vocabulary. And I just loved the idea of learning German, but since they didn't offer it, I went ahead and enrolled in Spanish.

Whatever their primary motivations for language study, several of the interviewees reported losing their initial curiosity about and enthusiasm for foreign language study in school and even temporarily discontinuing their study of a language. Allison, who later spent nine months studying Spanish in Bolivia, spoke of being so distressed at not being able to grasp "the concept of a foreign language" (verb conjugations, noun/adjective agreement, and so forth) that she gave up after one year of high school Spanish. Several, like Neil, who has since lived in two Spanish-speaking countries and completed a Spanish LAC immersion semester, quit basically out of boredom and frustration with classes. As he explained,

> In middle school, I didn't really have a whole lot of interest in Spanish. I started it just because it was a different language, and it seemed pretty novel at the time. . . . After [eighth grade] I dropped out . . . [because] in eighth grade, I felt there was no use whatsoever for Spanish, and I didn't know what my future career plans were, and felt it wasn't impor-

tant. . . . I dropped out and took part in more activities in music and other things that interested me more. . . . We didn't learn a lot of conversational Spanish. We learned just nouns—there were no verbs whatsoever—just a lot of nouns and basic phrases, things like that. I guess that was a large contributor to not being too interested, because I couldn't use the language. I just knew a bunch of nouns; I couldn't communicate in the language. I guess that just sort of pushed me away from wanting to learn anymore, or maybe I was just too impatient, because I wanted to learn all these other phrases and stuff more quickly. I had no interest. I just dropped out.

Yet, others, like Irina, who participated in an au pair program in France for a year and is currently planning for a second study abroad experience in Russia, continued their high school study of language, despite finding many classroom activities tedious or even ridiculous.

I knew I was interested in [languages], but I was never very excited by the class, by the teachers. . . . For example . . . I remember we saw this movie from the 50s, we went through this old poetry, we did these silly exercises in class that were just like: "Ask Rhona if she knows how to milk a cow." It was nothing that we could relate to, that our mentalities wanted anywhere near us.

But in reevaluating these experiences that a few years earlier seemed off-putting, Irina added, "But now I'd probably be interested in the kinds of things we did then, but I think [they weren't] the kinds of things that were attractive to our interests at the time."

No matter what their reasons for beginning study of a foreign language, all interviewees, with the exception of the two youngest participants, Camille and David, (aged 10 and 12, respectively, and currently enrolled in dual-language schools) experienced some spark, to repeat Owen's words once again, that piqued their interest. This spark provided the stimulus to continue their language study and to explore new ways of learning outside the classroom. For some, it was a special teacher, who through his or her example, made language come alive in the classroom. Gayle, entering her senior year of college at the time of the interview, spoke of being inspired by a high school Spanish teacher:

A lot of people complained that he wasn't a very good teacher—he didn't go by the book very much, but the interesting thing was at the end of the time [the two years that I had him], what people found was they actually could speak [the] language better. And it's interesting, because everyone was always worried . . . "Oh, am I going to be ready for the AP [advanced placement] test? Am I going to be?" And admittedly, people were not as thoroughly . . . prepared for the AP test as [those with] teachers who spent the whole year preparing for the AP . . . but the people who came out of our class were . . . able to speak better.

What made this teacher particularly special to Gayle was his ability to motivate students in a variety of ways, as she explained later.

> He was always having us do a lot of extra stuff like . . . keeping a diary in Spanish over Christmas vacation week, and just writ[ing] a lot of essays. . . . He would have a lot of discussions. He would say, "We're going to talk today about [this or that]." I remember one of the discussions was "Should women be in the army?" And then everyone was supposed to bring something in and talk about it. . . . I liked the way that he brought in topics and a lot of stuff from the outside. He really inspired me to . . . study languages, because he also told me . . . "You're going to be the type of student that comes back after ten years . . . that can speak ten languages."

Four years after graduating from high school, Gayle is working on her fifth foreign language.

For many others, what cemented a new or renewed commitment to studying a foreign language was their first experience using a foreign language to communicate with native speakers of the language, either in the United States or abroad. One of the most striking reversals in attitude among the twenty participants in this study is the story of Neil, who had dropped out of Spanish after the eighth grade because of boredom. His life changed when, in the eleventh grade, he traveled with his Boy Scout troop to Costa Rica for ten days to guard Pacific Coast beaches in order to keep poachers from snatching the eggs of endangered sea turtles before they had a chance to incubate and hatch. By resuscitating his limited junior high Spanish, Neil discovered the joys of using a language for real.

> I remembered some of the nouns and phrases, and I guess I could get my ideas across with my dictionary in hand. I could semi-navigate my way around, and I was just so interested. . . . I had a chance to use it [Spanish], I had a chance to listen to native speakers. It just *clicked!* I was pretty popular because I was the only one who was trying to speak. There were other kids who spoke Spanish, but they weren't interested in communicating. With the little bit of Spanish that I knew, I was . . . trying to communicate. I didn't speak too well, but I was trying my best, and I just got really interested. After I got back, I was determined to learn more Spanish, and that pushed me into deciding to go to Venezuela for a summer through AFS.

That summer, he did go to Venezuela for three months with the goal of "learn[ing] Spanish as best I could" in preparation for the following year's repeat patrol in Costa Rica. During his senior year, Neil was Senior Patrol in his Boy Scout troop. As the troop member entrusted with the highest level of responsibility for completing assignments, he was charged with helping solve communication problems in Costa Rica.

Reliving briefly his second stay in Costa Rica, after a summer of intensive Spanish practice in Venezuela, Neil marveled:

> It was great! . . . The first I time went, it was to see the *turtles,* and I didn't make many friends. And the next year I went back, I could speak Spanish, and the main reason I went was for the *people.* I was just talking the whole time. . . . I just spoke a lot and I made so many friends, it was just unbelievable. That was the best part of it. I went back, and I just spoke and spoke and made so many friends, and that's why Spanish is so important—I have so many friends . . . so it's really a necessary tool for me to have and I don't know where I'd be without it. It just felt great, going back, to be able to communicate . . . in Spanish and being an interpreter. . . . I just felt I was important, I was needed, and it was good to be able to have that skill.

Furthermore, Neil played the role of ambassador between the other Scouts and his Costa Rican friends.

> They [the other Scouts] saw me having so much fun with all these other Costa Ricans, and I guess I was sort of like the key . . . they were locked out, and they needed me to come in and break the ice between the Costa Ricans and them. So, they sort of hung around, and I would introduce them to all the people that I met. . . . Even though . . . the other Scouts that went . . . didn't speak any Spanish, once I broke the ice with them and sort of interpreted for a little bit, they just felt comfortable. . . . The other people [Costa Ricans] would do their best with Spanish or "one-act plays" to get their ideas across. . . . The rest of the trip went really well, because people at least knew each other and weren't afraid to communicate through other means.

Subsequently, Neil has become a Spanish major, has started studying Portuguese because of his interest in international environmental issues, and is currently looking toward a career as a bilingual fire fighter in a major metropolitan area after graduation from college. At the time of the interview in early June, he was hoping to spend a month during the summer in Costa Rica as a member of a rescue service/fire department to acquire the terminology needed to serve a Spanish-speaking clientele.

While not all interviewees' stories were as dramatic as Neil's, many mentioned trips abroad or foreign study experiences as high school or college students that changed their lives forever as language moved from the realm of the theoretical to that of the practical and personal. Others highlighted the rewards, and regrets, of discovering languages as adults when their language learning was oriented toward a particular professional goal. Elise, a graduate student in Renaissance and Baroque art history and a two-time participant in summer residential immersion programs, contrasted her attitude toward studying French in high school with that of learning Italian as an adult. In her words,

In high school, I had taken a couple of years of French, and I liked it, but I don't remember any of it now. . . . Of course, in high school at least, I was one of those students who was not really, really serious, and so I did . . . what I did to get by . . . and as soon as I finished what I had to do, I had no desire to continue in college, because I [fulfilled the requirement] with a couple of years of French in high school. So, I think that's part of the reason I became so enamored with it, because when I started Italian I was older. . . . I *wanted* to learn it rather than having it be some requirement that I had to . . . get out of the way, or something like that. And, just the experience, I realized, of learning a foreign language opens up so many new doors. I mean, just from two years of Italian, I've met people I never would have met had . . . did I not know the language.

Elaborating further, she continued her self-examination:

When you have [a] goal—like, I'm going to Italy next year so I really want to learn it—that's just a lot different than when you're in . . . high school . . . and . . . it's just another class . . . amongst many, where there's no real goal. And, I think a lot of times in high school, people think, "Why do I have to learn this? I'm never going to speak it. What purpose is this going to serve me later on in life?" And I kind of had that attitude, I mean, "I'm not going to France. I don't know anybody French that I'm going to speak to. . . ." Whereas, with Italian—and part of it, I'm sure, was being a little bit older—I realized, "Wow! . . . I know people that I can speak to!"

Other interviewees past the traditional college age echoed similar sentiments of the sheer joys of beginning or continuing language study as adults with well-defined personal and/or professional goals. More importantly, they emphasized the many ways in which their maturity made them especially capable of taking advantage of the many benefits that non-traditional language learning environments offer.

# Relationships between Conventional Classroom Foreign Language Study and Non-Traditional Learning Experiences

There's a program at [a local elementary school] now where kids are immersed in Spanish, and I think that's a really good idea, because [foreign language learning] shouldn't have to be torture. I mean, you shouldn't have to sit in a stupid classroom and have irregular verbs pounded into your brain.
—Teresa, student of German and language camper

With the exception of Camille and David, the ten- and twelve-year-olds who have thus far only studied their foreign language, Spanish, in dual-language schools, the volunteers interviewed for this study have all learned languages in a combination of conventional foreign language classrooms and non-traditional settings. These eighteen individuals have each had to forge links between their conventional classroom work and the other opportunities they have been able to take advantage of in the United States or abroad. Some have succeeded in weaving together a variety of language-learning experiences with relative ease, producing what they view as a coherent, well-designed pattern where each piece complements and enhances the others. Others have found it frustrating and at times overwhelming to try to fit together pieces that seemed to clash.

The four interviewees who were first exposed to a foreign language in dual-language schools did not face the challenge of integrating language study into a larger educational framework as children. The use and practice of a foreign language in multiple academic contexts was guaranteed by the nature of the curriculum. Yet, for three of these individuals, use of a foreign language was something that failed to transcend its academic applications. Through Kathryn's previous words, we have seen how Armenian was a language that she did not use socially until meeting native speakers of Armenian in college. Prior to that, English was the language of the playground, of extra-curricular activities, of friendships. Likewise, both Camille and David, currently enrolled in dual-language schools, affirm that English is the lingua franca outside class, despite the fact that their school is located in a predominately Puerto Rican neighborhood.[5] Valerie, the native speaker of Dutch who began her schooling in an English-Spanish dual-language school in Peru, learned two new languages simultaneously. Both in and out of class, however, she spoke of identifying with the English-speaking teachers and students (primarily, citizens of the United States, Great Britain, or the Netherlands) and preferring English to Spanish for social, rather than linguistic, reasons. In all four instances, what would seem to be an ideal setting for encouraging the natural use of foreign languages beyond the classroom failed to do so in any consistent way. Children's social interactions were—and are still—obviously subject to influences beyond the best intentions of curriculum designers. The language of instruction does not necessarily become the language of conversation and social relationships.

Teresa and Rachel also started language study outside the conventional classroom: Teresa at a summer German camp and Rachel at a summer French camp, after beginning informal instruction at home with her mother, a French teacher. Both thrived in the camp atmosphere. Language classes were interspersed among other typical camp activities—skits and plays, crafts, sing-a-longs, folk dancing, hiking, canoeing, swimming, and so forth—in the target language. Even meals and cabin life were organized to encourage the use of the language of the camp, without making it obligatory. Oftentimes, both Teresa and Rachel found themselves using the language spontaneously without realizing it until afterwards. Rachel raved about her camp experiences, contrasting the flexibility and informality of the camp atmosphere to the structure of later classroom experiences.

> As a camper, all I remember is seeming to hear more French or more Chinese than I ever did in an entire school year, and it was only for two weeks. I just remember it being great. It moved really fast, but it wasn't hard. And if it was hard, it slowed down, whereas in the classroom, it'd always be like you had to meet the deadline, you had to turn things in, you had to take the test, you had to do this, and that's not how I like to learn. And I don't know if it's because . . . I don't like to learn [that way], or it's because I started [language camp] so young that I'm used to [the camp system] and that affected me negatively at school. I had a real hard time with that [classroom language study]. I'd want to read texts in French—books. I didn't want to read verb forms and stuff. I wanted to just get right into it.

Teresa's comparison of camp and classroom experiences demonstrated an even greater level of frustration. She learned enough during her first two-week German camp experience that she was not challenged when she began actual German classes in the eighth grade. Because she had "learned enough at camp to take the entire first semester of German I," she dropped junior high German and enrolled in second-semester German at the high school. Two successive language camps increased her sense of the disparity between her ability to use German and the elements of the local school curriculum. Perceiving that her classroom work was a duplication of what she had previously learned at camp, she explained:

> We [hadn't] really straightforward covered it [the classroom material] in the camps, but you've heard it being used and you know how to use it correctly, and then they [classroom teachers] start going over these things. . . . German was kind of a study hall for me this year . . . the class seemed to be so stupid after I went to the camp, because it's so much more effective just to learn [German] by *using* it instead of picking it apart.

Not only was Teresa dismayed at her school's emphasis on learning the discrete elements of the German language rather than on the use of

German in more communicative activities, she was also disappointed at the minimal time devoted to language study in the curriculum. She summed up her feelings in the following way:

> I think school is one of the worst places to learn a language, because if you're getting it for a half hour for five days a week, it's obviously going to take you a longer time than if you hear it every day.

Despite her frustration at the pace of classroom foreign language instruction and the torture of having "irregular verbs pounded into your brain," at the time of the interview, Teresa was off to another two-week German camp, to be followed by a three-week family homestay in Germany. With two years of high school yet to go, she was applying to take German at a local college.

The majority of the interviewees, fourteen in number, first started learning a foreign language in a conventional classroom. For most of them, the initial classroom experience, whether it inspired them to continue on immediately or temporarily dampened their curiosity and enthusiasm, introduced them to a new realm that they would later explore in other ways with a passion. Thirteen of the fourteen who began their language study in a classroom participated in one or more foreign study experiences. For some, reentering an American foreign language class after being abroad was a real challenge. Although they may have been conversationally more fluent than other classmates, some found that their spoken language was too colloquial for the academic environment. For instance, back in the classroom after over a year in Mexico, Barbara realized that her Spanish was peppered with words she had learned from a young male friend, who she mused "was basically a gangster." Other interviewees saw that they were able to express their ideas confidently, but that their grammatical accuracy was less than that of apparently "less fluent" classmates who had not been abroad. Still others felt at ease when speaking a foreign language, but became frustrated when having to worry about the spelling, accents, or more formal sentence structure of written discourse. The majority of interviewees, however, were highly motivated to overcome these challenges because, as Neil explained,

> It was difficult [working on the grammar], but I knew I was going to have a use for it in the future, so I really tried and did my best to learn it all. . . . I know it's something that's necessary. I'm willing to learn it, and it's a lot more fun when you know you're going to have a use for it.

For two interviewees, returning to the foreign language classroom after studying abroad was particularly difficult, not for linguistic reasons, but for attitudinal ones. Some time after returning from a semester in France, Kathryn enrolled in a conversation class at a state university. Instead of a classroom environment that encouraged student language use, allowing her to build upon skills acquired abroad, she found an environment that either discouraged student talk or replaced it with other activities:

> [The class] was called conversation . . . and I dropped it because it was . . . absurd, ridiculous. I thought the teacher did not know how to teach this class, and I didn't want to waste my time. He would bring videos and put them on, and you would watch them, and then he would want us to discuss [them] . . . nobody spoke, and everybody was so scared. And he would call on you, and you'd be like "Oh my gosh!" And, he brought in speakers while we were supposed to be speaking, and he want[ed] us to ask these fluent French speakers questions! . . . And we even suggested, "We'd feel more comfortable if you'd put us in little groups." But, then, he did it once, and he didn't do it again.

Marisa reported even more disturbing feelings after returning to the American classroom after a semester abroad, also in France. She described her first French class back at her home institution, a public university, as "terrible." The professor, in her view, was the cause: ". . . her accent was terrible, she never finished her sentences." Moreover, she chose aspects of the literature under study that didn't interest Marisa:

> . . . the structure, like what kind of meter was in the poem. . . . That's simple, and I wanted to go more into literature and look at what was the situation during that time, what made them want to write this, because when I was in France, I had a lit class, and it was more like a history class.

Marisa's frustration did not abate after this course, however. She soon felt that studying French in the United States was futile:

> I guess I was just thinking that I wasn't going to learn any more French, and I'd have to wait until I go back to France, and that was my mindset. I felt that I couldn't learn French here, especially after being in France. But coming back, you just think it's worthless learning French from, in an American university. Or the whole aspect of it kind of makes you laugh!

At the same time, however, Marisa was so motivated to "be bilingual" that she realized that she had just hit a "roadblock," as she put it. She was reenergized after enrolling in an LAC immersion semester in French at her university.

Most interviewees, in contrast, gained a greater appreciation of conventional classroom language instruction after an experience abroad. Allison's story is a dramatic example. What she reported learning in her one year of Spanish in the tenth grade was how to sing José Feliciano's

"Feliz Navidad." Yet, although she gave up on Spanish in high school because she could not seem to "grasp" what learning a foreign language entailed, Allison continued to be fascinated with the idea of living in a Spanish-speaking country. After graduation from high school, she left for Bolivia, where a homestay experience had been arranged for her with the family of a student who had studied in her high school. Upon her arrival, her host family enrolled her in school. Because her background in Spanish was so limited, she just sat there. She recalled her first day with these words: "I felt like a complete idiot . . . it was terrible. I went home and cried, . . . 'Don't make me go back.'" Sympathetic English-speaking students took her under their wing, and her host family spoke English with her at home. With no comprehensible input in Spanish, however, Allison felt disoriented and anxious and was making little progress in understanding or speaking the language. Yet, her host family continued to think "that she [would] just absorb it." Finally after about a month, her host family recognized the need for some type of instruction and arranged private grammar lessons for her with a Spanish teacher. When the regular high school year ended after two months in Bolivia, Allison's Spanish was still not sufficient to enroll in college classes. Instead, she entered a private tourism institute, where, as the only American in a class of five people, she took classes in Bolivian geography, history, culture, and accounting and went on the excursions that a future tour guide or travel agency might arrange for clients. Reflecting upon this experience, Allison found that her classes in tourism provided not only an in-depth practical introduction to the country in which she was living, but an intimate atmosphere in which her Spanish (primarily speaking and listening) improved rapidly. In retrospect, however, she expressed the opinion that her nine-month stay in Bolivia would have been enriched by previous classroom study,

> 'Cause when you get down there and don't know anything . . . you're kind of wasting what little time you have. . . . I think that if I would have had . . . a good, maybe a year in college . . . or even a couple of years in high school . . . and then gone down, I would have improved so much more.

Since returning from Bolivia, she has taken Spanish classes at a community college and a public university, participated in an LAC immersion program in Spanish, started Portuguese, and was preparing to leave for Brazil when interviewed.

The majority of interviewees believed, in retrospect, that a combination of conventional classroom and non-traditional experiences was essential to their developing an adequate level of linguistic proficiency. For example, in an extended reflection upon her various language learning experiences in high school and college classes, in Mexico while participating in a fourteen-month study/mission program, and in a variety of LAC classes at her college, Barbara paid tribute to her high school Spanish teacher and program for starting her off toward language as experiences, and not only as books or collections of irregular verbs.

> I left high school thinking that I hadn't learned all that much in Spanish class. I enjoyed it usually, but I didn't feel like I'd learned all that much. Now that I've seen Spanish taught in a number of ways and now that I've had to teach Spanish, I've had a chance to look back on my high school experience and realize how good it was. Maybe I really wasn't conversationally proficient when I left high school at all, but I had the right kind of learning experiences, I had hands-on learning, it wasn't straight drill. Yes, we conjugated verbs on the blackboard, but we were very involved in our learning. We dramatized fairy tales, we did demonstration speeches, we taught the class how to make malts in Spanish, we did those things. We had a teacher who was willing to take us on trips abroad, to smuggle us out of the school and go for the Mexican buffet at the Holiday Inn, things like that. I really appreciate my high school Spanish classes and my Spanish teacher much more six years later than I ever did at the time.

However, even more important in her eyes than this initial high school experience was the ability to continue to weave together both in-class and out-of-class learning into a meaningful whole. Barbara explained:

> I really see my experience in terms of the model of experiential language learning because it was circular, cyclical. . . . I experienced the language and the culture, and then I had an opportunity to dissect it, to analyze it, to look at it in an academic light, and then continue to experience it.

The interviewees who reported most positively about the relationships between in-class and out-of-class learning were those six adult participants in summer residential immersion programs. In these programs participants do not have to forge links between multiple learning environments as much as take advantage of ready-made connections. Although all six made it clear that one or more summers in a residential immersion program could never substitute for an in-depth experience in the target culture, they viewed the apparently artificial atmosphere of the program as superior in many ways to foreign study at certain stages of language learning precisely because of these carefully orchestrated linkages. Several of them recalled the irony of studying in a foreign country, but lacking, or not taking advantage of, opportunities to really use the language or gain more than a superficial understanding of the target culture. Some lived with host families more interested in practicing their English than in helping their boarders improve their foreign language skills. Others spent too much time around American friends or classmates who refused to speak anything but English outside of class. Yet others found that the only people with whom they could have extended conversations in the target language were other foreign students who had no better grasp of the language than they did. Also, despite being immersed in the target culture, not all interviewees capitalized on the opportunities surrounding them. One person, reiterating comments made by a variety of other participants in the study, recounted that study abroad students' most frequent out-of-class activities often revolved about bars and night life, to the exclusion of other activities. Not only did this prevent students' becoming familiar with a broader range of cultural spaces, activities, behaviors, and/or values, it could often contribute to, as another person explained it, students' returning to the United States with prejudices deeper than those they had held previouly.

In contrast, all summer residential immersion program participants raved about the extensive coordination between in-class and out-of-class elements of the program. Classes are designed to provide a framework for rapid improvement in speaking, listening, reading, and writing; to integrate information about both the "Culture(s)" and "culture(s)" of languages being taught; and also to serve as a forum in which students can further process what they learn outside the class. A multitude of extra-curricular activities complement the structured classroom learning environment. Invited lectures by noted writers, cinematographers, scholars, or government officials; showings of classic or first-run foreign language films; performances by musicians or actors of renown; and art expositions bring the "Culture" of the countries where the languages under study are spoken to the program participants. Indeed, participants noted that such direct access abroad to the variety of invited lecturers or performing artists that one can meet during one summer experience would be impossible. Patricia, a student in a Spanish immersion program who has studied in Spain on three occasions, commented that although the program offered "a superimposed culture, [one that is] not true," it afforded an irreproducible wealth of opportunities. In her words,

> You bring all these people together into one area and they have so many different views. The fact that I've studied with a painter, I've studied with authors, I've met the ex-Vice President of Spain . . . these are things that I would not get if I went to Spain.

Furthermore, clear contexts not normally available in the target culture are provided for such events that enhance students' understanding and appreciation of them. Elise, a student in an Italian immersion program, described how the organization of the program's film series made the simple act of going to the movies a much richer linguistic and cultural experience for her:

> The film expert . . . speaks before every film and says, "Well, these are the things you need to look for. These are the themes, this is . . . [and so forth]." And so . . . it's more than just kind of sitting back and relaxing. You're learning something . . . he will say, "Well, this is spoken in Sicilian dialect" or things like that. So the films are always helpful to your comprehension of the history and the language.

In addition to attending formal events such as lectures, film series, and performances, students can participate in a broad range of activities conducted in the target language: talent shows, theater productions, choirs, informal sing-alongs, soccer teams, folk dance clubs, excursions, banquets, parties, dances. There are so many options that one participant acknowledged that one could be busy all summer without even registering for classes. Another participant spoke of feeling overwhelmed, at times, with the wealth of options available in and out of the classroom:

> The object of the program is to give us the best opportunity to take advantage of having all of these materials and all of these resources available, [but] sometimes I feel as if I haven't quite absorbed it, and I need more time and I need to slow down.

Continuing in the same vein, he commented on the need for more extensive individual reflection on learning activities that seemed to be whizzing by too quickly.

> Maybe that's one of the disadvantages of an intensive program. Everything comes at you so quickly you don't have time. . . . I sort of feel that I'm learning lots of things, and there's a lot of interesting material, but I almost say to myself, "That's nice. Now, I'm going to put that aside, and at the end of the summer when the program's over, at my own pace, I'll take a good look at it."

Yet, despite the pace, the link between out-of-class activities and classroom learning is clear to participants. For example, a student in an Arabic-language residential summer immersion program, Lee, spoke of the ties between performing in a play and mastering new grammar concepts in class:

> [I was in a] play; it was a history of Egypt, and I was the villain who murdered the pharaohs. . . . [It was good] having to memorize those lines. Even now, I'm learning new grammar, and I think, "Oh, that was in the play!" And those lines will stay with me for good.

Moreover, the value of learning in an environment where such connections are frequent versus the value of being in a foreign country was emphasized again by Patricia.

> A lot of people said, "Why don't you do a semester [abroad]?" I thought, "Am I going to be part of a chorus? Am I going to be in a theater? Am I going to do different things that bring me closer to other people?" I don't know.

But, in the view of the immersion program participants, the glue that holds this plethora of classes, events, and activities together is the requirement that students pledge not to use any language but the target language for the duration of the summer program. In the first place, as one person noted, this requirement guarantees that program participants will be genuinely motivated to use the language and dedicated to pursuing common goals. Furthermore, it maximizes opportunities for speaking and listening practice with sympathetic and responsive interlocutors, both native- and non-native speakers, of different age groups and professional backgrounds. Most importantly, however, it makes round-the-clock use of the target language seem natural. Elise commented on the significance of such a no-English requirement for her as a language learner.

> [It's] a really, really important part of the program, and a lot of people find that [it], especially at first, is very superficial. You're standing there, and you're struggling to get these words out, and you're speaking to someone who's also struggling to get these words out. And you're both thinking, "We could be speaking English right now, and we'd be communicating fine." And you feel a little bit uneasy at first, because you know perfectly well that everybody speaks English, and . . . you're sitting there, trying to express that you have to go to the store or something like that, and it takes [you] twenty minutes. But, it's a vital part of the program, because you are forced to . . . figure out a way [to express yourself]. . . . And so, it's really important. It's hard sometimes, I've noticed, in the dorms. It's hard in the morning when I first wake up being that I'm not speaking my native language. . . . But, then, after a couple of hours, you get used to it. The thing about speaking it in the dorms, in the cafeteria, is that after a certain period of time, you really build up a relationship with . . . people in Italian. . . . I would be more uncomfortable speaking English with [both students and teachers] than I would [be] struggling sometimes in Italian. . . . That's what makes it important—you build relationships in Italian. Probably the most vital part of the whole program is that you go to dinner and speak Italian, and you speak Italian in the dorms, and you wake up in the morning, "Ciao! Come sta?". . . it's really important.

No matter what type(s) of non-traditional learning environments the twenty interviewees had experienced, their attempts to weave them together with their classroom experiences always resulted in their developing personal learning strategies, techniques, or "tricks." Activities as mundane as reading every label, box, or scrap of paper with printing on it or intentionally eavesdropping on the conversations of native speakers on the bus, in stores, before and after daily Mass, provided a wealth of vocabulary that many interviewees recorded for future use. Many reported keeping notebooks of expressions or "million dollar words" that they could practice on their own and later interject into conversations. Frank developed a sophisticated personal dictionary system while studying in France:

> I bought a French address book that didn't have the lines that say name, etc., and I used it as a dictionary. . . . I would take a word that I wanted to remember [and] I'd write it under that letter in my French address book. . . . What I would do is I would write down the word, and I would write down a definition in French, so that I wasn't writing down an English definition unless I couldn't think of how to explain it in French. And, then, I'd write a context of how it was used so I'd remember how to use it, because oftentimes, it was familiar French phrases that I was learning, but there are certain contexts when you use them and certain ones when you don't. I wanted to remember how [a phrase] had been used in the past, so that if I ever went to use it again, I wasn't using it inappropriately.

Others kept diaries in their foreign languages, where they reinforced new vocabulary through writing. Many spoke of going to the movies, watching television, and listening to the radio as important means of improving their comprehension. As a student in Mexico, Barbara became aware that sympathetic native speakers were modifying their speech for her; listening to the radio helped her learn to deal with authentic language:

> I knew that I had arrived at some point when I could listen to the radio and I could pick out words to the songs, and I could—they would stick in my head—and I could sing along later, when I could understand what the announcers were saying, when I could understand the weather forecast, things like that that were meant for native speakers of the language. That really encouraged me in my comprehension because outside of that, people were still adjusting their speaking and their vocabulary for me, and [the radio] was the case where there were no adjustments made at all. So that was a major thing.

Frank acknowledged similar benefits from listening to the radio in France and worked to really absorb the language he heard by actually taking dictation from news broadcasts on a daily basis. While in Costa Rica, Neil would copy songs off the radio and translate them into English to work on both comprehension and vocabulary. Irina noted the immediate effects that watching television in France had on her ability to speak

French: ". . . if I'd watch TV for a couple hours, [then] if I'd talk on the phone or something, I'd be a lot more together, and it was just like so much good French in my head at once . . . it had a really positive effect on me."

But for the vast majority of interviewees, the thread that wove together all types of language learning was the opportunity to speak the language and use it to interact with people and build personal relationships based on common interests, trust, and shared experiences. It is this important facet of language learning, glimpses of which have been sprinkled throughout this chapter thus far, that we will explore in greater depth below.

## The Interpersonal Dimension of Language Learning and Use

> Often . . . I think you meet a person who is interesting . . .
> and that person sort of leads you in through a door that opens
> to the world of that language.
> —Lee, student in an Arabic summer immersion program

As the twenty volunteers for this study described a mosaic of experiences learning languages here and abroad, at camps or summer residential immersion programs, in foreign language classes or studying other subject areas through the medium of a foreign language, it became evident that for the vast majority, the most important dimension of all their experiences was how they facilitated or inspired interaction with other speakers of that language. For many, the most effective way of learning revolved around talking with friends or host family members. For others, sharing a language cemented bonds with classmates or made possible new relationships with native-speakers. For practically all interviewees, their most memorable experiences using their foreign language(s) were those in which real communication with people important to them had taken place. Finally, for the majority, the ability to build relationships through a language was the signal that a foreign language was no longer just a subject to be studied, but had instead become a way of life.

The only interviewees who did not share this enthusiasm for using their foreign language in interpersonal interactions outside the classroom were ten-year-old Camille and twelve-year-old David. Their previous comments on language use in their school remind us that, consciously or unconsciously, they and their friends at school have developed a pattern of using English in social interactions and other contexts in which language choice is not a function of teacher or school dictates. Despite this pattern, both David and Camille, like the other participants in the study, articulated the importance of being able to communicate with native speakers of other languages. Yet, neither could personally recount instances in which his or her Spanish had become a bridge to building friendships independent of an educational context. While on a family vacation in Central America, Camille reported that hearing Spanish all around her "felt normal . . . 'cause we hear a lot of Spanish [at school]." At the same time, she did not recall any situations in which she communicated personally with native speakers. David's face lit up when he spoke of using Spanish in class field trips in the Puerto Rican neighborhood surrounding his school, but his out-of-class use of Spanish was limited to watching soccer games on Spanish-language television. It seems likely that Camille's and David's ages have been the primary factor limiting their interactions with native speakers of Spanish outside school.

One of the most vocal and eloquent of all interviewees in emphasizing the interpersonal dimension of language learning and language use was Frank. Recalling his semester-long study abroad experience in France, he reflected on the value of the homestay component of his program, highlighting his interaction with his French family:

> I think learning with the family was probably one of the biggest experiences . . . so much of learning can go on outside of a classroom. Learning about mannerisms, and how French people view different world relations, their relations to the United States, and how I'm viewed as an American in Europe. . . .

Specifically, Frank focused on extended mealtime discussions as the arena in which his mind and his linguistic skills were challenged.

> I think a lot of my learning at home went on at the dinner table. The whole idea and concept of a meal in France is so drastically different from the United States. It's so much more than just *nourishment for the day*. It's *nourishment for the mind*. I had some of the most intellectual discussions I've ever had in my life in France with my family. I lived with a very intelligent family. The mother was the director of a school over there, and the husband was a retired salesman who'd traveled all over Europe. And so, I really had a unique experience living with them. We would discuss religion, we would discuss politics, the educational system in the U.S. versus France, telephone bills and how telephones works in the U.S. versus France, learning things like you put your hands here [on the table] where you're at the dinner table, or you fold them, you don't put them in your lap.

Reviewing the value of what he learned from his French host family, Frank summed it up in this way:

> I think it was a lot of vocabulary outside of the classroom I learned from the family, the familiar French that you really don't have a chance to learn, except in conversation with young people, with old people—words that aren't taught in textbooks, phrases that you can say with a very proper language, but you can also say very easily with a familiar language if you know the people you're talking to. Those are the types of things that I learned. It's like you wouldn't go to an English class in France and learn American slang, probably.

Mealtime in France with an exceedingly supportive host family became, for Frank, a time in which vocabulary acquisition, language use and practice, insights into customs and daily life behaviors, cross-cultural analysis, and interdisciplinary knowledge were integrated together in a natural fashion. Food for thought did indeed accompany sustenance for the body.

In other cases, classroom assignments set the stage for relationships that transcended the work at hand as interviewees bonded with others, united not only by their common language, but also by their shared experiences. Multiple comments from participants in summer residential immersion programs have already alluded to this as a daily reality for them. Yet, a variety of other interviewees, too, treasured such interactions. Barbara told of a research project to be based on interviews assigned while she was in Mexico on a study/mission program. Four years later, she chuckled at the grammar errors that pepper her final written project on the romantic and family lives of the Mexican women she interviewed. At the same time, she recalled the importance of the project for her as a language learner and a person.

> I was very excited [doing the project]. I was very excited that I could talk to, in this case, it was three generations of Mexican women, and a lot of them from the same family. I talked to a grandmother, mother, and daughter, and then the daughter had a baby already, so that was exciting because it was real communication. I was finding out very real things about these people, and they were women. It was an interesting move to make because I was used to spending time with them on an informal level and just talking about tortillas and food, but this was moving our relationship up to a different level. And, not only was that good for me, but I think they thought it was really neat that somebody was interviewing them about their lives, so there were a lot of really positive things about that project.

When asked if the project had any long-lasting consequences, she replied:

> It definitely had consequences in my relationships with some of them. The [women] that I normally had more contact with anyway—it really in-

creased the level of intimacy there. A couple of the women I interviewed I really didn't see on a regular basis, so it didn't affect those relationships. But the ones that I saw on a weekly basis and a few on a daily basis, it really did affect those relationships. I did interview my host mother as part of that, and she and I have maintained a very, very close relationship, and I think it does have a lot to do with that particular interview, because she shared things with me that she loved to talk about, but that she didn't normally have a forum to talk about. So, it definitely affected the relationship. I don't know that it affected my language skills or my language acquisition at that point. . . . It did [make a change in the way I felt about my language skills] because I was able to do something with my language skills that I hadn't considered doing before.

In a similar fashion, the four interviewees who had participated in multi-course LAC immersion semesters emphasized the relationships that developed among classmates as they worked and learned together. For the first time ever, those LAC students enrolled in large public universities actually got to know their classmates and socialized with them outside of class. "We had a bond, you know," explained Neil, ". . . they're [the program participants] all my best friends right now." They studied together before and after class, went to plays, movies, dinner, discos, speaking Spanish (or French) all the time. As Allison commented with regard to these group activities, ". . . every time you're speaking Spanish, it's helping." Even students at small colleges who routinely know a high percentage of students on their campus enjoyed a greater degree of intimacy with classmates. Barbara explained that the biggest influence her LAC experiences had on her related to her relationships with other people. In her words,

It made me much more willing to get together and talk with people, because I realized that we're not all getting the exact same thing from [a] text, so not only do we benefit when we get back together and speak in Spanish, practice our Spanish, talk about Spanish, but we're also sharing information. Before that, I wasn't always confident that my peers had much to share or I thought we were getting the same thing out of it, so there was no need to repeat . . . information. So, [the LAC courses] made me willing to work with groups and collaborate with people much more so.

In a particularly revealing example, she recounted with pride and fondness her experiences in a Spanish-language LAC immersion semester:

By the time the semester was ending, we were committed to each other, not to just the material we were studying, and for students who were normally very competitive, we ended up working together. . . . I remember very vividly studying for a final exam with some of the other women in the class who, I don't want to say they'd been enemies before, but they'd been more like political opponents before this course. Nonetheless

> . . . we'd learned these things together, we'd studied them together, we
> got together, and we continued to discuss them to prepare for our final,
> and it didn't matter at that point who got what grade because we were all
> in it for the learning . . . a lot of that was based on the shared language
> that we'd used, and [that] shared language being a language other than
> our own . . . I think it made the bond stronger.

As the various interviewees related their experiences developing new
relationships through the languages they were studying, it became apparent that perhaps some of the most satisfying ones were those that
were in no way linked to a specific program, course, or assignment. The
moment of triumph for many people was when they could connect with
native speakers on their own, when they were accepted freely by disin-
terested persons with no obligation to converse with them at the dinner
table, before or after class, or in a dormitory. For some, this moment
was a simple one. Gayle, who studied in China, spoke of mixed emotions. On the one hand, she felt isolated from the Chinese people in a
society where forced segregation between foreigners and the Chinese
was the norm. But, on the other, she came to appreciate the graciousness
and courtesy of the Chinese people, who, "in such awe to see people
with pale skin, tall . . . strange human beings that can speak their language," were effusive in their compliments. In her words,

> The moment of triumph in my life would have been . . . while we were
> sitting there waiting [while on a tour], and [a woman] started asking ques-
> tions, and she said, "Oh, you speak so well, so well." And, then . . . [all
> the Chinese people waiting there] were all saying, "Oh, [you speak] so
> well."

For others, like Barbara, this moment was when she was treated not
like a language student, but as "just another" member of the group.
While in Mexico, she was invited to give a sermon about Moses, based
on verses from Deuteronomy, at an independent Protestant church. She
recalled "pulling out all the stops" as she prepared it, pushing her developing Spanish-language skills to their limit and writing out the complete text in longhand. Afterwards, she felt:

> An amazing sense of accomplishment. . . . [The sermon] was very . . .
> carefully planned, and I felt pretty confident going up to give it, but . . .
> the thing that made me feel so proud of myself was that here in the United
> States sermons are about twenty minutes long. Well, in Mexico, they're
> an hour to an hour and a half long, and I knew I wasn't going to speak
> for an hour and a half, but I did speak for forty-five minutes, and . . .
> usually time doesn't mean that much to me, but being able to extend dis-
> course for forty-five minutes in that setting, I patted myself on the back
> and said, "That was good."

She had been treated like an adult and not as a study abroad student; she had been given a task that would be a challenge for a native speaker, had risen to the occasion, and been received as part of the community. And when feedback came from members of the congregation, they focused on the *message* of her sermon, not its linguistic features.

Yet other interviewees were most animated when speaking about relationships whose beginnings were totally serendipitous. Elise enthusiastically narrated such a chance encounter that changed her life during the Pope's visit to the U.S. in 1993.

> One of the most exciting things that happened [to me] was last summer . . . they had set up a little museum in a historical building called "The Vatican Treasures," where they [had] . . . all these little relics from the actual Vatican Museum in Italy. And the three girls that were working in the shop were all Italian, they were from Rome, and they had come over with all this stuff to sell and really needed help. So, I volunteered and helped . . . them, and we only spoke Italian the whole time. And, it was really one of the "funnest" experiences I've ever had, because I was really a translator for the first time in my life, because they knew some English, but my Italian was probably better than their English, and we ended up becoming great friends . . . we ended up doing quite a bit as well . . . going for cappuccino and coffee. They're in Rome now, and I'm going to be in Italy next year, and we . . . have plans to get together. . . . I would have never, obviously, [have] had that experience without knowing Italian, because it was my Italian that introduced me to them.

Not only will this experience possibly lead on to lasting friendships, but it and others she has had at summer residential immersion programs have also given Elise a new view of herself in light of her abilities to use Italian.

> It's just done so much for my self-confidence to see what I've accomplished in two years, with this language . . . that I can make speeches and act in plays and make friendships, and all that based on a language that I've known for two years instead of thirty.

The thrill of using language as a means to build interpersonal relationships permeated the stories of the interviewees. Moreover, it continues to motivate them to look for every opportunity to use their foreign language with others who speak it. Person after person spoke of always being ready for the fortuitous encounter with speakers of their foreign language(s) as well as intentionally searching for situations in which they can make use of their language skills. Elise, for example, goes weekly to an "Italian table" at a restaurant in the city where she resides to eat and speak Italian with those who gather there. As she said, "I've met a lot of people through that, and when you have the common interest

. . . in Italian, you already have a place to start to get to know these people." Furthermore, she revealed that she "will only speak Italian with people that speak it," no matter where she is. Many interviewees have become involved in volunteer activities in which their language skills are needed. A tally of some of these includes such diverse endeavors as: working with Russian-language Jewish refugees in the United States; volunteering at a day care center in Russia; and serving as hosts for Japanese visitors during Japan-America Week celebrations, for the Chinese national delegation for the Special Olympics, and for participants in similar international events.

Finally, several of those who are no longer full-time students have pursued careers in which they can use their foreign languages, either informally or as an essential part of their jobs. For example, Lee, an ESL instructor, uses his languages, when possible, to break the ice with his students. As he explained,

> There was one older Russian lady who came to class, and she said that had I not said anything to her in her own language the first day, she wouldn't have come back because she was too afraid, so [speaking their language] encourages them. And also, when they hear the mistakes that I make, it puts us on an equal footing, and I think that's good psychology sometimes. . . . Even the person with very little education at all knows more than I do in that language, and somehow that seems to create a new bond between us, as though, "Well, if he can learn my language, maybe I can learn his."

Helen, a veteran of several study abroad and summer residential immersion experiences, has used her foreign languages in a position with an advertising firm that specializes in ethnic marketing. At the time of his interview, Frank was preparing to begin a new job with an international accounting firm. Despite the fact that he had not yet finished his course work to qualify to sit for the CPA exam, his international experiences and proficiency in French were major factors in his being hired. As he embarks upon his career, he is looking forward to the opportunity to spend some time abroad and/or work in the firm's international division in the near future. Until that time comes, though, he plans to keep his French conversational skills from getting rusty by joining a local group of professional people who meet on a regular basis to talk about current events and converse in French.

The interpersonal dimension of language learning and use that interviewees described took many different forms: acquiring and maintaining language skills by interacting with others, feeling the joy of making oneself understood without intermediaries, bonding through shared experiences made possible by a common language, developing rewarding personal and professional relationships with native speakers, using a language to become good-will ambassadors between peoples of different national origins. The participants in this study made clear time and time again that people had opened the doors to new languages and that new languages had opened the doors to new people and new friendships. More than anything else, for them, effective language learning and use were social acts that led to being part of a community.

The interviewees' focus on language learning and use with regard to interaction with native speakers seems to imply that as a group they define "knowing" a foreign language in terms of being able to speak it. It is evident that for the majority of them, the doors opened by the native speakers they have met lead into a world of effective and rewarding interpersonal communication. Yet, this is not a world unconnected to other language skills—listening, reading, and writing—that may be less immediately oriented toward person-to-person interaction, but which may make possible another type of communication over time and space.

Repeatedly throughout this study, the majority of interviewees college-aged or older emphasized the multi-faceted and cyclical nature of language learning. Interspersed throughout their enthusiastic comments relating how they built bonds of friendship through speaking a foreign language were references to how developing other language skills has enriched their encounters with other people and cultures. Strengthening their listening comprehension, for example, through activities as diverse as in-class note taking and writing dictations and watching television news broadcasts live or by satellite in a language laboratory, made many interviewees feel more capable of engaging in true dialogues in a culturally appropriate fashion. As Lee commented:

> From my experience, I've learned that it helps to expose yourself to a lot of the language first, and then begin to speak. And that way you start from the way *they* say things, rather than from . . . [thinking] in English in this situation, "I need to use this expression, so how do I do that in Arabic?" Whereas in Arabic, they might not even say *anything* in that situation.

Acquiring new information through listening (to everything from popular music to television interviews to classical theater productions) and reading (from tourist brochures to current economic policy statements to a nation's great works of literature) was viewed as essential for enriching one's understanding of the culture of one's interlocutors. For, without a shared cultural repertoire, words may be exchanged, but real communication is unlikely to take place. Frank put it this way:

> I think reading texts in the original French gives you more of an insight
> into French culture, maybe a French mindset . . . because when you know
> [how to read] French, you can learn about the other culture, and there's
> a lot that language can tell you. Words that are important in one language
> may not be important in another language, and that shows you the value
> of . . . certain aspects that are prevalent in a culture.

Writing was seen as an activity that enabled learners to process new
cultural information while at the same time allowing them to practice
new registers of language. New ideas and new discourse together became part of active knowledge.

While interpersonal interaction through speaking was seen as the
most immediate entry into the world of those languages, it was certainly
not the only doorway. Several interviewees who had participated in either
LAC courses or summer residential immersion programs spoke of an
intellectual entry into these other worlds, too, through reading.

In many instances, an ability to read texts in the original language
was cited as the key to understanding other peoples and cultures without
the filter of one's native language. Marisa, for example, expressed her
excitement at taking an LAC course on the European Community with
materials in French so new that there had not even been time to translate
them into English. She felt that the information she learned through them
was more up-to-date and thus more "real" than any translation could
have provided. Barbara, a veteran of several LAC courses, discussed at
greater length the value of reading in the original language.

> I've seen translations; I know what they lose. So . . . I prefer to read . . .
> texts in the language they're [originally] written in. . . . I like to read my
> primary texts in Spanish, because there are a lot of nuances, especially
> about relationships and political underpinnings.

Such was Barbara's enthusiasm for learning through reading that her
response when asked how she would convince reluctant college students
of the value of learning a foreign language, was as follows.

> I would try to engage them in a conversation about the interdisciplinary
> nature of living. I would say, "You like philosophy? Oh, ever heard of
> Spinoza? Know anything about him? . . . Would you like to read some-
> thing . . . that he originally wrote, as opposed to something [written about
> him] down the line?"

Other LAC and summer residential immersion students echoed similar
sentiments about the academic dimension of learning and using a foreign
language. In another case, reading knowledge of a language—Arabic—
was seen as an introduction not only to the Arab world, but to other
cultures that had had extensive contact with Arabic-speaking peoples.

In Lee's words,

> To me, Arabic was the Latin and Greek of the Muslim world, and Persian and Turkish, Swahili and Malay, and Indonesian were extensively [derived] from Arabic. Even Spanish has a lot of Arabic words, and, so to me, [Arabic is] a key to other languages in a way.

One of the most striking reflections on the intellectual rewards of being able to use a foreign language was shared by Elise. Previously, we have followed Elise through various stages of her story: giving up on French in high school because of its perceived irrelevance, experiencing the joy of studying Italian as a motivated adult learner, and building friendships based through shared language. But for Elise, studying Italian not only welcomed her into a community of Italian speakers, it also illuminated her main area of professional interest—art history—and allowed her access to a much richer view of her academic discipline than would have been possible without it.

> I'd always been interested in Italian art, but now I'm able to do some research, obviously, in Italian, and . . . because I've continued with Italian, I've taken a lot of history and culture courses, which I . . . wouldn't have taken in the Art History Department, which have really given me a much more solid basis for what I've learned in the art history I've taken. And, I'm aware, much more aware of the literature, of the history, of the politics during the Renaissance, how Italy actually was established . . . how the development [progressed] from city-state to a unified country. And that is really important when you consider the art of one period, to consider it as a whole, and when you take an art history class, obviously you touch on that, but you're not totally immersed in it, because there's just not time.

Among the individuals in this study, face-to-face conversation was doubtless the most immediately gratifying and rewarding motivation for language learning. Nevertheless, these last comments by Elise and others clearly recognize the contribution of their other language skills, especially reading, in giving them access to fascinating worlds quite beyond the realm of personal encounters.

## What Is the Value of a Foreign Language?

> . . . I just feel like you're isolated if you just know one thing, one culture, one language. . .
> —Marisa, former participant in French-language LAC and study abroad programs

For the twenty people I interviewed for this study, the question of whether or not foreign languages were of value for U.S. society was not an issue. As a result of their meaningful personal encounters with other languages and the people who speak them outside of the conventional classroom, the great majority of interviewees were convinced that the ability to use a foreign language was important for them personally and for our society as a whole. Instead, the question was one of articulating the diverse aspects of the value of knowing another language: the personal, the academic, the practical, the professional, the abstract. Each of these is touched on briefly below.

Not only did the participants in this study speak of the multiple and diverse ways in which their study or use of a foreign language had influenced their lives up to the moment in which they were interviewed, all twenty visualized themselves in endeavors in which they would need one or more foreign languages in the future, both near and distant. To begin with, those who had made significant friendships through a foreign language assumed that they would continue those friendships—in the language of the first encounter. Person after person echoed Kathryn's view that a relationship is forever defined by the language in which it is first established, and that it would be simply unthinkable to envision the relationship in any other language. Underlying their comments was the feeling that they had been accepted into a community whose members were united by a common language and that they would continue to strengthen their ties to that community through maintaining current friendships and developing new ones down the road.

As the majority of those interviewed are still part- or full-time students, they saw continued, and very pragmatic, links between language learning and their academic life. Ten-year-old Camille thought that continuing to learn Spanish now would make it easier for her in high school. Julie, a veteran of multiple language camps, plans to continue her study of Japanese to qualify for an International Baccalaureate diploma through her high school. Successful completion of the IB program, she believes, will guarantee her admittance to the college of her choice and qualify her for Advanced Placement credit worth up to a year of college study. The other high school students and recent graduates look forward to continuing language study in college and going overseas, even if they do not yet know what major(s) they would like to pursue. For them, choosing a major will not force a choice between a language and some other discipline; it will involve selecting a major that will *complement* their foreign language(s). The current undergraduate students spoke enthusiastically of plans for participating in additional study abroad programs or LAC courses. Marisa, for example, highlighted how studying in France and completing an LAC immersion program in French at her university had changed her outlook on the effectiveness of different ways to learn a language. As she put it, "If I asked to take astronomy, it should be in French—that's what I feel, anyway." For her, "it's not the subject . . . it's the language" that is important in her studies. The graduate students, whose participation in non-traditional programs already demonstrated their level of academic and personal commitment to foreign language study, looked forward to the next stage awaiting them.

Most interviewees acknowledged very practical reasons for knowing a language. Foremost among these was the frequent opinion that ability to speak a foreign language both facilitates and enriches travel abroad in a world in which more and more people venture beyond the borders of their homeland for pleasure or business. Those who had already lived or studied in another country had discovered the textures in other societies that can only be perceived when one explores foreign cultures through the medium of the native language. Realizing that many, if not most, people who study languages in schools, colleges, and universities forget them soon after their studies end, others suggested that the experience of having studied another culture through its own language may leave important conceptual knowledge behind that may facilitate interactions abroad even after language skills have become dormant. In particular, Frank recalled a content-based intermediate language class he took that examined selected aspects of French culture. In commenting on the value of that course, he explained:

> For those people who only go through that . . . semester, [the culture] is what they're going to remember of French. They may not remember forever how to say, "My name is [Frank]," but they probably will remember things about the French people. . . . People who just wanted [to finish the foreign language] requirement, they're going to forget their French, but they're going to remember that France is based on a centralized theory where things come together, streets and roads in many cases go through a round center, they go through the center of the city, that there's a very hierarchical system there. They're going to remember those types of things and not necessarily the language . . . you learn so much about the culture and the people by learning the language. Even if you don't remember the *language,* you're going to remember the *people.*

Frank's comments remind us again that language learning is not only skills acquisition for face-to-face communication, but that it also involves higher cognitive skills and makes possible more diverse intellec-

tual endeavors than those available to individuals who inhabit a mono-
lingual world.

The ability to really profit from travel abroad was not the only practical reason mentioned for knowing a foreign language. Being able to
communicate effectively with native speakers of other languages within
our own national borders was also cited. Speakers of Spanish were
acutely aware of this need, as Spanish-speaking populations across North
America rapidly grow more numerous and more visible. Barbara, having
recently accepted a job as a bilingual elementary school teacher, felt that
her many experiences learning Spanish both here and abroad would make
her especially sympathetic to the affective side of the linguistic challenges facing U.S. Hispanics.

> Having experience living in Mexico and struggling to make the transition
> from formal [language] to informal and back to formal, it makes me more
> understanding of the kind of language [Hispanic children] use, because
> U.S. Spanish is—I wouldn't call it Spanglish, because it's something
> [more sophisticated] than that— . . . it's really hard to handle the type of
> language that those students use. I feel like I'm pretty well prepared to
> do that and not to say, "Well, you're saying this wrong," but to say, "Here
> are two situations and one situation needs this kind of language, and [in]
> the other 'blank' is wonderful."

The Spanish-speakers were not the only ones who noticed this need,
however. Teresa, a student of German, commented on the need to accommodate non-English-speakers in our society:

> We're kind of secluded in the thought that all you need is English, but
> things are changing. There's a lot more people coming from different
> countries and . . . [even in] a normal job you will be confronted by some-
> one who hardly speaks English some time, and just to be able to more
> easily communicate with them and have them feel like, "Everything's
> okay" [is important].

In regard to the specific professional value of foreign languages, with
the exception of ten-year-old Camille, all interviewees either have careers with some link to foreign languages and cultures or assume they
will be able to find such careers in the future. Although Camille acknowledged the importance of knowing a foreign language in some careers,
she could not visualize any possible links between her knowledge of
Spanish and her ideal future careers: paleontologist or trial attorney. In
contrast, when the other interviewees who are currently school or college students were asked to imagine their future, they all simply envi-
sioned themselves using a foreign language. Twelve-year-old David,
who aspires to be a television or movie director some day, thought his

Spanish would be a definite advantage to him. He could work with Spanish-speaking actors or actresses and be able to film on location without communication problems. Frank is already en route to a career in international accounting and business, and Neil, who knows the real needs of the Hispanic community where he resides, is actively preparing to be a bilingual firefighter/rescue squad member. Others still in high school or college may not have made definite career plans, but they take for granted that opportunities to use their foreign language will await them. Statements such as "I think I'll probably have an occupation where I'll need foreign languages somehow," "I guess I see myself being fluent in Spanish . . . and definitely speaking Spanish with whatever I do, be it business or international business, or teaching school or social work. I haven't really decided yet," or "I always want to have aspects of French culture or French speaking in my life; I definitely want a job where I will be using my language, whether it's here or in France. I feel like I'm pretty open to go wherever" were frequent. Whether or not such career opportunities will actually materialize in the future did not seem to enter their minds. The adult interviewees who were no longer full-time students all have careers in which languages play a role, either informally or formally. Yet, for them, their professional lives are just one more facet of a multi-linguistic and multi-cultural lifestyle that they have. They use foreign languages not only as job skills, but as "life skills," to borrow a phrase from Patricia.

Finally, those interviewees who went beyond the immediate personal, academic, practical, and professional importance of learning foreign languages to the realm of the abstract centered their comments around themes of heightened cross-cultural awareness and the values of broadening one's horizons in a world being made smaller by technology. Gayle spoke of the impact that her experiences learning Chinese and studying in China had had on her view of the world: ". . . it takes away the . . . sense of 'Well, this is how things are supposed to be, and this is the way things are.' . . . It just made me aware that the world is a really varied place, and that's just a reassuring thing to think about. . . ." Lee reiterated the same thoughts, but with different words:

> [Knowing a foreign language] makes you more broad-minded about the world in general, life in general. . . . It's like putting on a different color of glasses and looking at the world in a different way, or drawing a different map of the world. And I think that means that it gives you a chance to step outside your own cultural background and turn around and look at it from another point of view and say: "Oh, I never thought of it that way. Maybe that's right." You don't necessarily have to agree with that other

point of view all the time, but if you spend all your life in a well and you never go outside the well, you're just a frog in a well. You'll never see anything but the well.

But, ultimately, the real worth of "going outside the well" may be not only what one learns about the world beyond, but also what one learns about the world within. Learning a new language is not just an intellectual pursuit; it is an experience that transforms people, that leads them to explore the depths of their own lives as they enter the worlds of others. In his parting words, Frank left me with this enthusiastic exhortation:

> I'd tell everybody—students, parents, anybody I come in contact with— that if there's any chance that you can learn a foreign language and go to a foreign country, do it! Because you can learn so much more about the people, the world, you get to see a different vision of what a different media other than the U.S. media presents, you get to see so much more. Going abroad and living outside of the U.S.—or even outside of your normal community—is such a valuable experience personally because you grow so much internally.

# Conclusion

These voices from beyond the classroom tell rich and varied tales. Stories of inspiration and frustration abound: of being able to "soak up language like a sponge" and of not being able to remember those irregular verb forms, of moments of triumph when things finally click and periods of anxiety when nothing makes sense, of the joys of becoming part of a new community and the loneliness of isolation when language is insufficient for communication. These stories are the experiences of twenty individuals who, for a variety of reasons, experimented with learning languages beyond the confines of the conventional classroom. Without overgeneralizing based on this small, select sample, what can we learn from their experiences?

Without exception, all interviewees both value and enjoy being able to use one or more foreign languages. Furthermore, they envision for themselves futures in which the(se) language(s) play(s) an on-going role. Yet the path to the point where they began to appreciate and take pleasure in learning and using languages was neither uniform nor easy. Very few interviewees reported like Steve, a former German language camper, that "it never really felt like we were actually learning German. . . . It was all kind of [like] we absorbed it. . . ." Most emphasized the effort that it took to learn and, in many cases, to become aware of the value of learning a language. Indeed, many—those who struggled and dropped out, those who were bored in class, those who did minimal work, those who thought most class activities were corny or weird—were not the types of classroom learners that some foreign language educators might anticipate would become the enthusiastic language learners they are now. But, the plots of most interviewees' stories thickened when something—a special teacher, memorable class activities, a first experience abroad, connecting with a real native speaker of the language—piqued their interest. At that point, learning a language became useful, meaningful, and real. Moreover, except in the cases of those children who began their language study in dual-language schools or summer language camps, it was often at that point that they became particularly interested in continuing their study in one or more types of non-traditional learning environment such as those described in this chapter.

As the interviewees began to diversify the environments in which they were learning languages, the relationships between their in-class and out-of-class experiences became more complex. Those still in grade school or high school often found that their highly motivating "extra" experiences in language camps or short-term foreign study programs created situations in which they no longer fit into the limited curricular options at their schools. Those who could often ended up taking college-level language classes at local colleges or universities. Those who could not sometimes sat through classes that repeated what they already knew. College-aged interviewees returning from study abroad programs frequently came back with an increased appreciation for what they had learned—or could have, or should have learned—in conventional classrooms. Energized by the opportunity to use a language, many reentered the classroom with a strong desire to really work on the bits and pieces of language (read, grammar) that they now realized they needed to perfect their writing and speaking skills. Others found great challenges in adapting their fluent street language to the world of academic discourse or in adjusting to the linguistic limitations of their classmates and/or instructors. A few had to deal with their feelings that no learning environment in the United States could possibly contribute anything to their knowledge of a language and culture. For the latter, access to LAC courses or summer residential immersion programs helped bridge the gap between the conventional U.S. classroom and the experience abroad and allowed them to use their knowledge of a foreign language to explore disciplines outside the realm of the traditional language department. The post-collegiate adult language learners interviewed, all participants in summer residential immersion programs, found that these programs provided for them an ideal combination of effective classroom instruction, intensive language practice, a stimulating intellectual environment, and access to a concentrated wealth of cultural opportunities that could not be encountered abroad even by the most motivated learner. In short, this type of environment facilitated the weaving together of the "experiences" (interpersonal communication) and the "books" (intellectual dimension) of language learning into a masterful whole. Not to be seen as equivalent to extended periods of residence and study abroad, these programs do, however, fill an essential niche, especially for the adult learner with family and professional obligations that may preclude extended stays overseas.

Underlying much of what all interviewees recounted about their experiences was the importance of the interpersonal dimension of language learning. The sparks that motivated most of them to continue on with their languages involved real interactions with people with whom they felt some type of affective connection. And, ultimately, what makes them value knowing languages most is the fact that, through their foreign languages, they have become part of a community of people with shared experiences. Whether this community is an academic one or an extended family, a group of friends or colleagues or an entire society, they feel that they belong. Their languages are no longer simply a subject to study, but part of their lifestyle. Moreover, they live presents or imagine futures for themselves in which languages touch many, if not most, spheres of their lives—the personal, the practical, and the professional.

What impact can stories such as these have on the way teachers and administrators, textbook and instructional materials authors and publishers, and members of the general public view foreign languages in our society? A few final questions may stimulate our continued thinking on this subject.

## Motivation

How do we—or do we—communicate the rationale for foreign language study and requirements? Do our goals for classes and curricula include enhancing motivation in addition to teaching skills, covering specific content areas, and facilitating acquisition of language and/or cultural proficiency? Are we "de-motivating" too many students? If so, why? Can they be "re-motivated"? With limited resources, how can we incorporate more language "experiences" of the type that excite students about learning languages into classrooms too often perceived by students to be dominated by "books"? At the same time, if students perceive the study of "books" to be irrelevant or even detrimental to language learning for the purpose of communication, how can we modify student misconceptions and/or reorient foreign language programs so that "books" (in the sense of the "content" of literature and culture) enrich the multifaceted process of language acquisition in a more explicit fashion (see Henning, 1993)? Must the interpersonal and the intellectual dimensions of foreign language learning be in opposition? How can we help students explore outside of class the real-world uses of languages? Will we be more successful in motivating people to learn languages if we expand alternative types of language instruction, beginning with elementary school immersion programs and continuing on with more flexible, varied and affordable programs overseas and here in the U.S. for high school, college-aged, and adult learners?

## Articulation between Conventional and Non-Traditional Language Learning Environments

Since most language learners start in the classroom, how can we assist them in moving in and out of the classroom? Are our curricula so structured that people returning from language camps, foreign study experiences, or other immersion programs can no longer fit in? What alternatives can we provide for them? Even if our course offerings are limited, can we use such students as resources in such a fashion that they continue to learn at the same time they serve as role models for others? Can we encourage our colleagues in other disciplines to incorporate foreign languages into what they teach, thus broadening the realm of languages beyond the foreign language department?

## Language Learning as Interpersonal Interaction

How can we provide opportunities for more people to experience learning a language as a social interaction? Can we build closer ties between schools and local non-English speaking communities? Can we use the resources of such communities to the benefit of our students and yet provide some needed service in return so that the relationship is genuinely two-way? Can we promote closer contacts between U.S. and foreign students on college campuses? How can we dispel commonly held notions that buying such-and-such series of audiotapes can teach people to talk like natives in thirty days or less without ever having contact with real speakers of the foreign language? How can we use technology to bring more speakers who share a language together rather than to eliminate the human dimension of language learning and use? Finally, how can we better illustrate for our students that the academic dimension of foreign language learning ("the books" of literature classes, for example) aids language learners in developing the cultural—understood here in the broadest sense of the word—background that is an essential part of communicative competence at levels of interpersonal interactions beyond those of "narrowly pragmatic" transactions such as asking directions or getting a hotel room (Henning, 1993)?

## The Value of Knowing Foreign Languages

How can we better communicate the benefits of being able to use foreign languages to all sectors of society? How can we "display" this knowledge as something attractive? Can the media be persuaded to show-case people who use languages in a positive light (e.g., bilingual news reporters who do person-on-the-street interviews abroad without the assistance of an interpreter)? Do people hiring employees in different fields of endeavor value the ability to use foreign languages? Will the interviewees who aspire to future careers in which they use their languages, either formally or informally, find such positions not only because of the immediate, practical applications of their language skills on the job, but also because of the potential for their language ability to be a truly valuable "life skill" that transforms them into persons especially capable of dealing with a rapidly changing world?

These are not new questions. But the voices from beyond the classroom challenge us to think about them again.

# Notes

[1] The italics that appear in quotations throughout the chapter reflect the vocal emphasis that interviewees gave to specific words while speaking.

[2]Throughout this chapter, the acronym LAC will be used to refer to languages across the curriculum programs. Other commonly used acronyms in the professional literature include FLAC and LxC.

[3]Dual-language schools feature instruction in two languages. Various patterns of distributing instruction across languages exist in such schools. For example, morning instruction may be in one language, with afternoon instruction in another, or the language of instruction may vary from day to day. In other schools, some subject areas or classes are taught in one language, and others in the second language, according to overall curricuular goals or the lingusitic background of individual teachers.

[4]I wish to thank all volunteers who participated in this study, as well as the many foreign language educators who cooperated by identifying possible interviewees. Lack of explicit recognition by name of the many teachers and administrators whose collaboration was indispensable to me is meant not to diminish their valuable assistance, but to avoid compromising the identity of interviewees.

A very special note of appreciation goes to Jennifer Bergeson, whose careful and rapid transcription of many interviews greatly facilitated the completion of the study. Many thanks are due also to R. L. Karol for assistance with table design and final formatting of the chapter.

[5]David estimated that approximately 80% of the students enrolled are Puerto Rican, a figure which has not been independently verified.

# References

Curtain, H.A., & Pesola, C.A. (1994). *Languages and children—making the match: Foreign language instruction for an early start grades K–8* (2nd ed.). White Plains, NY: Longman.

Grandin, J.M., Einbeck, K., & von Reinhart, W. (1992). The changing goals of language instruction. In H. Byrnes (Ed.), *Languages for a multicultural world in transition* (pp. 123–163). Lincolnwood, IL: National Textbook.

Henning, S. D. (1993). The integration of language, literature, and culture: Goals and curricular design. *ADFL Bulletin, 24* (2), 51-55.

Hernández, L., & Terry, M. (Eds.). (1994). *Work, study, travel abroad: The whole world handbook, 1994–1995.* New York: St. Martin's Press.

Krueger, M., & Ryan, F. (Eds.). (1993). *Language and content: Discipline- and content-based approaches to language study.* Lexington, MA: D.C. Heath.

*Peterson's study abroad 1994: A guide to semester and year long academic programs.* (1994). Princeton, NJ: Peterson's.

Rosenbusch, M.H. (1991). Elementary school foreign language: The establishment and maintenance of strong programs. *Foreign Language Annals, 24,* 297–314.

Salomone, A. M. (1991). Immersion teachers: What can we learn from them? *Foreign Language Annals, 24,* 57–63.

Steen, S.J. (Ed.). (1994). *Academic year abroad.* New York: Institute of International Education.

Straight, H.S. (Ed.). (1994). *Languages across the curriculum.* Translation Perspectives VII. Binghamton, NY: SUNY.

# Native Speakers as Language Learners

María Teresa Garretón

*Chicago State University*

## Introduction

> I felt I had a more insistent reason for learning Japanese than
> other people because it is my background. It is not something
> I am going to gain, or is going to be an addition to me as a
> person, it is something I have to make up for because I've
> lost it. I'm not where I should be so that is why I have to
> learn Japanese.
> —Rika

This chapter will report on interviews conducted[1] with fifteen "native speakers" of seven languages: Chinese, German, Greek, Japanese, Korean, Polish and Spanish. For the purposes of this study, "native speaker language learner" was defined as anyone who grew up speaking a language other than English at home and studied it formally for at least five years. Twelve of the fifteen people interviewed were born and had lived most of their lives in the United States; the remaining three participants had been born overseas and moved to the U.S. at a young age.

To identify our sample we contacted foreign language departments in several universities in the Chicago area and asked if they had students who would describe themselves as native speakers of the language they were studying. This process helped us identify not only students at those universities, but other potential participants as well. Once we described the project, faculty members were very willing to share information and refer names of alumni and friends.

We interviewed eleven female and four male participants ranging from 12 to 48 years of age.[2] The table below summarizes the characteristics of the participants in this study. The great majority of them attended special language schools on Saturdays or Sundays as they were growing up and only two of them started taking language courses at the university level without prior formal instruction in their language.

| Characteristics of Participants | | | | |
|---|---|---|---|---|
| | *K–8* | *9–12* | *Undergraduate* | *Postgraduate* |
| Female N= 11 | | Stacy [Gr] Maria [Gr] Melissa [C] | Lorena [S] Miné [J] Rika [J] Carol [K] Kiyoko [J] | Christine [J] Maria [G] Rita [S] |
| Male N= 4 | Henry [C] | | Tom [P] Steven [C] | John [S] |
| Total Participants | 1 | 3 | 7 | 4 |

Note. The letters represent the following languages: C = Chinese; G = German; Gr = Greek; J = Japanese; K = Korean; P = Polish; S = Spanish.

As a native speaker of Spanish, the author had a particular interest in this group of language learners. We set out to discover the extent to which the lives of native speakers were affected by their experiences as learners—both in and outside the classroom—of their native language, and how these experiences compared to those of learners of foreign or second languages. As described below, we found that besides the benefits reported by many foreign language learners (e.g., better interaction with people of different cultures, interest in international events, etc.), many native speakers also felt that studying their language was part of an identity-seeking process. What may have started as an unwelcome parental imposition for many of the voices interviewed in this chapter, gradually became a medium to discover what it means to be a Japanese

American, or a Mexican American or a Polish American, in the United States today.

Whilemany factors influenced the participants' language experiences and their attitudes toward language learning (e.g., language, family expectations, socioeconomic status), we found several common themes in the fifteen voices represented in this chapter. The chapter has been organized around those themes, not intending to draw definitive conclusions from a small sample, but rather to focus on certain aspects which could be followed up by further research.

# Voices

Before reporting on the themes suggested by the research, we selected four participants as the main "voices" for the chapter. While the opinions of all fifteen participants are present in this chapter, the following four profiles exemplify the different backgrounds and personal histories we discovered in our interviews. These four individuals had given a great deal of thought to their language learning process and were able to articulate their beliefs and explain their reactions in ways that helped us understand some of the issues highlighted by this group.

These four voices continued the formal study of their native language beyond the level required by their parents and did it for reasons that only became clear to them when they immersed themselves in their language and culture.

## Tom

Tom is an 18-year-old freshman at a private university in Illinois. As the first born in a Polish family, he spoke only Polish until he started going to school; his memories of kindergarten and first grade are not unlike those of other students we interviewed:

> In kindergarten and first grade I really didn't know much English at all. I'd just look up and smile at the teacher and slipped through the class, basically. And I got A's and things, you know, I didn't get bad grades at all. But then again, there were other people who had gone through school illiterate so I can see how it would happen. . . .

Tom's parents have lived in the United States for about twenty years and have always lived in a Polish community in Chicago. Tom's description of this community reflects his exposure to his parents' native language and culture:

> They lived in like a Polish town so you didn't need to know English at all. It was
> a big Polish community so you could go to the Polish stores and if you had
> anything broken, you'd go to a Polish repairman and everything's Polish. So
> when my parents came over, they stayed only in that section. Basically, it's
> just like a small Polish town and my grandma still doesn't know any English
> at all. She's been here for like twenty-five years.

Living in the "Polish town" also influenced Tom's relationships with other
kids, as the following recollection indicates:

> I remember having friends at school; that is basically where they stayed though.
> Actually some of them did live around me. I didn't, I never grasped the idea
> of playing with these kids outside of school until very, very late, third or fourth
> grade. And then I realized: "Oh, you live across the street from me!" And I
> never knew that before because I'd never be outside. I'd stay in. If I did go
> outside it would be in our back yard which was fenced off. We had a three-flat
> [building with three apartments] in Chicago, there were fences all around us.
> I was perfectly content that way. Sometimes my cousins would come over, or
> my mom would bring one of her Polish friends over with their kids and that
> would be my exposure to kids.

Another aspect of Tom's family background that appeared in several other
interviews as well was the role he played in his parents' language learning
process:

> I taught them English. I would teach them what I learned in school every day.
> They'd go along and play with my little exercises and things and they kind of
> went through first through fourth grade that way. They didn't go at the same
> pace I did, you know. After they knew a little, they started going out and could
> go to the store and things and then they wouldn't have to just point at things.
> So they started learning on their own, too.

Tom started his formal study of Polish at age 5 when he attended a Polish
school for four hours every Saturday. The curriculum included four subjects:
grammar, history, geography, and reading. He continued to attend this school
until eighth grade. While in high school, Tom took Spanish and traveled to
Mexico and Poland. He plans to become a lawyer, practice a few years and
then teach at a university.

# Christine

Christine's parents are Japanese; she is the youngest of four children
and grew up in an Illinois suburb. When talking about her experiences
growing up, she recalls,

> We spoke Japanese conversationally at home. Well, it's interesting, the younger
> two kids, myself and my sister, spoke Japanese a lot more actively than the first
> two, my brother and my sister . . . I think because my mother was trying to be

very americanized with the first two kids. In fact, they have only English names, and they spoke only English first, but my sister and I who were the third and fourth, spoke Japanese and understood Japanese and have Japanese middle names.

Christine went to Catholic school until seventh grade and then attended public schools, where she took French for five years. At the same time, she explained that "since my mother was a teacher, I went to Japanese school from the time I was in second grade until I was in college." She laughed as she added "I never saw Saturday cartoons."

Christine attended a large state university where she selected Asian Studies as one of her majors and took intensive Japanese language for two years; she spent two hours a day in Japanese language class plus the language labs outside class time. She explains,

> I found this to be one of the best things I could have done. Japanese language school during my childhood, it was very . . . it was good for me to keep my ear attuned to the language and I think I enjoyed it, as much as a kid can; but, when I was in college I think the reading and writing really came together for me because it was intensive first of all, it was a daily class and the focus was very strong on the written Chinese characters which help you understand the language so much more, it's something like Japanese.

During her junior year, Christine went to Japan and, when she returned, she continued to take other independent study courses dealing with Japanese literature. She worked for Japan Airlines during her college years and has been working in state government for the past seven years.

## Lorena

Lorena is a 22-year-old Spanish major at one of the state universities in Illinois; she is the oldest of four siblings in a Mexican family. Her parents came to the United States in 1971 and have lived in the south side of Chicago since then. She recalls her schooling experience in one of Chicago's public elementary schools:

> I thought it was great, I had some of the best teachers ever, I think . . . I learned a lot, I could say that I learned more in grammar school than I did in high school. I really had these great teachers. High school to me, it's not that I didn't learn as much, but I guess I was scared to advance in the honors classes and I would've liked to change that if I could, but, well . . . I have to try my best now.

Lorena lived in a Mexican neighborhood in Chicago and after attending school for one year [kindergarten], her family returned to Mexico for two years. She recalls coming back to the U.S.:

> I had forgotten the little English that I did know so the only way to do it was to send me to the bilingual teacher, but I would only see her one hour a day,

I think it was three times a week or something, but it was only until fourth grade and after that I stopped going because I guess I didn't need it anymore. . . . For me it worked better, I know that there's a lot of students who have to stick to bilingual [classes], but I was able to handle it in English. I guess my teachers knew that.

Lorena started taking Spanish in her junior year in high school and took it for two years. Her memories are of experiences that, while not unpleasant, were not particularly useful to her:

My junior year I could say I learned a little more because my senior year all we did, and I am not lying, we watched movies and we just played around, we had parties . . . we actually watched soaps in Spanish. [The teacher's] idea was that if we watched soaps, that we would have a better understanding of the language, but we were all native speakers, we didn't need that and then we would watch movies that had nothing to do with education that were . . . some of them were interesting, like they were Spanish folkloric dancing, but they didn't have anything educational.

Although her parents did not speak English at all, they emphasized to their children the value of education.

My father, for one, didn't have a chance to study as he would have liked to because they used to live in the country and they had a farm . . . and he wanted to, but couldn't, so for him it was like his dream for us to go to school. It is not like he pushed us into it, because for a while there, I didn't know what I was going to do, but I knew I was going to college.

My dad, usually you think, oh, a Mexican, he's a macho, well, my dad is not a macho at all so he doesn't think like that. He's always told us, "well if you really want to better yourself, you should go to school . . . I am not forcing you; if you don't want to, you don't have to, but do learn something." Even though he couldn't go to school when he came here, he learned how to fix cars, he fixes transmissions. But, you see, that's something he had to learn and maybe he couldn't go to the university or whatever, but he wanted to better his family so he did something about it.

Lorena is planning to start teaching and then she would like to continue her education and focus on Chicano Studies. Her long-range plans include going after a doctorate and pursuing a teaching career at the university level.

# Maria

Maria grew up in a small German-speaking village in Romania; she was nine years old when her family emigrated to the United States. She states that,

. . . communism had taken over for ten years and my parents saw that the chance for my sister and I to receive an education was not in that country. My parents had come to the United States several times and once my grandparents lived over here, their desire was to emigrate to the U.S.

Her memories of school are not unlike those of other immigrants:

> They put us into third grade and they assumed—I'm guessing with all immigrants—that because we didn't speak English, they put us back a grade, which was ridiculous because in the area of math we were probably two or three years advanced to the kids here, so having to repeat a grade was not a good idea. But, at the time, I'm sure it was the best they knew how.

Maria remembers learning English as a "painful" experience. "English was painful for a whole slew of reasons, never feeling that I fit in because of the culture thing, because of dress, because of mannerisms, because of just all sorts of things. . . ." Comparing the study of German to the study of English, she states,

> English was just painful, very, very painful and even now, when I think back to the areas that are the weakest for me now are areas that people overlook, they just kind of assume, "well, you'll catch it by osmosis." And it didn't happen.

She remembers German being a part of her life as a little girl growing up in the US:

> . . . things that I had learned as a young girl: to play the accordion, to sing folk songs, and, at the time all those things were "oh, I can't believe I have to do this!"—take accordion lessons—and then whenever people came over, my parents would have to show us off . . . so I'm sure I knew every German folk song there was, but it was out of having to . . . I can remember riding to the North side and—being immigrants, we were so obedient, even in our teenage years—riding to the North side and singing all the way there and all the way back. Now, in an hour run in a car you can go through a lot of songs. . . .

Maria decided to major in German during her second year in college because of the impact of a particular German professor. This man, she recalls,

> really sparked my interest; his idea of teaching the language was to take us to local pubs and the requirement was always to speak German. We'd go to his home and other kids who had apartments and homes, and we'd eat and converse and we'd sing . . . that kind of awakened those things I had learned as a young girl; it wasn't until this man really kind of sparked an interest and all those things became alive and it became fun. I thought, "Wow! I have this wealth stored here, why not put it to good use?"

Maria currently teaches German at a public high school in a suburb of Chicago.

These four voices had very different experiences: Christine and Tom studied the language as young children because their parents mandated it. Lorena had the opportunity to study her language and had a less than satisfying classroom experience in the public schools. Maria was taught by her parents once she came to the United States, and only discovered her love for her native German as a college student when a professor helped her to make the connection between her cultural background and the language.

While each of the participants interviewed presented a unique set of circumstances, much of the data gathered seemed to cluster around four major categories or themes: their motivation to study the language, their approach to learning their native culture, their search for an identity as a native speaker of a language other than English, and their insights into the process of language learning.

# Themes

## Motivation

> I think if they are genuinely interested in learning the language and they want to, not just the grammar part, but the whole language . . . and if they work hard, the language will come, the grammar will come. But, if you are only doing it because your parents are pushing you into a language, or it is part of the school curriculum, then you can't expect to excel as much as if you were really genuinely interested, because it won't come that easily. And either you will lose interest or you'll get frustrated and stop studying.
> —Carol

In this section we report on the participants' recollections about their initial efforts to learn their native language formally. We asked why they took language lessons and how they felt about it; as they reflected on the reasons they had for studying their language, we asked them about experiences that motivated them to continue their language learning process. We hypothesized that while the initial reasons these participants had for studying their native language might be similar to those of many foreign language learners (e.g., it was a requirement), the motivating forces that were present in the native speakers who continued to study their language might differ.

While we found that the types of motivation reported in other studies of language learners applied to most of the native speakers interviewed, we also discovered unique issues related to the some of the participants' search for their own identity. Those native speakers who chose to continue their language study, or who achieved a self-reported level of language proficiency that allowed them to function with equal facility in both cultures, seemed to have the type of motivation that goes beyond what has traditionally been examined in the literature.

Most of the native speakers interviewed started their language training early on (kindergarten); they attended Saturday or Sunday schools, had tutors or attended full-time language schools. The decision to begin formal language instruction was their parents' and most of them did not enjoy their early experience. Miné, a junior at a private university in the east coast recalls, ". . . when I was six years old my father enrolled me in Saturday school to learn Japanese so I went every Saturday for about six hours. . . . I hated it, I really did. I was very jealous of my sister, she got to go to swim meets and I had to go to Saturday school." Rika, another Japanese American college student had similar experiences.

> Well, I missed the Saturday morning cartoons so I didn't like it at first, and basically all the kids, the attitude was the same thing: "oh, we're here because our parents forced us to come." There wasn't a lot of "let's try and keep our heritage, let's learn Japanese." It was more like "let's try and survive the two hours and go home."

As did Stacy, a Greek American high school freshman in Chicago:

> We went to a lady's home with my cousins in kindergarten till about second grade and then went to my aunt's house with a private tutor. . . . The first lady that we went to, I don't even know if I liked the lessons so much, but the cousins were my age so we had a lot of fun being together for the two hours we got together. And then the private tutor that would come to my house, I hated it. It was so boring, I did not like it at all.

Maria S., a 17-year-old Greek American, talks about learning Greek at their church and then with a private tutor: "Well, as a kid it was boring. If I took it now, I might enjoy it, but as a kid it was 'oh no, do I have to go again?'"

Gardner (1985) focused on issues of attitude and motivation as important variables in language learning. He explains that in his study, the term motivation refers to the combination of effort plus the desire to achieve the goal of learning the language plus favourable attitudes toward learning the language. That is, motivation to learn a second language is seen as referring to the extent to which the individual works or strives to learn the language because of a desire to do so and the satisfaction experienced in the activity (p. 10).

Many of the participants in this study put in the effort as young children, but did not express the desire to learn the language nor did they experience any satisfaction in the activity at the time. On the other hand, some of the younger participants expressed a desire to learn the language, but were not willing to expend the effort that it would take to learn. In the words of Stacy, "I wanted to [learn Greek] when I was younger. I wanted to know how to speak it, but I didn't want to go through all the stuff to learn the grammar and the vocabulary. I just wanted to be able to speak the language."

Those participants who chose to continue their language studies as adults expressed a clear purpose and a conscious decision to learn their native language and reported great satisfaction in the process. In most cases the change was triggered by an episode where they saw the connection between their culture and the language they were learning: Maria W. realized she had a "wealth of information." For Lorena, the link became clear when she took a course specially designed for native speakers and she realized she liked learning Spanish. Christine remembers the thrill of being able to read the newspaper in Japanese and Rika felt the need to understand the Japanese videos her grandparents sent her family.

Their varying levels of success can be related to several factors: motivation, exposure to the language, opportunities to use it, attitude toward the language community and others. Gardner and Lambert's (1972) extensive study of motivation in second language learning examined motivation as a factor of a number of different kinds of attitudes. *Instrumental* motivation refers to the urge to acquire a language as a means for attaining instrumental goals such as furthering a career or potential use in tourism or trade. Henry, a twelve-year-old Chinese American student, puts it this way, "my father says that when we're out of college and in careers, we're probably going to be doing a lot of international stuff so it would be helpful to speak Mandarin or even if we take vacations there, it would be nice." Miné, a Japanese American college student who is studying business in Japanese, explains her motivations this way:

> I had just decided that I wanted a career that would involve languages and in order to do that I would have to do even more studying like at the college level so I just decided on Japanese because it was the one that I was the most proficient in and it would probably be the most useful, besides Spanish.

> Next year I'll be in Japan for the whole year. . . . I'm going to try and maybe get an internship, but it's hard to say right now. If I can find a job hopefully in this country where I can use my Japanese in maybe marketing or advertising,

then that's what I would like to do, but if not, then I just plan to maybe do graduate studies in some area using my language in hopefully some aspect of business, I'm not really sure yet.

According to Maria W., all of her college classmates were highly motivated language learners, though their attitudes towards learning German had a clear instrumental focus.

I hung around a couple of girls who were becoming translators, they needed to become really proficient. . . . They were focused, much more than I was because I wanted the whole picture and they focused on what they needed out of the language to become an interpreter or to become a translator. And there was another girl who was not a native speaker and she, too, was much more focused on doing the homework and doing it right.

*Integrative* motivation, on the other hand, refers to an identification with the culture, an identification with the cultural group and a desire to become part of this society (Richard-Amato, 1988, p. 368). Kiyoko, a Japanese American college student, exemplifies this type of motivation.

I really felt that in myself, I wanted to stay connected to my heritage, my ancestors, and be able to speak it fluently, especially with my grandmother, I'm very close to her, but I feel like I can't communicate 100% with her like I would like.

This same awareness of the power of language to connect generations was also apparent to Carol, a Korean American college freshman.

We studied Korean poetry for about two weeks, and I went home, and I told my parents about it, and they knew who the author was, and we could talk. I felt like I could talk to my parents more, so this is worth it. I could actually have conversations with my parents about something intellectual. . . . I know a couple of older people who are trying to go back to school now and I think they feel a lot more desperate. They feel like they've lost a lot of things in their younger years, that they couldn't go back to. My cousin is in her thirties, and she scrambled to get back into classes. She had to find a class so she could learn [Korean] now because she feels that she is almost isolated from the family at family functions. Everyone speaks Korean, and she just kind of sits there and nods and says "yes" or "hi" and I see that in my parents' friends' children. A lot of the older ones are desperately trying to get into Korean now because they want to be in the family, they want to have interaction with the family.

Many of our interviews reflected a combination of both types of motivation. Participants expressed a desire to become part of their cultural group and also to be able to use the language for business and career opportunities. For example, Carol clearly felt that studying her native language could have pragmatic as well as emotional value for her:

At some major universities they do have Korean classes, but it's still very limited. I know some of my friends are going to study Korean, but they do not have it at [this university]. I'll probably [study it] independently to learn a little more since

I know I'll use it when I grow up, for my career.

Carol further explains her own motivation,

> What I don't want is [to be like] other Korean friends who don't speak Korean at all, or who don't know anything about the culture. I think that is kind of correlated, learning the language is learning the culture. . . . Since I know I am going to Korea, I think I probably have more interest in that area than some of my other friends, so I think I am going to pursue an Asian studies minor. I'm not sure, but I always thought about maybe something international, for my career.

Richard-Amato (1988, p. 369) explains Graham's (1984) distinction between integrative and assimilative motivation. According to Graham, integrative motivation has been defined too broadly in previous research. He makes the distinction between the desire to learn a second language in order to communicate with or find out about members of that culture (integrative motivation), and the drive to become an indistinguishable member of that speech community (assimilative motivation). The former does not imply direct contact with the second language group while the latter requires prolonged contact with the second language culture (Richard-Amato, 1988, p. 369).

Tom, a Polish American college student, expresses his sadness at the realization that he somehow had ceased to be an "indistinguishable member" of the Polish-speaking community:

> In fourth or fifth grade, [my English skills] started to surpass my Polish, I was upset about that . . . now I have no accent in English, but I have an accent in Polish, so that distresses me that I switched over. I suppose that at the same time that I lost my English accent, I gained a Polish one somewhere and that was around seventh or eighth grade. . . . I felt stupid I suppose just because I was born here, but I still consider myself Polish and I feel like an idiot that I don't speak as good Polish as I do English. I try to go back and read Polish literature and go through the grammar books and things, but nevertheless, I still have an accent.

In addition, Tom feels that the change from "indistinguishable" to "distinguishable" member of his native community represents a far more profound loss to him than it does to his parents.

> I don't think that it ever really bothered them. They were proud that I was doing well in school and I suppose they had accepted that I was American and that I was going to be brought up American and be American, but I never wanted to be that, you know. So, to me it was distressing; to them, it was good. I mean, I'm sure they didn't like the fact that I was losing my Polish. To them it was just a slight thing, but to me it was pretty distressing. And I didn't know I had an accent which is why I don't know when I really got one until my grandmother told me that I said something funny, and I was like, "What do you mean I said it funny? I said it the way I always said it." And

then, out of curiosity, I ran back home and I tape recorded myself and played it back and listened to it and there was a definite accent and I was upset.

Oxford and Shearing (1994) explain that while most of the research on second language learning motivation has focused on integrative and instrumental motivation in the past twenty years, recent research has raised questions about other kinds of second language learning motivation. Findings of their study on motivation of high school students learning Japanese include about twenty distinguishable motivation categories; among these, they list intellectual stimulation, personal challenge, showing off to friends, and so forth (p. 13). In our interviews, we found that while most of the participants cited integrative (e.g., communicating with relatives) and instrumental (e.g., career) motivations, some of them had other reasons that did not clearly fit within those two types. Tom talks about the thrill of learning languages, "I like learning languages. It's exciting when you do find links that pierce through several languages, it's just kind of a thrill in a way. I suppose I could use them for a purpose, but mostly it is for personal enrichment."

Christine explains how the satisfaction and excitement developed during her college language learning experience:

> I'm not sure why I took [Japanese]. Actually, when I first signed up for the 101, the very simple, basic, or the 102, second level . . . I guess it was to keep Japanese in my world, but when I realized how easy the level was and I went into the advanced, I enjoyed it so much, learning it as a science and I guess in a real aggressive way it made me realize that everything I had been doing in my past with Japanese was less than dabbling, it wasn't even real almost, but at least it had kept my ears open to it. So, I'm not sure what initially made me sign up, but once I started the intensive level, I just loved it, I loved the language and I loved to learn more about it.

After an unsuccessful language learning experience at the high school, Lorena had not thought about taking more Spanish.

> I was in Fashion Merchandising, but the reason I went into it was that I like cloth and I like to sew, and I thought "wow, this is great!" But when I was in there, I didn't feel right. It did not feel like it was my calling, but I did not know what else I would like. So when they offered Spanish for Native Speakers I decided to take it 'cause I thought, "well, it's something interesting, I wonder what I'll learn." And I loved that class! I really liked it. So from then on I started taking more Spanish and then I got a job tutoring and I got more involved and I really started liking the language. So at first I double majored, but then I just dropped Fashion Merchandising and just concentrated in the Spanish.

Maria W., a Rumanian American who made the decision to study her native German when she was in college, recalls that the breakthrough experience for her was discovering that learning German could be fun.

> It wasn't until my second half of second year in college and it was at a point where I had to decide on a major and a professor at the university, a native speaker, really sparked my interest and it was in the area of culture. It was not until this man really sparked an interest and all those things became alive and it became fun. I thought, "Wow! I have this wealth stored here, why not put it to good use?"

Rita, a Spanish teacher, had different reasons for majoring in Spanish,

> I think it was a question of what I could do quickly and get to work. I had to get to work—there were kids behind me, I had brothers in Catholic High School. . . .
>
> So seeing that I could get myself through college relatively inexpensively and quickly, and teaching was something I thought I could do. I think that under different circumstances I might have pursued a degree in business or in medicine, but there wasn't the opportunity and there wasn't the time. My parents needed to have me out . . . although they didn't say, and probably would have supported me if I had decided to do it.

Sadow (1994, p. 243) explains that intrinsic motivation acts as both cause and effect since the more language is used, the more confident one becomes, and this in turn results in more language. This seems to have been the case with many of the participants interviewed here. Once they became involved in their language learning, their motivation increased. For Lorena the involvement included tutoring non-native Spanish students, Maria W. saw the possibility of teaching German, and Rita had the opportunity to study at the University of Guadalajara. Tom also perceived learning languages as a way to develop greater cultural understanding and cognitive flexibility:

> I do think it has helped me in my life, through growing up and now, it has given me perspective, a different one anyway, and I think it is one of the reasons I did so well in school too. It was more of a general mind-set. It's just a way you think because I do think that with different languages, people think differently. . . . So that I think would be one of the advantages if you knew so many languages, you could also skip between all these manners of thinking. You wouldn't be just stuck in one rut. You would have a lot more to base your judgments on and your thoughts so it makes you more wise I suppose.
>
> I try to establish some sort of influence on [my friends] because I do think it's an advantage when you're exposed to a lot of these different cultures and languages. It's more like a light knowledge, like wisdom versus knowledge. You could have knowledge, but I think you'd gain wisdom with that, not the slow way either. It prepares you later on for a lot of different things. If someone were to remark about something they just saw for the first time, they'd go, "oh, they eat cows' stomachs!" and they'd be thoroughly repulsed and they'd never ever think of things like escargot or calamari or things like that. I'm just

speaking of foods because it's the most obvious. The people with only one language behind them find that as repulsive or foreign or something they would never try, but I've always tried to try everything I could. Like when we were in Greece and Italy . . . I tried all the food, no matter how repulsive everybody else thought it was, just because I wanted to try it, just more of that cultural immersion going on. And thinking that the more you know about other cultures, the more you know, period.

Rika, another Japanese American college student, explained that she decided to study Japanese when she realized that her language skills were not as strong as they were when she was a child, "the Japanese became less and less until I was almost forgetting Japanese so I thought, 'well, I may as well try and keep what I started out with.'"

Rika's interest in learning the language reflects the complexity of the different types of motivation experienced by several of our interviewees: a mixture of identity seeking, need to communicate with relatives as well as curiosity about their culture:

I felt I had a more insistent reason for learning Japanese than other people because it is my background. It is not something I'm going to gain, or is going to be an addition to me as a person, it is something I have to make up for because I've lost it. I'm not where I should be so that's why I have to learn Japanese. . . . My cultural background is very much integrated into my identity so I think as a whole having learned Japanese is just one more anchor to know who I am, what my identity is and not having to worry since my eyes are almond-shaped that I'm going to feel strange walking in and speaking Japanese somewhere. . . .

. . . but, I think a lot of the reason that I probably chose to take [Japanese] again in college was that we'd be getting a lot of videos from my grandparents—their Japanese programs—and you can't understand them if you don't keep practicing, so I think it was a lot of interest in the Japanese culture . . . I take karate and I take Japanese classical dance and that very much brings the language into play as well.

When looking at the different clusters of motivation, Oxford and Shearing (1994) explain that students' motivation can change both in kind and in degree. Maria W. reflects on the point in time when her motivation changed.

I remember sitting in a pub singing folk songs and it was probably the first time that it was fun, up to that point it seemed to be something I had to do and had to learn . . . I knew I was going to use the language and there was a connection between really learning it well and learning as much as I could and using it because I had decided I was going to teach German. I'm going to become proficient as far as teaching and explaining it, because I want to teach it, for my students. For many of them the only connection they have is to get into a university or college so the connection is not there, and it's not immediately applicable, it's not immediately relevant. As far as a difference in learning, I'm not sure there is a difference in learning, it's just the desire is definitely different.

Miné, a Japanese American college student studying business in Japanese explains the process this way:

> After a point, it's kind of like learning to play the piano. For like 12 years I had to go to Saturday school. No matter what, I had to go and I didn't enjoy it. But just then I just learned to enjoy it. I think it was after going to Japan for several summers and developing friendships and becoming proficient enough to where I felt comfortable speaking it and so I wanted to learn more and I just felt like I don't have much longer until I can be totally proficient in it so I should keep working and then it will be very helpful to me and I think that was really why I decided to keep studying it. I also feel like I've spent twelve years studying it, why wouldn't I? Especially remembering everything I went through for Saturday school every week.

## Culture

> There wasn't any kind of emphasis on making any kind of home connection and seeing that culture as valuable in a classroom sense. It was kind of quaint, like "who cares." At times it was very insulting for people who were not living our culture, to tell us, "This is how Hispanics see this." Like the whole idea of being chaperoned was very much part of how I grew up, I wasn't allowed to go out by myself, but this was a "quaint custom." I was always too embarrassed to tell people it wasn't a quaint custom, it was how I grew up.
> —Rita

While culture and language are so closely intertwined that it is difficult to conceive of learning one without the other, most of the participants interviewed in this chapter stated that their early experiences as students of their native language did not include culture. They explained that since Saturday or Sunday classes were designed for "native speakers," the target culture was assumed to be present at home and did not need to be a formal part of the language classes. As a result, most of the participants found these classes boring and did not see a connection between what they were learning in the classroom and what they were living at home. In general, only those participants who had attended full-time language schools felt that they had had appropriate exposure to their culture. Nevertheless, debate as to the value of formal vs informal instruction in culture remains a constant throughout their discussion of how and when they learned about their culture.

Scarcella and Oxford (1992, p. 183) explain that "people's perception of the world is expressed largely through language, although it is also expressed in many non-verbal forms such as cuisine, art, religion, music and dance." Several learners reported on additional, extracurricular activities such as taking karate classes, having informal talks with native speakers or visiting relatives overseas that taught them about their culture. Their comments implied that these activities had a much greater impact on their learning to appreciate their own culture than the formal classroom activities. Rika, for example, found that learning karate helped her learn Japanese.

> I think that one of the big things my mother had me do, and it indirectly had me wanting to learn Japanese more, was getting me into martial arts and into the dance. Both of them, it's like the mixing of the cultural activity and the language put together . . . I think they complement each other.

Crawford-Lange and Lange (1987) assert that "to study language without studying the culture of native speakers is a lifeless endeavor" (p. 140). Many of the participants interviewed described their early language learning experiences as boring. When pressed for details, it became clear that the focus of the instruction had been on vocabulary and forms and not on the culture. Stacy, a 15-year-old who attended Greek school for about three years and then had a private tutor for another three years, describes how lifeless the experience seemed to her:

> My dad would always tell me things about the people or things that used to happen [in Greece], the history, but never in the actual lessons. I think that if I had gone to my church, they had a Greek school program, I think I would have learned more about the history, but I learned just the grammar and vocabulary.

> I think I would have liked [Greek lessons] a lot more if they would have talked more about the culture or if it was more, not so much out of the book. I'm sure I would have tried a little more, it could have been a little more fun, but it was so boring. . . .

Henry, a Chinese American seventh grader, explains that ". . . we didn't learn anything about the culture at all, just the language. My parents tell me a lot, but it probably would be more interesting if we were told about the culture." Melissa (Henry's 15-year-old sister) had a different learning experience, suggesting that Henry's insight was right:

> I had this one teacher who, instead of using the book, he would talk about the culture. He told us how the words were derived and some of the customs, the Chinese customs, and that was very exciting because I realized how the words came [to be].

Sometimes, learning about culture in the classroom had unexpected consequences. For Tom, the experience of learning about the culture of Spanish-speaking countries in his Spanish classes made him more appreciative of how he learned the culture of his parents' native Poland in his Polish classes.

> In the Spanish class, they tried, they showed movies and we talked about different rituals and what they did in the culture, but that was kind of like a second-hand kind of thing, enrichment basically. And that is how it was treated in the book. It was just a little side kind of by-the-way kind of thing. But in the Polish class, it was twenty-five percent of the whole class, well much more because there was one section that was called culture and that ended up being all your readings and lectures, but that's what the section was called.

> In kindergarten, it was like regular kindergarten where you got an hour to play, but then they'd get into basic grammar, language, history, geography and things. They'd have a big map of Poland and we'd have races where they'd say a city and we'd have to run to Poland and hit where it was and we'd get points. They found ways to teach us.

For Rita, on the other hand, finding her own culture the object of classroom lessons was an uncomfortable and unsettling experience. Here she describes a gap between the real life culture of the kids in the school (mostly Mexican American) and what was taught in her high school Spanish class.

> There wasn't any real connection between what was happening in the home and what was happening in the classroom. *Quinceañeras* [the Mexican equivalent of "sweet sixteen" celebrations] were seen as "oh, that's a quaint custom." Being in a high school that was in a Mexican neighborhood, the connection was not made, Mexicans were not encouraged to come to school to share things about their culture. There wasn't any kind of emphasis on making any kind of home connection and seeing that culture as valuable in a classroom sense, it was kind of quaint, like "who cares." At times it was very insulting for people who were not living our culture, to tell us, "This is how Hispanics see this." Like the whole idea of being chaperoned was very much part of how I grew up, I wasn't allowed to go out by myself, but this was a "quaint custom." I was always too embarrassed to tell people that it wasn't a quaint custom, it was how I grew up. . . .

While some of the native speakers recall learning about their culture through books—Carol, a Korean American college freshman remembers that in her language classes she and her friends "had books on Korean culture, or, as we got older, they had books on government or different aspects of Korea"—most of them credit less formal measures. Steven, a Chinese American college freshman, talks about "picking up" the culture:

> It was more on a subconscious [level]. Well, in other words, it wasn't as

obvious that here they bring out a cultural thing, but you slowly pick it up because you are in that environment. Especially during New Year time, we wouldn't have class, we'd usually have a party. Some of the classes might prepare skits, there's usually a dragon dance and there's that kind of atmosphere. I think the more you pick up on little things, the more you say, "Wow, that was kind of neat!" that there are different ways to look at something, especially in terms of values. Back then when I was in third or fourth grade, you don't think about values but you can see some of the finer points of the American value in society and some of the finer points of the Chinese value in society.

Steven regrets not having been exposed formally to more Chinese history and culture and would like to learn more about it. " I'd be more interested in taking a history and philosophy course," he says, "to learn more about the culture. The history is a lot longer than American history and it goes very deep and that is where the language originates. . . ." Nevertheless, in general, learning about their native culture outside of the classroom seemed to be a common experience across language groups. Maria S., a Greek American college freshman, started attending Greek school when she was six years old and continued for seven years. "Sometimes," she recalls, "we would have a special program where we'd recite poems from the culture, but not as much as we [studied] the language actually. . . . When I went to Greece, I learned a lot more, just talking to people everyday." Maria W. also recalls learning about her culture informally.

. . . there was another professor, a native speaker from Berlin, he seemed to zero in on food—I love to sing and I love to eat—and he lived across the street from us and would have us over for dinner which was like picking his brain, he just loved to talk about Germany and Berlin and foods and people . . . he was into the arts and the plays and he was just a wealth of information, but all I learned from him was across the table, not in the classroom.

For Miné, also, learning about her native Japanese culture was more experiential than intellectual:

. . . I feel like everything I know about the culture and the people came before I went to college because I used to spend some of my summers as a child in Japan and I would go to school and that is where I really learned about the culture. I guess the way that [the classes] have made me more knowledgeable is like I took a course in Business Japanese and I hadn't known anything about that beforehand, but there are all these separate terms and these expressions and just specifically for business and I didn't know them, but as far as learning about the people . . . no. I think you have to experience it first hand in order to learn it, you can't really learn it from a class that much.

She added that learning the culture becomes an even greater problem when the opportunity to experience it first hand is not there:

There are a lot of Japanese Americans who really don't know anything about the Japanese culture because they've been here their whole life and even their parents, while they might speak Japanese, are very limited on what they can teach their children because as long as you are in this country, it is just very limited . . . you really have to go and experience it.

Christine agrees with Miné's opinions about the importance of experiencing the culture first hand,

One thing I felt very strongly about when I came back to the States, was that it's a pity that the Japanese Americans that I know in the Chicago area rarely go to Japan. I think that is such a crucial stage of development for Japanese Americans to go and realize how American they are. I felt like, because the community is so small here and because of camp and a lot of psychological things that have come up through the generations, Japanese Americans, specially my generation, if they don't go and realize their place here, they are never quite at a stage of empowerment that I feel is real important for Japanese Americans to take advantage of [American] society, to be active participants.

# Identity

> I thought, "OK, people are looking at you differently because you are Asian, so then you have to find out, what are they thinking about? What is it to be Asian?"
> —Rika

The previous discussion of culture makes clear that the individuals we interviewed experienced this topic in a uniquely personal way. In fact, while "culture" and "language" seemed at times to be separate learning experiences for them, "culture" and "self" were definitely much more closely connected. A very powerful issue for many native speakers of other languages living in the United States is identity. As first or second generation in the United States, many individuals have to deal with questions about who they are and what it means to be Korean American, Greek American or Mexican American. While the quest for identity lead ultimately to great personal satisfaction, the journey often involved a painful coming to grips with who they are not.

For many of the interviewees, the quest for identity involved some identity confusion. Rita calls it a "cultural dilemma."

Some of my best memories are with people that were caught in the same cultural dilemma I was, when we were sent to Mexico, we were American and when we were here, we were Mexican . . . we didn't really belong here because we were Mexican, but when we went to Mexico we were clearly not Mexican because we didn't have the same rules . . . in some ways the culture that came with our parents was kept in a bubble for some things and never got really developed, and yet, in other ways our own exposure to what were norms for

American women shoved us ahead....It made for a lot of heated discussions and a lot of tears too, it was a very traumatic time to go through.

Rika recalls the first time she had to think about her identity.

I always considered myself to be Japanese American. It's kind of funny, I never thought of myself as Asian until one time my father had some freelance work at a hospital in Iowa, my mother and I were waiting at a playground for him to come out. It was kind of farm land—not too many Asians in Iowa, I don't think—I was playing in the playground and a station wagon drove by and this Caucasian boy stuck his head out and went, "Hey, Chinese!" and I looked to where he was pointing . . . I didn't know he was referring to me. And then I thought, "Oh, everyone thinks of me as Asian." From there on—I was in sixth grade—from sixth grade on, I thought "OK, people are looking at you differently because you are Asian, so then you have to find out, what are they thinking about? What is it to be Asian?"

For Japanese Americans, the issue of identity as a group poses some problems when dealing with Japanese natives. Kiyoko explains it as a tension: "Because I look Japanese, Japanese people expect me to speak [Japanese] perfectly—that is a lot of the tension that I feel." She recalls one specific instance where she had to address the congregation at her temple.

I went to this Buddhist meeting, everyone was Japanese, except for me—I was considered American I guess. They conducted the meeting in Japanese. This was the hardest, the most frightening experience I had had, trying to speak Japanese in front of all those other Japanese people. Some of them didn't really know my background, others knew more; I stuttered, I felt like I could have spoken a lot better had I been more comfortable in the situation, but the tension was there.

Dorinne Kondo, a Japanese American anthropologist, writes about her experiences: "I created a conceptual dilemma for the Japanese I encountered. For them I was a living oxymoron, someone who was both Japanese and not Japanese" (Kondo, 1990, p. 11). The same dilemma was painfully apparent to many of the learners we interviewed. Christine talks about her experiences this way:

The Japanese would give me a hard time because all my friends were Caucasian and even though I spoke much better Japanese than they did, I wasn't up to par with the Japanese natives of my age, so they thought I was really strange if not dumb—and they are very comfortable at making people feel stupid if you are not up to their speed. . . .

. . . there were people who just got real angry if I told them I wasn't from Japan, I was from Chicago and that is why I don't understand, could you please speak slower. I would have people just "huh" and walk away and I swear it was because they didn't believe me. If my Caucasian friends said exactly the same thing, they would bend over backwards and do anything to accommodate them.

This reaction is also described by Kondo (1990), who writes about the treatment encountered by Japanese Americans in Japan.

> White people are treated as repulsive and unnatural—*ben na gaijin,* strange foreigners—the better their Japanese becomes, while Japanese Americans and others of Japanese ancestry born overseas are faced with exasperation and disbelief. How can someone who is racially Japanese lack "cultural competence"? (p. 11)

Rika reflects on similar feelings:

> I feel very defensive, because I look Japanese. Their eyes, their mentality is going to be that I am Japanese and that I can speak Japanese and all the assumptions that come with being Japanese and then if I say something a little bit differently, or the level is a little bit lower, then they're like, "What is wrong with this person? There must be something wrong with her mentality, her educational level must be low." And it is always something to fight against, even with my family. . . . The rest of my family is in Japan, and even with my grandparents or cousins, they can't see it as "Wow! she speaks English *and* she can also speak Japanese." They have to judge you at the level of Japanese that you are at, otherwise they might feel a little offset because they are studying English.

Many of the individuals we interviewed shared experiences that had much in common with those documented by Kondo (1990) while in Japan:

> I became all too familiar with the series of expressions that would flicker over those faces: bewilderment, incredulity, embarrassment, even anger at having to deal with this odd person who looked Japanese and therefore human, but who must be retarded or deranged, or—equally undesirable in Japanese eyes—Chinese or Korean. (p. 11)

Although the process of finding one's own identity is often a difficult one, the results can be, in the words of Christine, a "sense of discovery that [is] very empowering and strengthening." She explains how she came to that understanding after having spent a year in Japan.

> When I went to Japan I really considered myself a Japanese person and I guess because growing up I don't remember many bitter experiences of being discriminated against or made fun of for being different, but I was aware of the physical differences—that I was not a white American, therefore I must be Japanese, or that's how I identified myself—and obviously when I went to Japan I realized how American I was and it was very empowering as an Asian American to go over and kind of realize who you are and that the limitations of the strictness of Japanese society don't bind us. Even though I look like them, I'm a very, very different animal.

Another dimension of Christine's personal search for identity can be seen in her description of her relationship with her mother. She credits the emphasis her mother placed on language and culture for the preparation she needed to deal with issues of identity.

The language training, the cultural values that my mother instilled in us all was very appropriate training, I think, to be [in Japan] and then to have that year mean so much to me. It kind of answered a lot of questions I did not even know I had.

In turn, Christine found that her year in Japan helped her understand her mother's cultural identity and therefore her own.

Being in Japan and also studying the language more gave me a great advantage of insight into my mother, which I wish my other siblings had, and I remember trying to explain a little bit, but you can't really explain nine months or twelve months of digesting that type of culture.

. . . there are more internal values and internal processes [in Japan] that aren't real common in American culture. It was with those values that I identified very strongly in Japan, never being aware that I had that in me, but it made clear a lot of my mother and herself to me when I was in Japan. There were so many times throughout the year [when] I felt like "no wonder I feel this way, because my mother grew up in that country and that's part of them." It was nice, I felt very close to her through that year.

## Language Learning

I was too young for them to start teaching me grammar and a lot of it was just "Well, this sounds right, you don't have to learn how to conjugate the verbs, this is how you say it and it just comes out." I think I was lucky in that sense, I didn't really have to learn the grammar for it. When I started taking courses I even had to learn the names of the tenses!—"Oh, that is what it is called!"—but I knew how to use them. In a way it was interesting how people had to look at Japanese as a language to be learned while I was looking at it as just labeling all the parts of the language and I already knew how to use the language.
—Rika

All the participants interviewed had strong ideas about their own language learning experiences. As we saw in the culture section earlier in this chapter, they were often dismayed to find that their language classes included little cultural information. Many of their negative comments also focused on the role of grammar and on the difficulty of learning their language as children in non-formal settings (e.g., Saturday school taught by volunteers). Several learners remembered the excitement of taking formal classes in their language as college students, and some of them were motivated to take an additional language as well. Others, faced with the pressure of grades and their own uncertainty about the value of the study of their own language compared with that of other more "academic" pursuits, decided not to pursue the study of their native language after high school.

Most of the individuals interviewed felt that, as native speakers, they had an advantage over foreign or second language learners; but there were also times when they felt an added burden. Kiyoko recalls her first year studying Japanese.

> I should have focused more on learning vocabulary. I figured, "Oh, as I hear it more often, I'll learn it," but I found out that I really didn't learn it as well as other students did. It was my first year, I thought I knew everything! There was a lot of vocabulary that I knew I didn't know, but I didn't bother studying as hard as I should have.

Like Kiyoko, Lorena found that being a native speaker had its advantages and disadvantages as far as formal language study went.

> . . . because we grew up speaking [Spanish] and we know it, but we don't know the rules and I have had trouble actually learning them because I just let it go and say, "Well, I know this." If they say "past" I know what the past is, I don't have to look it up. And I guess that's a disadvantage for me because I notice that the students that have to learn Spanish from the beginning, that don't know anything, at least in that aspect, they are on a higher level than I am. For them it is sort of like a process where first they learned these rules of grammar, then the next set of rules . . . and for me I still get stuck a little when they ask, "What is this part of speech?" while the other students had had to learn it already.

Grammar was a challenging learning experience for Rika, too.

> One of the major reasons I wanted to take lessons at this university was because it is formally taught. All of the Japanese I had learned, even at the Buddhist Temple, even the tutoring, it wasn't exactly formal teaching. I was too young for them to start teaching me grammar and a lot of it was just "Well, this sounds right, you don't have to learn how to conjugate the verbs, this is how you say it and it just comes out." I think I was lucky in that sense, I didn't really have to learn the grammar for it. When I started taking courses, I even had to learn the names of the tenses!—"Oh, that is what it is called!"—but I knew how to use them. In a way it was interesting how people had to look at Japanese as a language to be learned while I was looking at is as just labeling all the parts of the language and I already knew how to use the language.

Several of the native speakers interviewed expressed dissatisfaction with their early learning experiences. Henry's description of his Mandarin lessons sounds sadly familiar: "I can't think of any memorable learning experience," he said, "because there wasn't really anything, there was just always homework. We went from one chapter to the next chapter, there wasn't anything unique." Steven gives credit to his mother for helping him keep up with his Chinese lessons.

> Every year I'd want to quit, but she'd tell me to take another year. Sometimes you'd have to memorize this story and then go up and speak it. It was kind of hard at times memorizing it and my mom would help me. She'd cut it down to segments, I'd memorize a few segments . . . she would spend a lot of time helping me.

In some cases, the problem had more to do with what the young learners perceived as unrealistic expectations. Miné explains why the way the language was taught at the Japanese Saturday school was a problem for her.

> One of the reasons I hated [Saturday school] so much was the way they taught it, the way the teachers acted—I always felt very intimidated and very scared to raise my hand and say something unless I knew I was absolutely correct and I think that if they hadn't been that way I would have learned a lot more because I went into school every week with the attitude that I hated [it] and just, "I have to come here because I have to come," and I just hated it so much. I did my homework and everything, but I just feel like I would've learned so much more if they had been different about the way they taught it. In college, I feel like I've just started learning how to speak freely, I'm not really scared about making mistakes and I don't care what I sound like and I never felt that at Saturday school so I feel like if the teachers had been [like my college teachers] I probably would've been better off.

In most cases, however, their dissatisfaction was due to what they saw as a tendency to "follow the book" too closely, as well as a narrow focus on the forms of language. Rika found the focus on memorization of forms uninteresting, and wished things could have been different:

> I always wished I could have gone through the Japanese school system, I think I would have retained a lot more Japanese. It's much more disciplined. I love how the Japanese teach Japanese to their little kids—the little drill books—versus how it is taught here . . . it was just, "Here is this character, here is this verb, this is how it is used, learn it, memorize it." Where in Japan they had word games or match this with the picture or the character part is wrong, pick it out and it just seemed a lot more fun the way they taught.

Sometimes, as Rika's thoughts indicate, the spark that seemed to be missing in their lessons was not apparent except through contrast with other language learning experiences. Maria S. also recalls that she became much more enthusiastic about learning Greek after visiting Greece.

> . . . yeah, because you are not just reading some stupid book. You are actually talking to real people so I think that makes a big difference, you pick up a lot. You know somebody says something you don't know and you ask them, and you understand. But here, just reading vocabulary, is not real exciting. You learn for the week and then you forget.

For Stacy, a positive experience learning Spanish in 8th grade highlighted what had been wrong with her experience learning her native Greek as a child:

> I think that my tutors for Greek were just right out of the book. We would always work from the book. My [Spanish] eighth grade teacher would relate everything we learned to something. If we were learning about fruits, we would throw fruits across [the room] and we would catch them and say them. We were learning about houses, outdoors, nature words, we would do a play about people going through forests. She would always relate it to something that was more fun than just sitting in a desk and writing or reading out of a book. And I think that's just a lot of the reason why my Greek school was just so boring for me because I just had to sit there for hours listening to people talk.

If the participants had bad memories of their childhood language learning experiences, most of them were considerably more positive about their experiences as adults. Here, too, the exposure to study of a third language was often the catalyst. Maria S. recalls the excitement of understanding Greek while taking Spanish.

> During my freshman year in high school, when I was taking Spanish, that's when a lot of stuff, when they explained it in Spanish, a lot of stuff in Greek clicked in. Like the tenses, perfect tense, imperfect tense, that kind of stuff really hit me. Even these last few years, I kind of understand . . . I never understood pluperfect and those seven or eight different tenses because we don't have them in English, so when I started taking Spanish, it really started to kick in, they are very similar.

Carol explains the difference between learning her native Korean and her third language, Spanish:

> I think in Korean class you had to kind of speak it already in order to follow the class so it made it a lot easier, because when you have conversation skills, you may not be able to write it down, but you can hear yourself speaking it, then you could at least put the idea down and then you can work on the grammar later. Whereas with Spanish, those people taking the class, they didn't have the conversational skills in Spanish to begin with and so you had nothing and the teachers had a lot longer way to go before you could get comfortable.

> When I started Korean, well it was my first language so I did not have any expectations. But in Spanish, I just assumed that it would be as easy to pick up Spanish as it was for me to pick up English. And when it didn't happen that way I was kind of disappointed. I kind of thought that I had this—well, because I hung around people who only spoke one language—this special gift so when I failed in Spanish, and I didn't do as well as I thought, that was a real disappointment and I think that is a big reason I am not pursuing Spanish because I did so badly and I expected so much.

Tom's love of languages started as he was studying his native Polish, and was increased when he discovered Spanish:

> Yeah, I'd find little things—like the word for "end" is the same in both languages. Certain words are the same, "library" is the same. I'd be sitting in

Spanish class and they'd say something and I'd be like "Yahoo! It's the same thing in Polish! I know this!" And I'd always bring it up in class, too. I'd always be excited to tell my teacher, "It's the same in Polish!" And she'd always nod and say, "That's good." I don't how what interest they [my classmates] had . . . I had great, great interest in the fact that I was finding all these similarities between the two. I'm sure the rest of the class thought, "Oh, please. . . ." I wasn't thinking about it at the time though, but in looking back, it's kind of a natural reaction.

[Learning Spanish] was easy. I suppose they geared it for American students and English speaking students so they went at a slow pace, but I caught on incredibly fast and I didn't need much time to understand it all because it was all essentially the same. But then again, there were things that were completely different too, as in any language, but the similarities helped me a lot.

As we saw earlier, the more language learning connected to culture, the more enjoyable it became for these individuals. But other factors contributed to success as well. The participants who enjoyed their college language courses talked about the characteristics of those learning experiences. Kiyoko describes it this way, "I thought it was good, the way the teacher taught it, she spoke a lot, almost everything was in Japanese except when she had to explain a concept, and I thought it was good." Miné recalls one Japanese professor who really made a difference in her learning experience.

He asked a lot of questions and he made us learn how to express everything in Japanese which is different because I was used to just having to answer factual questions—which is pretty easy after a while—but he made us express our opinions and do everything in Japanese.

. . . even when we got frustrated, he just was very patient and when you try and express something and you say, "I don't know," he'd just bring out one thing that you said and say, "Well, expand on this." He would help us along, he wasn't one of those teachers that just said, "Oh, you don't know, okay, just forget it." He made us learn how to carry out what we were trying to say.

Christine talks about a Japanese professor who had a "scientific" approach to teaching the language.

I'll never forget the time he told me that Japanese Americans are usually the worst students of Japanese language because they are so comfortable with their ear, with the language, but it makes them lazy, or somehow not as good learners of the full language as a whole. I think he meant that they depend on their ear more so that those who have never heard Japanese before, they learn it as a science and Japanese Americans don't.

. . . I feel he was a very holistic teacher of the language and I guess what I liked about it is his approach was a very scientific approach to the language and I think in the past I had been very comfortable with teachers who presented language as almost like a social science or an art. While that makes the language very interesting and enjoyable to learn, I think that is limiting too, and I can't say that one is better than the other because when you are teaching someone a second language often times it is more important to hold their interest than anything else, but by the college level, especially on an intensive level, it was very rewarding I think to learn it as a science.

For several of the participants, the experience that resulted in their taking a closer look at their native language was their becoming language teachers themselves. Maria W. recalls the extra challenges she faced in assuming the role of teacher of her native language.

When you learn to speak a language, you are not taught why something is the way it is; we were taught correctly, but I never understood why. When it got to teaching—specially student teaching—and I had to teach students, and of course all their questions are why, why, why? It was like, "I don't know, it's just the way it is." And my cooperating teacher lost his hair that year because I could never explain anything and he was just totally frustrated with these native speakers who had the audacity to teach the language. My response was, "Wait a second, shouldn't we be the ones to teach the language?" but he was frazzled to no end. . . . But, it taught me that I really needed to learn that stuff and it wasn't until I started teaching that I began to learn the stuff, the rules and regulations.

Now, I think I almost go overboard in teaching my students rules and regulations almost to the point where they have to say, "Foul, enough, can we just do the fun stuff?" I guess because that man put such a guilt trip on me and made me feel like simply because I knew how to speak it and read it and write it, just wasn't enough.

Like Maria, all of the participants who have taught their language commented on the fact that it wasn't until they had to teach it, that they really learned certain aspects of their language. Lorena recalls her tutoring experience.

At first I was scared, and I said, "Oh my God, what am I going to teach them?" And that is when I found out that I really didn't know. I mean, if I am teaching, if I am trying to tutor someone and I don't know what I am talking about, well I have to learn it first. While I was tutoring, I was reinforcing myself and I learned that way, so I think that is one of the major things that helped me.

For many native speakers, the most difficult aspect of learning their language often centers not on speaking, but rather on the special rules and conventions associated with the written language. This was the case for John, a Spanish American educational consultant, who also found that having to teach the language was what finally enabled him to master it.

The only thing I found problematic was accents, learning where to put the accent marks, spelling was never a problem for me—I have noticed in teaching Spanish in a bilingual classroom that new world Spanish speakers sometimes have more problems with spelling Spanish than Castillians do because it is pronounced differently—but, that wasn't a problem, it was the accents and I think that everyone who has learned in a communicative way has problems with the accents.

I had always been aware that Spanish was accented orthographically and knew in speaking it that words were accented in Spanish and then finally looking at the rules and trying to connect that to the spoken language. . . it was very enlightening to understand that *agudas* are accented on the last syllable and you can hear that when you say them, and then there are the rules as to why they would be accented orthographically. I only learned them when I had to teach them to my students.

A number of the individuals we interviewed decided not to pursue their language study beyond high school. They cited a number of reasons for this, often revealing that the study of their native language was becoming less of a priority than their regular academic subjects. Maria S. recalls,

Right now, I think Spanish is easier because you had it more, you had five days a week every day for an hour. You had it more and it was for a grade, you had to do it. Whereas Greek was not, was like a pawn, you use it to learn, so I think I picked up more Spanish just because you had it more. Greek was once a week for an hour, this was five days a week, really studying.

She recalls her parents' attitude towards Greek and other school subjects:

I think they wanted me to learn Greek more so that I could talk to people, but when I took Spanish, it was a grade so it was kind of important and they wanted me to get a good grade. It was probably equal, but in different senses. It was more, "take Spanish so you can get the grade and go to college." Greek was so that you could talk to grandma.

Carol recalls similar reactions from her parents regarding Korean and other academic subjects:

I think they gave me support, even when I messed up or something like that in the Korean class. They always said, "Oh, it doesn't matter, you just try again." But when it comes to other academic subjects, they are not that supportive because they don't know. They just assume you are supposed to get A's [in Korean] and so they are not as supportive. They are a lot more strict with academic areas.

The participants who decided to continue their language studies beyond the time required by their parents had a very different perception of how their language studies connected to the rest of their schooling. Miné sees a difference between learning Japanese and other subjects as one that includes how one studies.

I guess it depends on what you compare it to, but language courses I think most of the time they are more time consuming just because it's the kind of thing where you have to spend a little bit of time every day. Like for history, you may have to read a chapter, if you have a week or something it can wait. But I think for languages, in order to learn as much as you can, or keep up with it, you have to spend a little time on it each day either on memorization or just like reading, speaking, writing and so I know I spend a lot more time on my Japanese classes than on history or philosophy. A lot of times I spent more time just because it was something I liked because I knew exactly what I was doing, so I just liked spending time on it.

The concept of language as a "vehicle for explaining or expressing culture" (Scarcella & Oxford, 1992, p. 183) is emphasized by Christine when talking about her preference for Japanese over other subjects in college.

Well, I guess I found it much more rewarding because there's a real practical use of it. It was a tool to converse with Japanese nationals and to learn so much more about a country and a world and a way of thinking that was very different than ours so I found it much more interesting first of all than any of those other subjects . . . but I guess it was very empowering too, because as a tool you can open so much with the language and what I found real interesting in Japan too is that most of my friends were coming from very different backgrounds and regions, sometimes countries, yet our interests and love and all for Japanese culture and language really brought people together that would have never been together.

# Conclusion

The main purpose of this chapter was to find out more about the experiences of language learners who are native speakers of languages other than English. While we cannot reach definitive conclusions based on the fifteen voices who make up the chapter, we found that the participants, most of whom studied their native language while they were in elementary and/or high school just because their parents required it, fell into two distinct groups: those who stopped studying their native language when it was no longer required; and those who continued their studies because of their own need to understand who they are.

Participants in the former group did not see any need to continue their studies and cited reasons such as, "everybody speaks English in Greece" or "I really don't see that big an advantage just because I have two languages, we never use [my native language] in school at all." These participants did not perceive a connection between their native language and their identity; having studied their language did not influence their view of themselves or of the world around them. From their comments one might speculate that the type of instruction these language learners received did not help them understand the relationship between their language and their culture. In most cases their native culture was present in their homes, traditions were kept and even the language continued to be spoken; for the members of this group, this seemed to be enough.

While all the participants realized that having two languages was something that not everyone has, this group did not show enthusiasm or excitement when discussing their language. They seemed to look at their experience almost as a "condition" that one must accept in order to move on and not as a characteristic that made them special. Their language learning experiences were not very satisfying, several of these participants wished they could have learned more about their own history and culture and not focused exclusively on the language.

The group of participants who decided to continue studying their native language focused on identity issues and explained that learning their languages has given them "new insights" into their parents, grandparents and themselves. All of the native speakers in this group seemed to enjoy learning their language and were excited when discussing issues related to their learning experiences. They saw the study of foreign languages as an "empowering" experience and as a way to understand themselves, as well as an opportunity to craft a place as a native speaker living in the United States.

While the great majority of the learners interviewed for this study had negative memories of their early language learning experiences, the reasons were clearly related to their age (i.e., Saturday/Sunday school meant missing out on "fun" activities) and to the way language was often taught, "following the book." Once these students became older and saw the relationship between studying the language and understanding who they were, their opinions and view of language learning changed. They still found the studying of vocabulary and grammar boring, but they acquired a more "holistic" view of language. They focused instead on how language and culture relate and on what this means to them as native speakers.

These data seem to suggest that rather than giving credit to native speakers for knowing their language and focusing on areas which would motivate them and add to their sense of self, we seem to ignore their accomplishments by having them go through boring or unchallenging experiences. Images of native speakers watching soap operas to learn culture, memorizing vocabulary or going "from chapter to chapter" are very disturbing; in the words of Maria S., "you learn for the week and then you forget." As language teachers we need to realize the implications of the type of classroom instruction we provide for our students and must seriously examine the expectations we have for this group of learners. The participants interviewed in this chapter are no different from other language learners. We found native speakers wishing to talk to "real people," hoping to relate what they discussed in class to their lives, or getting excited when they were asked to express their own opinions rather than answering just "fact questions." It is our responsibility to provide a learner-centered classroom where students will have opportunities to develop their language skills, experience the culture and ultimately discover what that language and culture mean to them.

The role that teachers play in the motivation of native speakers to continue their language learning process cannot be overestimated. Many participants reported having a teacher who helped them establish a link between the language they brought with them from home, and the culture of their parents and ancestors. In one case it was a professor who loved to talk about the foreign food, people, music; in another a teacher who held his students to high standards, thinking them "lazy" because they relied on their ear when they could do much better; or one who kept pushing them to "expand" and would not let them give up; while in yet another it was a professor who taught the language as a science. In every case, the teacher played a key role in helping the student make the connection with their culture, and ultimately with their own self-esteem.

Personally, the data collected through the interviews served as a tool for introspection. As a native speaker of Spanish, mother of two children who are now formally studying their native language, the data forced me to realize that my own responsibility goes beyond encouraging and supporting my daughters' language learning experience. I must help them understand that Spanish is a very important part of who they are; that rather than being just another subject, it plays a key role in the search for their own identities.

The role that native language and culture play in the development of native speakers' identity is one that should be further investigated. We need to look at different languages, educational level, and socioeconomic status as well as the personal circumstances that brought the native speakers and/or their families to this country.

Regarding our role as foreign language teachers, the data suggested two areas that need to be studied further:

1 Motivation: What should our role be regarding the motivation of this particular group of learners? In what ways are they similar to the traditional learners in our classroom? In what ways are they different?

2  Instruction: What kind of classroom instruction should we use to help this group learn their native language? What kinds of learner strategies should we help them develop? How can we provide them with the experiences that will help them understand their culture and the role that it plays in their search for their own identity?

Native speakers, as other language learners, recognize the importance of learning other languages and value what these languages bring to their world. In Tom's words,

> And as people, I think, they [individuals who know more than one language] are a lot more open minded, a lot more worldly, a lot more knowledgeable on these languages and that gives them an advantage. They just know more about the whole world.

# Notes

[1] Interviews were conducted by the author and Mary Ann Mackey, a graduate student in the Bilingual Education Program at Chicago State University.

[2] We are very grateful to all fifteen participants who were very generous with their time. With their permission, we have used their first names and a general statement identifying their current occupation.

# References

Crawford-Lange, L.M., & Lange, D. (1984). Doing the unthinkable in the second language classroom: A process for the integration of language and culture. In T.V. Higgs (Ed.), *Teaching for proficiency: The organizing principle* (pp. 139–177). Lincolnwood, IL: National Textbook Company.

Gardner, R.C. (1985). *Social psychology and second language learning.* London: Edward Arnold.

————, & Lambert, W. (1972). *Attitudes and motivation in second-language learning.* Rowley, MA: Newbury House.

Kondo, D. (1990). *Crafting selves.* Chicago: The University of Chicago Press.

Oxford, R., & Shearing, J. (1994). Language learning motivation: Expanding the theoretical framework. *Modern Language Journal, 78*(1), 12–28.

Richard-Amato, P. (1988). *Making it happen.* New York: Longman.

Sadow, S. (1994). "Concoctions": Intrinsic motivation, creative thinking, frame theory, and structured interactions in the language class. *Foreign Language Annals, 27,* 241–249.

Scarcella, R., & Oxford, R. (1992). *The tapestry of language learning.* Boston: Heinle & Heinle.

# Voices from down the Hall: The Reflections of Non-Foreign Language Teachers

Frank B. Brooks

*The Florida State University*

## Introduction

In this chapter I report on the conversations I had with ten teachers who are *not* teachers of foreign languages, but who have, at some point in their educational experiences, been foreign language learners.[1] The purpose was to cull the voices of teachers who had experienced foreign language learning in various school settings in order to uncover their views on the impact of foreign language study on them as individuals as well as on the place of foreign languages in the educational landscape in the U.S. The ideas, viewpoints, experiences, and suggestions of teachers in other content areas—our colleagues down the hall—can bring an interesting and worthwhile perspective to foreign language educators, enriching our understanding not only of ourselves as educators but of our particular circumstances as well.

Hammadou and Bernhardt (1987) have argued that in many respects foreign language teaching is different from what many of our teaching colleagues do in other content areas. We deal with things, people, and ideas that are "foreign." For example, in many schools the foreign language teacher is left alone to do his or her own thing with no colleague with whom to interact regarding professional concerns, to share teaching ideas, or to collaborate, for example, on advertising National Foreign Language Week to the school community or on ways of teaching about any given topic. At the elementary and secondary levels, our colleagues may be able to "stay up" with their discipline by going to a local museum, to a local theater, or to a lecture. We, on the other hand, are frequently unable to improve or maintain our content proficiency without leaving the country.

Despite such differences, we share many common concerns with our teaching colleagues in other disciplines. We tend to hold similar beliefs about why education is important, about the value of particular instructional practices, as well as about the vagaries of classroom life and the varied learning outcomes that emanate from it. Like foreign language teachers, our colleagues in other disciplines also want to help learners construct positive images of themselves as learners of a particular subject, as members of society, as individuals, and as human beings. The similarities and differences in our circumstances suggest that examining the viewpoints of our colleagues in other disciplines may help us more fully understand our place in schools and in the overall curriculum. In short, our colleagues can be at the same time our best critics and strongest supporters.

These particular teachers represent a broad sweep across different levels of instruction in public schools. They speak from the dual perspective of professional educators and language learners who harbor very vivid, personal memories of those experiences. These memories have enabled them to construct attitudes toward what foreign language study entails. Although their language learning experiences are quite varied (for example, they studied different languages at different times in their formal education), there are some common issues that emerged during the interviews, and some unexpected news as well. For example, despite what were often difficult and frustrating personal experiences as language learners, these individuals as a group appear to be overwhelmingly positive about the value of foreign language study.

The first part of the chapter reports on the data collection procedures used in the study, characterizes the teachers whom I interviewed, and provides an overview of how the interview data were analyzed. Following these preliminary points, the second part of the chapter discusses the findings of particular relevance to the field of foreign language education. In the third and final part of the chapter I offer some concluding remarks as well as some suggestions for further investigation and pondering.

## Data Collection and Analysis

This chapter is based on interviews with ten teachers from varying subject areas, levels of classroom instruction, and years of teaching experience. Although I asked all the teachers the same basic core questions (see Appendix A), there were times when I felt it necessary to ask other questions for further clarification of issues and concerns that the teachers expressed. The format and process for each interview followed the general procedures outlined in the Introduction to this volume (p. xviii).

I employed various means to locate teachers within the local district who would be willing to participate with me in these interviews. In several cases I called a friend in a local school who located volunteer teachers. In other cases I spoke with a colleague, such as the school principal or some other administrator, who put me in touch with teachers who had agreed to participate. I also located one volunteer teacher in the local area quite by chance through a computer bulletin board service.

The interviews were audiotaped and fully transcribed. I read all the transcripts a number of times searching for recurring issues of interest and concern across the ten interviews, generally following procedures found in Spradley (1979). Once recurring themes were identified, the process of thematic identification and analysis across the ten interviews became an interactive-reactive process, involving multiple passes through the transcript data (Brooks, 1992; Erickson, 1986; Evertson & Green, 1986; Green & Smith, 1983).

## Participants

The interviews reported on here represent the voices of only a small number of teachers, primarily at the middle and high school levels. Nevertheless, these particular individuals represent a broad sweep across different disciplines and different levels of instruction in public schools. In this regard, the voices of these teachers resonate quite well together in that, despite their differing ages, social groups, teaching situations, and academic concentrations, they seem to have had similar things to say regarding the teaching of foreign languages as part of the curriculum. There are no drastically different voices to be heard among these teachers. Their opinions and perceptions are remarkably similar.

In many respects, then, the voices in this chapter are probably not unlike those we would hear from others who are of similar backgrounds and experiences. It is important to note, however, the one quality which may set them apart from other samples: the teachers whose voices we will hear on these pages live in Tallahassee, the capital city of Florida.[2] In this, the fourth largest of the fifty states, people who speak other languages abound; Florida is most assuredly a multilingual and multicultural state. Although Tallahassee is quite a distance from the more populated areas farther to the south, news of legislation regarding other cultures and languages and language education is readily available in the local newspaper, on local news programs, on special television and radio documentaries, among colleagues, neighborhoods, friends, and so forth. News of refugees from Cuba and Haiti, among other countries, is almost constantly in the headlines. The multilingual and multicultural nature of the Sunshine State affects its tax structure (how those taxes are spent on education), its legislative decision-making (how laws are developed that have a direct impact on schooling and education vis-à-vis language education), and its social forces (how people of different ethnic or linguistic backgrounds either do or do not get along).[3] Given that their perceptions of language learning combine classroom memories with perspectives drawn from other life experiences—a tendency these interview data suggest—it is important to keep the "geographic identity" of the participants in mind in interpreting their remarks.

Tables 1–3 summarize some of the background information about each teacher. Three males and seven females from varying cultural or ethnic backgrounds agreed to participate in the project. Three of the participants were African Americans, two males and one female. One was a Japanese American female, one a Hispanic, the remaining five Caucasian females. Their respective teaching areas also varied: two were third-grade teachers in area public schools, one was a university professor of finance at a historically African American university. Four of the teachers taught primarily at the middle school level, and the remaining teachers taught at the high school level. The languages they had studied also varied, although the majority had elected either French or Spanish. The majority of the individuals in the sample had studied their languages at the high school level and/or the postsecondary level; two (the university professor and one third-grade teacher) reported having studied a language at the middle school level, one teacher reported a brief foreign language learning experience at the elementary school, and one teacher also reported that her father had taught her some Spanish at home as a young girl. Most teachers studied a two-year high school sequence or a several-semester sequence at the college or university level. The university professor and one other third-grade teacher were the only interviewees who reported achieving any real fluency and actual use of the languages studied beyond the classroom. The Japanese American teacher reported that she still maintained her Japanese language, which she had learned in the home, to interact with family members. In addition, one of the third-grade teachers reported that she still remembered some of the German (and Yiddish) that she had learned at home, though she rarely uses it now. One of the young male teachers, born in Panama, claimed to be bilingual, Spanish and English, although he appeared to be English-dominant at this point in his life. For example, he revealed that he probably spoke more English with his family now, even when his Spanish-speaking grandmother addresses him in Spanish. As he commented, ". . . it's just easier for us to speak in English . . . the majority of the time I respond to them in English."

| Table 1. Languages Studied in Various Environments[a] | | | | |
|---|---|---|---|---|
| | *spoken at home* | *middle school* | *high school* | *college* |
| Female N = 7 | 1 G 1 J | | 1 F 1 L 1 R 4 S | 2 F 1 G 2 S |
| Male N = 3 | 1 S | 1 F 1 S | 1 G 1 S | 1 G 1 S |
| Total | 3 | 1[b] | 9 | 7 |

Note. The letters represent the following languages: F = French; G = German; J = Japanese; L = Latin; R = Russian; S = Spanish
[a] the totals are greater than the n because individuals typically studied languages at more than one point during their education
[b] same person studied two languages in middle school

| Age | Sex | | Race | | | |
|---|---|---|---|---|---|---|
| | *M* | *F* | *W* | *B* | *H* | *A* |
| 20s | 2 | 1 | 1 | 1 | 1 | |
| 30s | 1 | 2 | 2 | 1 | | |
| 40s | | 2 | 1 | | | 1 |
| 50s | | 2 | 2 | | | |
| Total | 3 | 7 | 6 | 2 | 1 | 1 |

Table 2. Demographic Profile of Interview Participants

Note. The letters represent the following groups: W = White; B = Black; H = Hispanic; A = Asian

Table 3. Current Professional Context of Interview Participants

| Age | Subject Area | | | | Level | | | Experience, in Years | | | |
|---|---|---|---|---|---|---|---|---|---|---|---|
| | Lang. Arts | Math, Sci. | Soc. Sci. | Art, Music | K–8 | 9–12 | 13+ | $0^a$–3 | 4–10 | 10–20 | 20+ |
| 20s | 1 | | 1 | 1 | 2 | 1 | | 3 | | | |
| 30s | 1 | 1 | 1 | | 1 | 1 | 1 | 1 | 1 | 1 | |
| 40s | 1 | 1 | | | 2 | | | | | 1 | 1 |
| 50s | 1 | 1 | | | | 2 | | | | 1 | 1 |
| Total | 4 | 3 | 2 | 1 | 5 | 4 | 1 | 4 | 1 | 3 | 2 |

[a]includes one teacher interviewed during teaching internship

Spanish was by far the most widely studied language. This is perhaps because most of the teachers attended schools in Florida, a state with a comparatively large number of Spanish-speaking citizens, especially in the southern parts of the state. Not all the teachers, however, attended schools in Florida. One, for example, had attended school in Massachusetts, though she taught for only two years in that New England state. She also taught for four years in Atlanta and some nineteen years in Naples, in southwest Florida. One of the teachers hailed from Alabama and another from Missouri. Four of the teachers were originally from Florida, having spent the majority of their lives in the southern part of the Sunshine State.

The next section of this chapter presents the four major themes that emerged as a result of the interviews. These themes are important for our profession in that they represent what some of our teaching colleagues believe and perceive regarding what it is we as foreign language teachers do and what we set out to accomplish.

# Themes

The first theme deals with motivation: the reasons these teachers decided to study a foreign language. The second theme deals with their recollection of experiences as classroom language learners. The third theme explores the perceptions of these teachers regarding the benefits of studying a foreign language as part of the regular school curriculum. Finally, many of the teachers were able to supply their own recommendations to teachers of foreign languages with regard to what it is we should do in the classroom.

## Motivation

> I had great interest in learning another language . . . just to know how to speak and say something they [my parents] wouldn't understand.
> —Bernard[4] [student intern in middle school band]

The ten teachers revealed a variety of motivations for studying their respective languages. Two reasons emerged most frequently. First, the desire to learn a foreign language was often tied to achieving pragmatic purposes such as completing a school graduation and/or entrance requirement, enhancing job marketability, or developing the ability to use the language for interacting with family or members of the community. Second, some individuals were drawn to learn a language out of intellectual or artistic curiosity.

Among members of this sample, examples of pragmatic or instrumental motivation were the more frequent. Connie, a middle school language arts teacher, expressed a strong desire to learn Spanish because, as she said, "I also have relatives in Miami [who] were taking Spanish in elementary school and middle school and it was something neat that we had in common even though I was in high school." She also stated that she had decided to take Spanish while living in south Florida "mostly because it was kind of doing what everybody else was doing." Katherine, the teacher who hailed from New England, also revealed an initially strong instrumental motivation. She had decided to take Spanish in high school because at that time in her life (the 1960s) she thought she wanted to be "an airline stewardess" and felt she "had to have foreign language to travel around the world." In contrast, Bernard, a student intern in middle school band who hailed from South Florida, was very aware of the important influence of the Spanish-speaking population in that region. He decided to take Spanish so that he could "speak and say something [his parents and friends] wouldn't understand" and because he felt a foreign language would "help me get a job in places; it would be a boost up if I could put it on a job application that I speak a little Spanish." As a young lad, he said that he "had a great interest in learning another language [and thought that] knowledge of another language was really important to me." Bernard commented that in that part of the state others around him spoke at least two languages "and that was neat," he said.

Also originally from South Florida, Isabel, a third-grade teacher with many years of experience teaching in the classroom, was required to study a limited amount of Spanish in elementary school: 15 minutes a day over the school's public address system. This learning experience in her elementary school days was brought about as a direct result, she said, of the "tremendous Cuban influence" in that part of the Sunshine State in the 1960s. Isabel went on to study Spanish for two years in high school, a decision she recalls being due to two things. First, there was a requirement to study two years of a foreign language in order to go on to college or university. Second, she was aware of the growing Spanish-speaking population in Miami and was already somewhat familiar with that language.

Although several of the participants talked about their experiences growing up in South Florida as having been a strong influence on why they chose to study Spanish in school, Beverly, a new third-grade teacher, was rather unique. During her childhood, her parents traveled a great deal to various countries in Central America because of an organization in which they had direct involvement. In the sixth grade, after her father had taught her a limited amount of Spanish informally in their home, she experienced her first visit to a Spanish-speaking country, El Salvador. This and other subsequent travel out of the U.S. solidified her interest in languages and being able to speak them, though she commented that "the only language I've ever *studied* is Spanish, from elementary school on to high school and college [and] it was always in a classroom setting" (original emphasis).

Hank, a new social studies teacher, also studied Spanish, but only at the university level as a university requirement for his degree. He revealed that he decided to continue studying Spanish because of his Hispanic background. He was already fairly fluent in Spanish and therefore needed to take only nine credit hours of upper-division courses to fulfill the arts-and-sciences foreign language requirement at his institution.

While most of the teachers were primarily motivated to study a foreign language because they thought it was a useful thing to do, some of them studied their respective languages more out of intellectual or artistic curiosity. Margo, for example, who studied French at the university after two years of studying Latin in high school, stated: "I took my two years of Latin my first years in high school and I almost turned around and right after that took my French because . . . I just wanted to take French." These remarks are similar to those made by the middle school science teacher, Keiko, who also studied French. She revealed that her choice of language in high school was recommended by her mother who was ". . . an artist, and she just thought that French was a beautiful language." Likewise, Louise, also a mathematics teacher, studied Russian in high school because "it was just unique and novel and because it was different . . . off the beaten path and it was available . . . and I thought [it] was an opportunity not many high school kids had."

The two types of motivation were not mutually exclusive within the sample. As we saw earlier, Bernard decided to study Spanish as much because he thought it might enhance his job opportunities as because he considered it "neat" to be able to speak two languages. At times, one or another motivation became primary as a reflection of changing interests and needs across an individual's life. Charles, for example, is currently a university professor of finance who grew up in Huntsville, Alabama, where there were many Germans involved in the space and science industry. He was interested in the sciences in school (he said he was a "science nut"), and became very interested in German because as a youngster he had been given sophisticated chemistry and other science sets whose directions were provided both in German and in English. Although as a youngster he studied both French and Spanish in middle school, his older sister had studied German in school and she, too, was in the sciences. Charles concluded that German would be the logical language to learn, and he ended up studying it for a total of six years, four in high school and two years in college. Charles's current interest in international business and finance has motivated him to maintain a working knowledge of his languages, especially German, though he also learned Italian in Italy. As he stated it rather bluntly during the interview, ". . . the U.S. is not the only place where people write business and financial reports, and those reports are not written in English." He also reported that he enjoyed travel and found that knowing another language was quite helpful.

Interestingly, a rather stark contrast emerges between those who elected Spanish in school and those who chose to study other languages, such as French, German, Italian, and Russian. Spanish was generally perceived as a very practical language for these teachers, especially for those who lived in areas where there were great numbers of Spanish speakers. Those who studied it saw a real-life or pragmatic need for its use with their families, in their jobs, and with friends in their neighborhoods. By contrast, the teachers who decided to study languages other than Spanish did so out of intellectual curiosity or artistic interests. The one apparent exception is Charles, the university professor of finance. Initially attracted to German out of a perceived connection between this language and the intellectual world of science, his motivation to maintain his languages, especially German and Italian, developed out of the recognition that foreign language skills can be very useful for him in his daily professional life. And even now, he continues to travel for both business and pleasure, and, as he says, "it's really handy to be able to speak the language of the country you're in, even if just a little bit. Every little bit helps."

## Recollection of Experiences

> Who wants to sit around and talk about verbs?
> —Charles

These teachers had both positive and negative things to say about their experiences studying foreign languages in school. The best and the worst of their experiences were invariably connected less to methods than to persons, less to what they learned than to the atmosphere in which they learned it. The classes they remembered positively were associated with relaxed feelings, and with teachers who were "fun" or had a sense of humor. The classes they remembered negatively were recalled in black terms indeed: "terrifying," "stressful," "petrifying." Their recollections group themselves into four broad categories: learning activities, classroom atmosphere, classroom vs. the real world, and learner strategies.

### Learning Activities

One characteristic of language classes noted more than once was the quantity of work required. Given that most of these teachers were language learners during the 1960s and '70s, the type of work they described will sound familiar to many of us. For example, Charles, the university professor, characterized his middle school French and Spanish classes as "lecture, drill, lecture, drill,"—a format he found unappetizing: "who wants to sit around and talk about verbs?" he asked. High school and college German classes were more to his liking because they were more "interactive," involving the use of visuals and discussion.

Bernard, the middle school band intern took both Spanish I and II in the tenth and eleventh grades respectively, having a different teacher for each level. He felt that his Spanish I class was "more positive" than his Spanish II class. He further explained that his Spanish I teacher, who was also a football coach at his high school, "used a lot of English and everything, he just explained and broke it down to us in a nice way." Later in the interview, with a chuckle, Bernard contrasted his two Spanish teachers. After having the football coach as his Spanish I teacher, he laughingly referred to his Spanish II teacher as "Miss Piñata" because, from his perspective, she was "the all around Spanish II teacher" and because she "put it on us as far as Spanish II was concerned." He elaborated further, saying that "people worked, I mean, it was tremendous." Bernard provided the following account of what life in the Spanish II class was like.

> We had to, we had paragraphs in the Spanish book we had to translate, write out in English and vice versa, when it was in English we had to write it in Spanish, conjugate verbs, um, change around and saying this to that, making it backwards, making it passive, making it present, you know, it was a lot of work, you know.

## Class Atmosphere

It was the atmosphere in the classroom that triggered the most vivid memories. Katherine, now a veteran English teacher with over 20 years of classroom teaching experience, recalled her two Spanish classes in the ninth and tenth grades in high school in the 1960s in Massachusetts. When I asked her whether she still harbored any memories of those early foreign languages classes she said immediately and with a great deal of affective force: "It was frightening, terrifying, awful, awful memories." Her Spanish teacher, according to Katherine, seemed to have taken "great delight in picking on the freshmen and sophomores" in her high school. She further added that her Spanish classes were characterized by "no humor, there was no give and take. It was Señorita T on her throne giving her students an awfully hard time." Katherine reminisced:

> She was very, very strict . . . very old fashioned . . . there was no humor. It was either yes or no; there was no encouragement. You knew the answer or you didn't. There was no give and take. She wouldn't ask you, or try to pull something out of you, you know. You got it wrong, you would have to sit down, and she would go on to someone else and almost always would start at the left-hand side of the class. We all sat alphabetically—my name, right up front!—so, inevitably, I would start. I might have the word ending wrong, maybe in feminine as opposed to masculine, the pronunciation. I had a terrible time rolling my r's and she got very upset with that. . . . I had to memorize words and I just had a terrible time . . . it was very stressful, it wasn't pleasant [and] I rarely heard her speak any, yeah, anything conversational.

By contrast, Katherine's college German courses with Herr D.B. were certainly more positive, interesting, and motivating. As she commented with a bemused look on her face and a certain twinkle in her eye, "I was in love with my German professor . . . he was a fun person." This particular professor spoke "a good amount of German during the day." Moreover, she said, "the whole feeling of the class was relaxed [and] I realized that was the best way to learn it."

Another of the ten teachers, Margo, reported that she took two years of Latin in high school and later went on to study French for four semesters at the university. She, too, harbored strong memories, especially of her French classes. As this middle and high school mathematics teacher revealed, "[those classes] made profound impressions upon me. I really can remember my French; I can remember my teachers, I mean, and this has been many years ago." Her most deep-seated memories were about her professor in her third semester of French. This particular professor, she recalled, "was a very nice, pleasant man until you walk[ed] in the classroom, [and then he] was very demanding, and I had trouble." In this professor's class, Margo remembered that she felt "petrified" because, as she recalled, "I would literally memorize the questions in addition to the answers so that I would understand the question when he called upon me." Her fear appeared to be so great at that time that when she went to the next class immediately following this particular French class, she said "I would be so upset, I would miss the first . . . ten or fifteen minutes of the next lecture because I would just still be so scared after coming out of [French] class."

## Reality vs. Expectations

Several of the teachers were disappointed about what they perceived as a lack of connection between the classroom curriculum and the "real-world" goals that had initially triggered their interest. Isabel, a third-grade teacher with over 20 years' teaching experience, related that her first experience studying Spanish occurred with a teacher presenting brief, fifteen-minute "phrase-book" lessons over the school's public address system. Although the content of those lessons clearly was intended to be useful and usable, ironically there was no person with whom the young learners could interact directly, one-on-one: students in class repeated key phrases that an unseen individual read and translated aloud over the public address system. Later in high school, where she studied Spanish for two years, Isabel described the program as "canned speech [or] *'Hola María, ¿cómo estás?'*" She further added, "I mean it came directly out of the book and that's how we memorized it and there was very little transfer to any kind of creativity." There appeared, in her recollection, to be no "practical application," to use her words, no using the language "to intermingle." Living in Miami in the 1960s, Isabel wanted to learn Spanish for pragmatic reasons: Spanish speakers were increasing in number in the city and she felt it was important to know that language. However, her memories reveal that she was conscious of not getting what she wanted out of her classes, that is, the means to "intermingle" with the growing Hispanic population of that city.

For Beverly, who studied Spanish for four years in her high school in West Palm Beach, Florida, the "disconnect" between the language classroom and the real world took a slightly different form. This third-grade teacher, who was just completing her first year of full-time teaching at the time of the interview, had spent some time in Central America with her parents, learning Spanish from her father as well as from interacting with native speakers. In telling about her experiences learning Spanish as a formal academic activity in high school, she commented that in the beginning classes "it was hard to remember all those rules. It would get frustrating 'cuz I would say something and say it in the completely wrong tense." Making grammatical errors in the classroom was an uncomfortable experience for Beverly because of the way her teachers reacted to her: "Teachers in school, you know, it was just something marked wrong." Moreover, vocabulary learning was "just isolated vocabulary, lists of vocabulary words, usually in alphabetical order." She further added that "it [Spanish] wasn't taught to me to be fun and exciting. Our teachers did not motivate us to want to learn the language. It was, like I said, textbook material." In fact, for Beverly, "there really wasn't any difference between a history lesson and Spanish lessons. . . . We talked about [the Spanish lesson] in English. We talked about the stories we read in English."

Beverly's disappointment with her Spanish classes was heightened by the contrast between the classroom and her experiences traveling abroad with her parents and on special trips, such as a home-stay experience in Spain one summer while still in high school. As she put it,

> I wanted to learn the language. I wanted to be able to speak a second language. I was just a motivated person. I think I went on to learn four years of Spanish not because I really liked the teachers and the way it was being taught. I did it because I liked the language.

One may wonder about Beverly's experiences beyond the beginning levels of Spanish. Did she have a more positive experience as she went from second, to third, to fourth years, and was she able, for example, to read more literature and use more pragmatic kinds of language skills in discussing the literature she was reading? Unfortunately, this appeared not to be the case. Rather, she related that

> When I went to my junior and senior years, my honors courses, [the teacher] was an American, an English-speaking woman, and we, you know, she had studied the language. It wasn't her native language so she didn't speak it natively to us. I don't think it helped me very much.

In reflecting upon these experiences learning Spanish as a formal academic subject, Beverly was, sadly enough, quite aware, even at that time in high school, of things she could do in Spanish that she was nevertheless not able to do in Spanish *class*:

> I couldn't communicate. It was just, you went from basic [language] to literature. You didn't go to discussion at any point. It was very much the same as you read a chapter, you talk about it, you write the answers to

the questions. I mean, we went to a very structured school, very textbook, rows, you know.

Connie, the middle school language arts teacher with relatives in Miami, definitely wanted to learn her chosen foreign language, Spanish, to be able to communicate with others. She quickly realized to her chagrin, however, that the Spanish she was hearing around her in her daily life outside school "wasn't the same kind of Spanish that I learned in the book." In other words, Connie realized early on the discrepancy between what her teacher taught in the classroom and the language the native speakers spoke in the South Florida neighborhoods and streets around where she used to live. Although Connie's public-school experience with learning Spanish was not what she had originally expected, a conversation class in college turned out to be closer to what she had in mind:

> I enjoyed it there, but it was more conversational than the book stuff, and it was stuff that I could use wherever I went . . . you could actually sit in a room and discuss and talk and decide why you weren't pronouncing things correctly or what was the problem, you know, grammatically. I enjoyed it even though it was just two semesters.

## *Learner Strategies*

Foreign language instruction, as in other kinds of classes, is a differentiated process (Green & Smith, 1983) with teachers and students constructing different relationships with and environments for one another. Margo, for example, alluded to this when she spoke about her fourth semester of French at the university where she was a mathematics major. Her French instructor at the time was a native speaker of the language who taught the course "almost completely in French." In this regard, she revealed that

> it was almost an in-house joke that she [her French teacher] wouldn't call on me, and I wouldn't answer because I didn't speak it well. I could usually keep up with what was happening, you know, because I would have the book and . . . so you know . . . generally what type of questions are going to be asked, so I could follow along with what was being said.

Katherine's strategy was to focus on assignments that involved reading and writing instead of speaking and listening:

> The dictation, the listening and interpreting quickly and then giving it back orally was the hardest thing of the foreign language to me and so I would always make my grade reading. I mean, I could read, I could translate, I could write you a paragraph or a page or whatever you wanted in French but just to carry on a conversation was not my strong point.

The same strategy also "saved" Margo. Once she transferred out of the class of the professor whose classroom manner frightened her so, she found herself able to manage—if not actually enjoy—her French classes.

> They were never unpleasant classes. I mean I never hated to go to French class and I generally did well in the classes. Except when we took dictation tests and other things like that there would be a portion of your tests that had the dictation but then the rest of it was written. Well hey, I would shine on the written part and so, therefore, I always survived.

In recalling their experiences as language learners, several of these teachers indicated that they felt that at least some of the difficulties they encountered were due to a "lack of seriousness" on their part, an attitude which was reinforced to some extent by what their school counselors had told them. For example, Connie said that she did not feel that her foreign language was deemed by her high school counselors a "real" subject area, like science, math, and social studies.

> This [the Spanish class] is a real class like every other class and I don't think that was stressed to me enough, um, it was almost seen as an elective when I went to high school, but when we registered for classes it was, you know, "You've got to take math, you've got to take English, you've got to take social studies, you've got to take science. Oh yeah, and a foreign language. . . ." So it seemed more like an elective as opposed to a real class.

Now, as a result of her personal experiences and frustrations in high school Spanish, she feels compelled to counsel her own middle school students, who are about to move on to the high school level, to construct a different perspective on foreign language classes. She said that she typically tells them

> "You guys, this isn't just PE, you know, this [foreign language] is a class, this is just like being in English, but it's a foreign language." And they're [her students] like "Oh no, don't worry about it Miss T, don't worry, it'll be fun." But it's not, and they get there and they're shocked, you know, their maturity level isn't at a point where they're ready to take the foreign language.

For this teacher, foreign language should be considered an important academic subject just as any other. As she said about her own rude awakening with regard to foreign language and its academic importance, "it was an eye-opener for me . . . it was the first time that I really had to sit down and say 'look, this is something you've gotta get, this is something you're gonna need'."

The notion that status as an "elective" might have some bearing on how one perceives the importance or value of a particular subject area was an issue that also surfaced during my interview with Bernard. For this young band teacher, who was at the time of the interview involved in his student teaching internship, courses such as foreign language and music, which was his own particular area of concentration, were not really viewed as important because they were electives.

> English and math [are seen] as more important than the Spanish class . . . they look at Spanish as another elective 'cuz the curriculum presents it as an elective . . . as cooking, French, band . . . you know, these are classes that . . . they call it, you know, workshop, tool shop whatever.

At this point I posed an analogy for him to see if he agreed with me. I said

> So . . . you think that's really sort of how foreign language is packaged, you know, in marketing terms. That foreign languages is packaged in such a way that it is kind of in the gourmet section as opposed to where you gotta go and get bread, meat, and potatoes and that these are the staples. But if you've got a little extra, then foreign language is there, too? Was that a fair characterization?

To this, Bernard quickly responded, "yes, it is . . . at the time that's what it was." This young intern was also rather shocked to learn that, although Spanish was an elective in his and others' minds, "I had to use a lot of analytical thinking . . . I had to do work there . . . but then it counted as an elective, but I saw English and Math as more important than the Spanish class." In this way, then, it may be that what people get out of or put into studying a foreign language as a formal academic subject area is a function of how the subject area is "packaged" and "sold" to individuals who are required to take it. This attitude seems similar to that expressed earlier by Connie. As an "elective," then, foreign language is perceived by some, perhaps by many, as being "fluff," something that is really not all that central, something that one has to "get through" in order to complete a required set of credits (i.e., language proficiency as measured by seat time in a required number of courses) in order to gain entry to a college or a university.

In sum, the above discussion indicates that these ten teachers remember their experiences quite well, even after being out of their foreign language classrooms for over twenty years in some cases. This is not to suggest that they do not also harbor strong memories about their mathematics, English, chemistry, biology, physics, social studies, or physical education classes. All these individuals indicated that they could recall many aspects of their formal schooling experiences, some being more positive than others. There is nothing to suggest that foreign language is necessarily so unique that it sticks out in their minds any more or any less than other learning experiences in school.

## Perception of Benefits

> So you get a broader view of just, you know, people and the
> way people think and the way they can view things . . . be-
> coming acquainted with another culture and see[ing] what
> life is like some place else, you know. It prevents people from
> being so egocentric.
> —Louise [middle and high school mathematics teacher]

Despite the fact that many of the individuals in this sample had some negative memories of their time as language learners, they all concluded that the experience of learning another language had been beneficial to them in important ways. The positive outcomes they attributed to foreign language study fell into four broad categories: acceptance of others, awareness and appreciation of other cultures, cognitive benefits, and linguistic benefits. For these and other reasons, the individuals in this study were firmly supportive of language study; they all expressed the belief that foreign languages should most definitely continue to be part of the American educational scene.

### Acceptance of Others

One of the benefits of having studied another language that several of the teachers talked about was achieving a level of understanding and acceptance of others who might come from different linguistic and cultural backgrounds, an important issue these days, especially in the Sunshine State. Isabel, for example, who had studied Spanish in the 1960s in Miami, said, "I see in myself that I am far more tolerant of children from other languages and other dialects." Reflecting further, this third-grade teacher, who has been working in a school where there are increasing numbers of limited-English-speaking children, commented:

> I still see some teachers [at my school] not very tolerant, not very patient
> that learning a language takes time. . . . But, I think it's real important
> to accept other people, no matter where they're from or how they speak.

In this sense, Isabel believes that the difficulties she encountered in trying to learn another language have helped her deal with thorny issues she now faces as a teacher: accepting, understanding, and working with children who, upon arrival at her elementary school and her classroom, have limited English proficiency.[5] Her experiences have allowed her to construct an understanding of and an appreciation for what it takes to learn or to have to use another language, no easy feat when one is quite literally dumped into a new school in a new country where the native language is not spoken. In other words, a certain empathy for what people have to struggle with while learning another language is developed. Moreover, Isabel feels that her experiences having to figure out how to say something in another language through simple translation activity in the classroom helped her understand that English is only one language among many, an important point that Charles also raised in my discussion with him. As Isabel said:

> It's important for [people] to understand that there are foreign languages; it's important for people to accept the idea that people do speak different languages. I think it would be important for children to learn or at least be exposed to the majority languages in the world, and I'm talking about those languages, not only English but maybe French or Spanish, the major languages that are spoken in the world.

Connie also observed greater tolerance among the students in her middle school language arts classes who have studied other languages or who speak other languages at home. According to Connie, those students who have had opportunities to experience other languages in elementary school ". . . accept people differently. They're more expressive than most of the other children . . . enough that you notice." In her view, interestingly, it was the male students who seemed to demonstrate these effects the most. She said that "their outlook on things is not local as much as it is global. . . . They look at things as it relates to the world, not just . . . Tallahassee." According to Connie, the students who know other languages or had language learning experiences in earlier elementary grades generally appeared to her to be "more global . . . and much more accepting."

## *Awareness and Appreciation of Other Cultures*

Louise felt that one of the by-products of her experience in the foreign language classroom was that she understood better and thus was better able to accept individuals from other cultural and linguistic backgrounds who also inhabit this Earth of ours. It was in this way that she expressed her perspective on some of the benefits of studying other languages in the school:

> I think it helps expose you to another culture. . . . Well, say you study psychology and do some interesting sort of psychological implications of language and the way we think that come out when you learn another language. So you get a broader view of just, you know, people and the way people think and the way they can view things . . . becoming acquainted with another culture and see[ing] what life is like some place

else, you know. It prevents people from being so egocentric.

For Beverly, a personal story summarizes the benefits of learning other languages and cultures. This new third-grade teacher told about her husband's "opening up" as a result of studying Spanish for three semesters at the Florida State University, an educational experience which seems to have opened up an otherwise closed door to the world.

> [My husband] was born and reared here in Tallahassee. Never moved outside of this state before. He took Spanish at the university and . . . it just opened up a new world to him. That, you know, there is not just the United States' way of life. That there's another way of life out there and you know, makes him more open, I think a lot more open than he used to be about other cultures. And now he wants to learn and he wants to travel . . . before when I first met him . . . [he was like] "Eh, I'm happy here." Yeah, I mean he was really happy being here. . . . I mean, I if I had all the money in the world then I would just use it to travel and go all over the place whereas [my husband] was just really content being here. But I think communicating with people from another culture, and going to [the university] and taking Spanish, he just *loved* his [Spanish teacher]. He'd always come home with ideas and things, and now he just can't wait to go to a Spanish-speaking country. So I think there are some positive things that people get from studying foreign languages.

Another teacher, Keiko, felt that foreign languages "would help them [the students] understand the world better." In her own experience, taking French was eye-opening in that she "learned more about France and the French in French classes than in any other classes." And this comment is similar to statements made by Hank who felt that one of the benefits of learning other languages was "to be able to cope in a multicultural world. The awareness that other languages exist." Isabel and Charles seem to echo these comments. Isabel commented that "our culture has not impressed upon the citizens that there is a world out there . . . it's fine to be proud of their country but it's not OK to be narrow-minded." For Charles, who deals with international businesses in various respects, the repercussions of this failing are obvious and acute:

> Dealing with business in particular I deal on a global basis. I don't deal with just the United States. We just think of ourselves [the U.S.] as being wonderful, the end-all. We're not the end-all. There's a huge world out there and our students, our kids, need to learn how to appreciate this great world. When you're talking face-to-face you really can't hold meaningful negotiation. You really can't have a meeting of the minds. Therefore, you really can't enter into a contract. . . .There are nuances of American culture that you cannot understand if you don't understand American English. Likewise, there are nuances within British culture you don't understand unless you understand the Queen's English.

## Cognitive Benefits

In addition to developing an acceptance and understanding of others from different cultural and linguistic backgrounds, these teachers also recognized that studying foreign languages developed thinking skills. Connie, for example, observed that "children with second languages tend to want to explore more. . . . They like to learn, they ask 'how' and 'why' questions . . . a lot of higher-order questions." When I asked Katherine, the veteran English teacher whose high school language classes had been recalled rather negatively, whether or not she felt this experience had been beneficial to her in any way, she responded with an immediate and very firm "definitely." "I think I'm a better person because of that," she explained. "I think I'm more insightful and creative, accepting of many things because of the experience. . . . Everybody should study foreign language. Just, you have another dimension of thinking. You think from a different point of view, you see it's more rounded, it's more . . . you see all the corners."

Margo, a high school mathematics teacher, also expressed feelings regarding certain cognitive benefits that stem from studying another language as an academic activity in school:

> I think it is a good thing for [kids] to do foreign language . . . whether they ever use that particular information or not. It's the same type of thing that there's many many students that graduate from high school who may never use Algebra 1 but that doesn't mean that it's not a course that they shouldn't take. . . . Just the basics of knowing you have different endings on words or you have a different way that they're put together, or the different types of meanings. Having studied a foreign language, I think, would help you no matter what foreign language you would study later.

## Linguistic Benefits

In addition to the social and cognitive benefits that some of the teachers discussed, there were also certain linguistic benefits that were mentioned. Katherine felt that her experiences talking about the languages in class, having to look at the structures of the languages she studied in comparison to those of English, all made her more aware of and sensitive toward her own language and, consequently, made her think about the other languages of the world. She feels as though she has a deeper understanding of the differences among languages as well as the similarities. Foreign language study in school helped her learn to look at language differently. Katherine further commented that, in retrospect, although her Spanish teacher did not encourage conversation in the language, she still feels as though she learned a great deal about the structure of language by conjugating verbs in class, writing sentences, translating, doing workbook activities, and so on. This knowledge, she felt, lead to a certain appreciation of language. For these reasons, she feels that, although individuals may not ever use in any way the particular language being studied, the activities associated with its learning are beneficial. She further suggested that the experience of studying another language in school probably helps in learning more about one's own language: "It's hard to really understand language if you really only know one language, or you've only encountered one."

Although she recognized that "some of the teachers [in my school] feel like our kids can't even, are um, even having problems with English and basic Math," Keiko, the middle school science teacher, remarked that she felt that foreign languages would "enrich" the school curriculum: "I think it [foreign languages] is just another aspect, maybe another part of the brain." These comments can probably be summarized best by Bernard who concluded by saying, "Hey, it's good to know another language."

The above statements clearly indicate that these teachers believe that there are beneficial outcomes to foreign language study and that foreign languages should be part of the school curriculum. However, one is immediately struck by the seeming discrepancy between the values these teachers attribute to language study and the generally unhappy particulars of their own experiences. What accounts for this contrast? A closer look at two of the individuals is revealing.

Isabel, who spoke eloquently about language study leading to greater tolerance and empathy, herself experienced an extremely impoverished foreign language learning environment in high school. She characterized her classes as repetition *ad nauseam* with no "application" of the language in any kind of real-world sense, such as interacting with native speakers of Spanish. How, then, does she reconcile her apparently negative learning experience in the classroom with the perceived benefits of the experiences that she discussed above? With this question, I returned to Isabel several months later. Her response was that she saw the foreign language classroom as having "the strong potential" for helping individuals understand the multilingual and multicultural nature of modern life, that the U.S. "was not the only country in the world, and that other languages are important as well." She further added that her foreign language experience was influenced not only by the Florida public schools but also by what her grandmother was experiencing at that same time. Isabel saw the struggle that her grandmother—a native speaker of German who came to the U.S. at an advanced age—endured while studying and learning English. And it was indeed a struggle, according to Isabel. The empathy, understanding, patience, and tolerance that Isabel developed, then, seems to have arisen out of a combination of experiences, both academic and personal, at a particular moment in her life.

Katherine's recollections of high school Spanish were described in vivid and unequivocal terms: "frightening, terrifying, awful, awful memories." At the same time, however, she maintains positive beliefs about the importance and benefits of foreign language study in school, and even feels that foreign languages should be required along with such subjects as mathematics, science, and social studies. In order to explore this apparent opposition, I went back later and asked her to characterize again both her foreign language experience as well as her feelings with regard to the math and science classes she took in high school. About the former, she quickly remarked "at the time, it was worthless." Her reaction regarding math and science was quite different. She said "no, because I liked to manipulate it and make it go and make it come out and I could, I had some beginning, and I always had closure, and ending to the problem or what have you." For this teacher, then, the value of some of her other classes was tangible and immediate, which can be noted in the following comment: "I suppose I could do it [mathematics] when I got through, like I could balance my checkbook and could do these things." Foreign language study, by contrast, was "worthless" because at the end, she admitted sadly, "I couldn't do anything with my languages." Interestingly, even though Katherine felt as though she could not "do anything" with her languages specifically, we have already seen that she attributes certain qualities of her own outlook directly to her foreign language learning experiences. Katherine also reported that her foreign language learning experiences, despite the fact that she did not take these classes throughout all her years of schooling, somehow stuck more in her mind than those in other subject areas because "foreign languages were different." It is quite possible, then, that some of the benefits that stem from studying foreign languages may not be immediately apparent but rather manifest themselves over time. In other words, in the years since taking high school language classes, Katherine has had time to reflect on her experiences and to draw conclusions for herself. As she commented, "I'm in education and have been for many years. Things change with time, they smooth out."

Apart from Katherine's rather blunt remarks, one important comment that I did *not* hear from any of the teachers was that studying another language in school was a complete and total waste of time, that nothing beneficial ever came from studying another language, or that foreign languages should be deleted from school curricula. Quite the contrary, the perceived benefits of learning other languages lead these particular teachers to conclude that it is indeed a worthwhile endeavor.

## Suggestions for Foreign Language Teachers

> Make it fun!
> —Keiko

Toward the end of each interview I asked the teachers to pretend that I was their former foreign language teacher. I asked them to give me their suggestions, if they had any, for improving foreign language instruction. Practically all of them had one suggestion or another to offer. The suggestions that came forth directly reflect the frustrations and inadequacies that they perceived as learners.

By and large, most of these teachers thought that foreign language classes should be focused more on pragmatic or "survival" skills. Margo, one of the mathematics teachers, for example, had some specific things to say about what students in foreign language classes should be able to do upon completion of those courses:

> In whatever language they choose . . . you should be able to, uh, in my case go to France or someplace else of speaking French or . . . in a Spanish class you should be able to survive in Miami or someplace else. Just like I think you should be able to use math when you come out of math class, when you come out of a Spanish or a French or German classes, you should be able to use it if necessary.

Here, Margo also mentions similar outcome expectations with regard to her own subject area, mathematics. Pragmatic skills or being able to do things such as solve problems with the language are what she feels are important outcomes.

While Margo spoke about broad outcomes with respect to attainment of some functional level of proficiency in several skills, several of the teachers offered suggestions with respect to actual classroom activities. These activities involved using the language in some real or meaningful way. Isabel, for example, suggested that foreign language teachers should make their teaching "applicable to the real world." In her view, this can be accomplished in at least one way by "showing the children in the classes how this [the foreign language] is important." In other words, as she said,

> Don't give them a book and make them memorize a dialogue, the way I learned. Let them have fun with the language, let them do a little of maybe writing in English and translating to another language, or, exploring how they could learn this language in the real world or having people from these countries coming in and um, talking to American children, or children in American schools. Get out of the ivory tower and make this real to the kids and don't be so dry and boring.

And this was not the only individual who reacted in this way. Keiko, the science teacher, wants foreign language teachers to "make [foreign language learning] fun . . . emphasize the survival skills . . . or more practical aspects." This individual, then, argues for more oral language activity in the classroom. She further suggests that teachers use "[repetition] and drill and oral work in the classroom . . . you know, you [should] speak it in class."

"Fun" was a descriptor that Bernard also used in his suggestions. "Make sure it's fun," he said, and "make sure they're going to learn something." He further added that he hoped that foreign language teachers would move away from "just giving instructions, you know, what to do in the classroom books, and just assigning . . . just giving homework assignments, telling them to conjugate verbs, just telling to study this vocabulary, know it, because Friday we're going to have a quiz on so and so." In this young teaching intern's view, the way to make foreign language classes more interesting is by "bringing things in the classroom, showing them to the students, field trips, uh, looking in, I guess, newspaper articles or something." More specifically, he suggested "making like a news report room and everything . . . making plays, writing out, you know, making it interesting like making a play or something that's in Spanish." In this way, he suggested that the language being taught could then become more contextualized and "you can conjugate verbs and everybody knows what you're talking about here." Beverly, the third-grade teacher who had rather extensive foreign language study experience, especially at the upper levels in high school, said that she would encourage her former Spanish teacher "to do a lot of discussion, a lot more discussion in groups, in Spanish . . . communication in Spanish instead of reading literature. " She further added:

> Reading literature is wonderful. But then, sit around in a circle and talk about it in Spanish . . . instead of answering the questions out of the book. You can always find the answers in the book.

Katherine was more succinct: "Lots of conversation. Groups. People talking, rather than rows and alphabetical seating and things like that. Noise. "

Based upon their experiences as foreign language learners, what these teachers are suggesting is that the foreign language classroom be more engaging and pragmatic. For them, learning and knowing about other languages and cultures is important. However, foreign language study decontextualized from the real world of language use is, recalling Charles's words, "not very interesting at all. Who wants to sit around and talk about verbs?" While several of the teachers used the word "fun" to characterize their suggestions, "fun" seems to equate to outcomes associated with real world abilities and understanding. Learning to survive in real world contexts is important for these teachers. Interestingly, their suggestions coincide precisely with the changes now sweeping our profession. Educational policy makers, researchers, and writers of textbooks and other instructional materials, all are calling for real world, functional outcomes.

# Conclusions

> Language is the key to everything . . . it's the key to build literacy, it's the key to writing . . . it's the key to communication.
> —Katherine

It is safe to say that studying other languages has had considerable impact on these ten teachers as individuals, as citizens, and as professional educators who are thinking about the total curriculum. These teachers all seem to feel good about their experiences despite the negative classroom scenarios they at times described. There are several broad issues that emerged from these conversations that are worthy of further discussion and exploration.

The first of these is the issue of experience. The teachers here reported, to varying degrees, less than ideal learning situations, and referred, in particular, to the decontextualized nature of their language study. What they studied or what they did in classrooms, at least in their recollection, was often neither "fun," nor "applicable" to the real world. In my view, this indicates that the consumers of our foreign language classes want their language study experience to be relevant to them, they want to experience something exciting, interesting, and, more important, meaningful. That is, they want to see a connection between what they are doing in the classroom and what they may possibly experience or encounter in life outside the classroom. Language study, to these teachers, should have applicability and not be an activity done in a vacuum. Language study is not an end in itself, but rather is a means to be able to achieve certain pragmatic goals in interaction with other human beings who speak the target language.

Although these teachers painted in some cases rather dismal pictures of their experiences in foreign language classrooms, all of them reported personal, positive outcomes from their learning experiences. Those benefits ranged from knowing more about other people who share our planet to greater understanding and awareness of their own native language and the apparent structure of language in general and general cognitive enrichment. Empathy seems also to have derived for these teachers from their efforts to appropriate another communication system. In other words, formal language study in school, at whatever level, and in spite of less than opportune learning environments, seems to have functioned as a mediational activity that helped these teachers reflect upon themselves, their neighbors, their education, their world, and their communication systems (cf. Donato & McCormick, 1994). As Katherine concluded, "language is the key to everything . . . it's the key to build literacy, it's the key to writing . . . it's the key to communication."

It is important to recognize that perceptions of language study may change over time and that at least some positive outcomes sometimes do not manifest themselves until sometime later in life. After being away from her foreign language classroom for many years, one teacher, Katherine, could reflect back and look beyond the negative, frustrating, and disappointing aspects of her experience as a learner. As she said in a subsequent discussion, "time heals all." As we become distanced from the activity, we are more able to extract what are positive outcomes. Isabel, another of the more experienced classroom teachers, suggested that while hers was a less than ideal experience in high school, she nonetheless recognized that the foreign language classroom has a great deal of "potential" for developing positive attitudes and perspectives regarding others who do not speak English or who are of a different cultural group. Of course, if she had been asked immediately following her foreign language classes in high school what she thought or what her opinions were, we would probably have a different picture entirely. After a number of years and a host of life experiences, one is able to see the potential for what can be. But then, this third-grade teacher has a vested interest in and concern for children who speak other languages. She believes that studying other languages can "encourage children to work together and accept each other."

While the suggestions of these teachers appear to validate current changes in language pedagogy, this should not imply that we as foreign language educators can rest. It does appear that ours is an important area of education, and the voices of these ten teachers have helped me to realize that we do have a positive impact on many aspects of our students' lives. We may not be so marginalized from the rest of our colleagues as we may sometimes think. Nevertheless, we still need to reflect on our classroom practices, on their impact on learners, and on how they can be improved to enable us to more consistently achieve the outcomes our profession espouses.

As with any kind of qualitative study, the interpretation is left to the writer and reader of the report. My interpretations of these interviews are a reflection of my own experiences learning and teaching Spanish as a foreign language and as an individual who has asked many questions about life in foreign language classrooms (e.g., Brooks, 1990, 1992, 1993; Brooks & Donato, 1994; Donato & Brooks, 1994; Platt & Brooks, 1994). In my mind, these interviews have been positive in that the voices are clear, articulate, and relevant. The findings are far from complete, however, and more research is clearly needed. One particular area for further investigation that emerges from these conversations is the notable gap between experience and outcomes. To what extent were their reflections influenced by the sociology of the geographic area in which they live and work? Is it possible to identify specific kinds of activities these teachers can connect to the positive outcomes they expressed? For example, one of the teachers, Katherine, feels as though she is now more "creative" as a result of her foreign language study experiences. What classroom activities or experiences specifically can she remember participating in that may have developed in her this creativity? Also, in what specific ways is she more creative? Is this creativity in terms of problem-solving ability or in terms of artistic creativity? Another teacher, Isabel, indicated that she felt she was now more tolerant of others who have difficulty appropriating another language or who speak English from a different cultural orientation. Can she tie these perceptions back to any specific kinds of activities that she remembers participating in as a student in her Spanish classes? Unfortunately, I did not enter into these issues during my interviews. Further investigation is therefore warranted to explore these important questions. If we can capture and know more about what specific kinds of classroom learning events lead to the kinds of positive outcomes these teachers expressed, we might be in a better position to effect change.

Another area for further research is how these teachers felt about foreign languages compared to non-elective subjects in school, say, mathematics, science, and social studies. What are their memories like for these classes? Did they particularly enjoy the classes that were in their current teaching areas? Are these areas inherently more important than foreign languages as one of the teachers hinted? If so, why are they considered more important? What arguments are put forth to substantiate a requirement for any set of courses while others are not required? Are the suggestions these ten teachers made for improving foreign language instruction similar to or different from suggestions they might make to other teachers in other content areas? In particular, would they make similar kinds of suggestions to teachers in their own discipline?

For me, writing this chapter has been rewarding and worthwhile. I have learned a great deal about doing research through interviews. It is not easy. But, hearing the stories of colleagues in other content areas and weaving them together to create a new understanding of what I do as a foreign language educator has helped me to appreciate our discipline more and to understand it and its place better.

# Notes

[1] I wish to thank Sangeeta Dhawan, a graduate student at the Pennsylvania State University, for her valuable assistance in transcribing the interview audiotapes. The Northeast Conference generously provided funding for the transcription and I thank them as well for their support. I also wish to thank Trisha Dvorak and Richard Donato for their insightful assistance in bringing this chapter together.

[2] I made no special efforts to interview teachers who lived outside of the Tallahassee, Florida, area since it was not necessary to gather a statistically representative sample of teachers from across the U.S. for the purposes of this volume.

[3] The Department of Education of the State of Florida recently implemented a mandate that requires all teachers in the state to participate in various inservice programs to prepare them to teach the increasing numbers of limited-English-proficient children who are

entering Florida public schools at all levels. This consent-decree mandate has been met with differing degrees of resentment, misunderstanding, and, in some instances, hostility. Nevertheless, the point is that the linguistic and cultural diversity found in all Florida classrooms is now affecting all teachers in the state, causing widespread discussion among all those concerned and affected. Editorials have appeared in all the newspapers in the state, letters have been written to the editors of these papers, and public discussion still continues.

[4]The real names of the interviewees in this chapter have been replaced with pseudonyms to protect the confidentiality of the individuals who so graciously agreed to participate in the study.

[5]This particular teacher, along with Beverly, teaches in an elementary school where many children from other linguistic backgrounds who are in the US for one reason or another find themselves placed. These limited-English-proficient (LEP) children are quickly mainstreamed with pull-out ESL programs, a fact that causes some teachers to react negatively simply because the children have, in some cases, extreme difficulties with English in the beginning.

# References

Brooks, F. (1993). Some problems and caveats in 'communicative' discourse: Toward a conceptualization of the foreign language classroom. *Foreign Language Annals, 26,* 233–242.

———. (1992). Communicative competence and the conversation course: A social interaction perspective. *Linguistics and Education, 4,* 219–246.

———. (1990). Foreign language learning: A social interaction perspective. In B. VanPatten & J. Lee (Eds.), *Second language acquisition—Foreign language learning* (pp. 153–169). Clevedon, UK: Multilingual Matters.

———, & Donato, R. (1994). Vygotskyan approaches to understanding foreign language learner discourse during communicative tasks. *Hispania, 77,* 262–274.

Donato, R., & Brooks, F. (1994, March). "Looking across collaborative tasks: Capturing L2 discourse development." Paper presented at the annual conference of the American Association of Applied Linguists, Baltimore, MD.

Donato, R., & McCormick, D. (1994). A sociocultural perspective on language learning strategies: The role of mediation. *Modern Language Journal, 78,* 453–464.

Erickson, F. (1986). Qualitative research on teaching. In M. Wittrock (Ed.), *Handbook for research on teaching* (pp. 119–161). New York: Macmillan.

Evertson, C., & Green, J. (1986). Observation as inquiry and method. In M. Wittrock (Ed.), *Handbook for research on teaching* (pp. 162-213). New York: Macmillan.

Green, J., & Smith, D. (1983). Teaching and learning: A linguistic perspective. *Elementary School Journal, 83,* 353–391.

Hammadou, J., & Bernhardt, E. (1987). On being and becoming a foreign language teacher. *Theory into Practice, 26,* 301–306.

Platt, E., & Brooks, F. (1994). The "acquisition-rich" environment revisited. *The Modern Language Journal, 78,* 497–511.

Spradley, J. (1979). *The ethnographic interview.* New York: Holt, Reinhart, Winston.

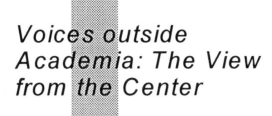

# Voices outside Academia: The View from the Center

Susan Terrio

*Georgetown University*

Mark Knowles

*University of Oregon*

## Introduction

. . . We stopped at the first café [in Marseille] we came up to, and entered. An old woman seated us at a table and waited for orders. The doctor said: "Avez-vous du vin?"

The dame looked perplexed. The doctor said again, with elaborate, distinctness of articulation: "Avez-vous du—vin!"

The dame looked more perplexed than before. I said: "Doctor, there is a flaw in your pronunciation somewhere. Let me try her. Madame, avez-vous du vin? It isn't any use, doctor—take the witness."

"Madame, avez-vous du vin—ou fromage—pain—pickled pigs' feet—beurre—des oefs —du beuf—horse radish, sourcrout, hog and hominy—anything, *any thing* in the world that can stay a Christian stomach!" [sic]

She said: "Bless you, why didn't you speak English before? I don't know anything about your plagued French!"

—Mark Twain, *The Innocents Abroad or The New Pilgrim's Progress*, 1895

This chapter highlights voices outside academia and centers on individuals from business, government, law, journalism, private foundations, and the arts. Interviewees span the range of these professional activities and share a number of characteristics. They are all well-educated, successful in their respective fields and largely unanimous in recognizing the value of second language acquisition despite a widely diverging set of personal experiences related to it. In formulating the research design for this group we divided the chapter into two separate sections based on two distinct research sites and samples. Thus, one set of interviews was conducted by Terrio in the nation's capital, Washington, DC, and a second by Knowles in the nation's heartland, two large Midwestern cities.

Two research sites were deemed necessary in an effort to determine what, if any, attitudes related to second language study differentiate professionals in a large metropolitan center from those in a smaller regional one. Recent comparative research conducted among members of the American and French upper-middle class in the Midwest/provincial France and in metropolitan New York/Paris is suggestive in this regard (Lamont, 1992). For example, although upper-middle class Americans seem to share similar overall attitudes with regard to the role of education, intellectualism and the legitimacy of high cultural pursuits, this consensus is mediated to a certain extent by the different outlooks of Easterners in important "cultural centers" like New York and of Midwesterners in "cultural peripheries" like Indianapolis (1992, pp. 124–126; 131–132). In this chapter, we wanted to determine the extent to which the attitudes of Midwesterners dovetail with or differ from those expressed by Easterners in self-consciously important and sophisticated metropolitan centers like Washington and New York. With both its literal and more figurative meanings, the "center" in the subtitle for this chapter thus references both groups whose voices are heard here.

## Data Summary

The data analyzed in this chapter were gathered from a total of 21 interviews conducted from April to August 1994. Twelve of the interviews were conducted on site in Washington, DC, or via telephone by Terrio. Knowles interviewed nine professionals in their offices, homes or by telephone in two large Midwestern cities. Both Terrio and Knowles targeted a balanced representation of fields as well as of gender, age, race and ethnicity but found this impossible to achieve for the reasons outlined below. In the end, both samples are broadly representative in only two areas: professional activity and age.

In Terrio's sample, five of the twelve interviewees are women, seven are men. They range in age from 30 to 66 and represent the arts (1), high level government service including both branches of the legislature (3) and the civil service (4), business (1), journalism (2) and a private educational foundation (1). Nine are Americans, one is a naturalized American having come here from Switzerland at the age of six, one holds dual German-American citizenship, and one is Argentinean. None is African American, Asian, or native American. With one exception all hold university undergraduate B.S. or B.A. degrees in humanities and/or social science disciplines. One interviewee began but did not complete college. In addition, six of the twelve hold advanced degrees in political science, economics/business administration, French litera- ture, international studies and design. One interviewee holds advanced degrees in journalism and English literature. All of the interviewees are widely traveled and claim at least some functional proficiency in a lan- guage other than their mother tongue. Eight of the twelve claim that they use a foreign language occasionally or frequently in their work. Many had a prolonged contact through travel or residence with cultures and languages other than their own at a very young age. As adults most lived (or currently live) in a foreign cultural setting for extended periods of time for personal, educational or professional reasons. Most explicitly described or implied that their parents' social milieu is middle or upper middle class, with one exception. That interviewee depicted her family background as largely blue-collar.

In Knowles's sample two women and seven men represent the arts (2), politics (1), law (1), business (2), publishing (2), and private foun- dations (1). All are Americans; nine are Caucasian, one is African American. They range in age from 35–60 years of age. All interviewees graduated from undergraduate institutions and five hold advanced de- grees in law, chemistry, Oriental studies, and English. Another common- ality among Knowles's respondents was attendance at private schools; six of the nine mentioned private school experiences in the course of the interviews.

In contrast to Terrio's sample, the people interviewed by Knowles had not all had prolonged contact with a foreign language and culture as youngsters or traveled widely. Seven of the nine claim some functional proficiency in a second language but only four of the nine have used or currently use it in their work.

## Constitution of the Samples

Both Terrio and Knowles encountered a number of constraints in constituting a sample composed of professionals outside academia. Gaining access to these individuals often posed a challenge. Similarly, a research methodology built around one-hour interviews with the possibility for follow-up questions posed a formidable problem. It was sometimes unrealistic to ask legislators, senior government officials or other highly paid professionals like attorneys to devote an entire hour of long, tightly scheduled days to one interview. This was particularly difficult for Terrio who sought prospective interviewees based on the high structural positions they occupy within institutions and on the predominantly national or international perspective their work demands. Some of the individuals she contacted had to decline despite their interest and others accepted on the condition that the interviews be shortened. For example, five of the interviews, those with Senator Paul Simon, Congressmen James Oberstar and Sam Farr, Deputy Secretary of Education Madeleine Kunin and journalist Susan Stamberg, averaged 20 minutes. This format did not allow for the in-depth questioning or follow-up so critical to the gathering of rich data in projects of this kind. The constitution of her research sample was largely determined by both the interest of prospective interviewees in the research topic as well as the time constraints imposed by their professional schedules. In the end only those who felt strongly about the importance of language study agreed to be interviewed. Those who did not see its importance would not allocate the time to be interviewed.

Knowles was also faced with the problem of time constraints. However, once the interviews were underway, Midwest respondents were generally more willing to allow the interviews to extend beyond the one-hour limit agreed upon in advance. In addition Knowles faced the problem of being new to the Midwestern locale where he conducted the interviews. For this reason, he relied primarily on three colleagues for his contacts outside academia. One of those colleagues was located in the public relations office of his university, a second was a theatre professor, and a third teaches in a local branch of the Alliance Française. Their understanding of the nature of the research project necessarily influenced their choice of prospective interviewees for Knowles to contact. This may explain why some of the interviewees in his sample had very strong connections to foreign language use. For all these reasons, we make no claims to having constituted a representative sample or one whose results could be externally validated.

Knowles changed all but one of the interviewees' names for purposes of confidentiality. Only Tom Barrett, an elected public official, is identified by his real name. Terrio gave the interviewees in her sample the choice of anonymity or identification by name. Those who preferred to retain their real identities include: Senator Paul Simon, Congressmen Sam Farr and James Oberstar, Deputy Secretary of Education Madeleine Kunin, Susan Stamberg, Karen Moody, and Jeff Munks.

## Foreign and Second Language Study in the 1990s

The discourses of professionals within and outside academia must be situated in a specific sociocultural and economic context. It is a context marked by a preoccupation with a number of challenging domestic issues: educational and health care reform, mounting social fragmentation and urban violence, change in family and gender roles, economic polarization, diminished government resources and renewed debates concerning the appropriate scope and role of government on the local and national levels. With respect to language education, this is a climate marked by contradictory trends. On the one hand, ambitious educational initiatives like Project 2000 include foreign languages among the critical core academic subjects. In addition, a series of recent public hearings held by Senator Paul Simon drew national attention to innovative bilingual programs in schools at the elementary level. Similarly, in November 1994, National Public Radio highlighted a special public school curriculum in Northern New Jersey featuring an immersion French program in the context of an Afrocentric curriculum. Debates in American universities on the issue of multicultural diversity have provoked a rethinking of the assumptions informing the official canon in a variety of disciplines. In some language departments this has stimulated a broadening of traditional offerings which had previously focused exclusively or primarily on literature and high culture.

Outside the United States the mounting contestation and blurring of national and cultural boundaries in many areas of the globe has drawn attention to different sets of languages and emphasized the sociocultural, political as well as economic benefits to be gleaned from mastering them. For example, the dismantling of apartheid in South Africa has had a number of unforeseen consequences. One such consequence includes the effort on the part of some whites to learn the languages of indigenous Black South African peoples in the interest of both increased cultural understanding and better business. The fall of the Berlin wall and the opening of vast new markets in Eastern Europe represent important economic opportunities for those with international expertise, both linguistic and cultural.

Yet, the shifting international circumstances notwithstanding, we all recognize that the current educational climate here at home is characterized by serious fiscal constraints and deep social problems which demand difficult programmatic decisions. In an era when politicians win elections on the strength of promises to reduce income and property taxes, it is important to examine the sociocultural attitudes which inform the decisions regarding which programs will inevitably be cut when tax revenues shrink. In the press of daily events, languages (both traditional and innovative courses) and arts programs are often the first to be downsized or eliminated. As one interviewee put it, "Here we are talking about a language requirement and what the teachers in this city [Washington, DC] really want are bullet-proof vests to wear to school."

We began this chapter with a quote from Twain's *The Innocents Abroad*. It recounts only one of several failed attempts by Twain and his fellow American travelers to communicate with foreigners in their own tongue. Although first published in 1869, it sounds contemporary and familiar more than a century later. Indeed, many of the feelings and descriptions Twain so amusingly conveyed for his readership still have much to say to us today. In spite of his mocking wit, Twain revealed his attraction to and unabashed awe of many aspects of the "Old World." In the chapters on France we see him eager to get a glimpse of the French emperor, Napoleon III, "the representative of the highest modern civilization" (p. 126) and to claim recognition of Parisian art, architecture and important urban landmarks. Despite his self-deprecating humor, his descriptions also reveal the frustrations of Americans not able to communicate in a second language on even a rudimentary level as well as their embarrassment in the face of the attendant cultural misunderstandings arising in such situations. In a humorous but revealing passage Twain explains that despite their resounding failures at communication, he and his friends relentlessly continued "to put unoffending Frenchmen on the rack with questions framed in the incomprehensible jargon of their native tongue, and while they writhed, we impaled them, we peppered them, we scarified them with their own vile verbs and participles" (p. 113).

In the following chapter we will hear the thoughtful voices of professionals who, in many cases, have been irresistibly drawn to foreign civilizations and the languages spoken there. We should pay close attention as they share both their triumphs and their failures in the struggle to master languages other than their own. These are the voices of individuals who, in some cases, wield considerable power in those arenas which affect us most directly. Their voices allow us to explore the perceived benefits, expectations, and motivations of pursuing language study as well as the complex nexus of class, ethnicity, gender and political economy in the determination of what languages are "best" to study and why.

# Part I: Washington, DC

Susan Terrio, Georgetown University

## Introduction

I conducted interviews among individuals who all qualify as elites by virtue of their education and the high structural positions they occupy within public and private institutions. These individuals are regularly part of policy and decision making processes with potentially far-reaching impact within their particular fields and beyond. In an era of mass communication technology elites in highly visible positions in government, the arts, business and journalism frequently appear in print and visual media and have heightened power to shape and mobilize public opinion on particular issues.

The theoretical issues I had in the back of my head while seeking out and interviewing people for this project arose from a number of sources. First, as a longtime student of France and professor of language and civilization in a university French department, my personal experiences informed the interviews I conducted. So did my training in cultural anthropology, my experience conducting ethnographic fieldwork and my understanding of the issues raised in recent ethnographies of elites in complex societies (Marcus, 1983; Giddens, 1973). Previous research on elites, corroborated here, indicates that there are a number of important issues which readers should be mindful of as they listen to these voices. A brief summary of these issues follows.

A dominant strand in the research on elites developed in American social science after the Second World War. Informed primarily by political theory, this research attempted to chart the organization of mainly political elites in an effort to understand the actual power they exercised as leaders and to what degree they influenced social processes. As Marcus notes (1983, pp. 7–57), this research was marred by significant lacunae. Its principal aim was to prove or disprove the existence of a society-wide organization of interlocking elites. As a result it presented a monolithic view of all elites as political elites who pursue their goals and exercise power through conscious, systematic calculation and strategizing. At the same time, this research relied too heavily on external manifestations of elite power and organization as seen from the outside. Elites in this research seem to exist apart from culture; their agency allows them to appropriate and deploy it at will. It is not clear how culture shapes and constrains their practice in unself-conscious ways.

As Marcus has shown in his own work on American dynastic families, it is important to consider the internal culture and identity of elites manifest in their family relations and background, world view and practices. How do elites talk about themselves? How do they conceive and construct the boundaries which separate them from people in other social classes? As Bourdieu (1984) has shown, one's place in a given social order is reflected and maintained by the consumption of symbolically valued goods. The choice of cultural goods like art, music, and food are related to complex symbolic struggles for social differentiation. These struggles for differentiation beg an important question for this study. Are certain foreign languages considered to be cultural goods in the sense that studying or knowing them is a marker of distinction and thereby consolidates or elevates class status?

Marcus also notes that conducting research among elites is complicated for a number of reasons. First, they are frequently called upon to justify what they do and to demonstrate how they arrived at particular decisions. As a result, they become highly skilled at representing themselves, their work, and their politics. In Washington in particular the art of representation is highly elaborated and demands exhibiting multiple selves and identities in specific, located situations for particular ends. Sorting out personal views from political agendas on certain issues can be difficult. Second, research on elites in complex societies reveals that they manifest attitudes that, ideologically at least, mask privilege and eschew elitism (Giddons, 1973). This discourse can obscure the strategies actually pursued in an effort to reproduce elite status or ensure social mobility. A third and final complication regarding research on elites concerns gaining access to them (see page 146). This part of the chapter includes four sections related to language study: positive and negative experiences, benefits, motivations and interviewees' analysis and prescriptions related to both language teachers and the profession as a whole.

## Experiences

The interviewees in this sample experienced language study in a variety of settings. All studied language for varying lengths of time in their native culture in a structured school setting as elementary, secondary, university or night school students. All of the interviewees also had an immersion experience with language in a foreign culture in a formal school environment, informally as resident "street" learners or a combination of the two. Despite this richness of linguistic experience and a complete faith in the value and importance of foreign language study, interviewees were not exclusively positive about the learning experiences they encountered. Many expressed strong criticism of some of their teachers, foreign language pedagogy, the educational system as a whole, and American cultural attitudes related to language study.

Eight of the interviewees were predominantly positive when describing the overall impression they retained of their language classes. It is interesting that in all but one of these eight interviews positive impressions of the language experience were directly tied to a specific language teacher. Interviewees spontaneously mentioned these educators by name along with the distinctive traits that marked them as "great" teachers: they were "rigorous" in the demands they made of students, "passionate" about their subject, experienced and completely sure in the knowledge of what "worked" best. For example, one interviewee, an international economist with the Foreign Commercial Service who expected to be posted to China in October 1994, studied Mandarin Chinese in Taipei and at the Monterey Institute for International Studies. He remembers his teachers in both settings with fondness. He described his instructor in Taipei in this way:

> When I first started out, and I sat there in that classroom—I'll never forget this—we just studied the tones. You do that for two hours and then you try and make an assessment of how far you've come that morning. That teacher, he taught us respect. He really did. We had drills that we would go through again and again. It was very structured. Sentences would get longer and then a bit longer. I think for beginners it was the right way to approach it and I give him a lot of credit.

In a similar vein, Susan Stamberg of National Public Radio fondly remembered her French teacher after a hiatus of 35 years:

> Mme N, boy, I can see her. You are making me think of her after all these years. . . . I was so intrigued. I mean she really wasn't like anyone I knew. She was always demanding and very precise. I remember how tough it was, so in a way it's memorable.

Congressman Sam Farr had very disappointing experiences with Latin in high school and German in college taught in what he described as a "dead, grammar book-based" approach. After graduating from college he entered the Peace Corps and studied Spanish intensively in a small, conversational format which he found very effective:

> The teacher who taught me Spanish really wanted us to learn. He was so excited about what he was doing. He made up games, he would take us on walks. He would point to things and give us the Spanish word. All of a sudden, you quickly learn vocabulary . . . bird . . . car . . . and you see language as a real, living thing.

These educators are depicted as playing a pivotal role in motivating the interviewees to begin, to continue and to perfect their language skills. They often provided a watershed experience for the interviewees. Interviewees had the sense that they were at the beginning of a long, arduous but worthwhile quest for linguistic and cultural competence that would probably extend a lifetime. Congressman James Oberstar credits his fluency in French and Creole and some of the recognition he has received as a bilingual member of Congress to his ninth grade French teacher who insisted that he take her subject and his own talent seriously:

> I was 14 years old and interested in foreign language but my friends were really more important at the time. So we were about 20 in French class and I would systematically sit in the back of the class with my buddies and goof off. After the second week, Madame Y took me by the scruff of the neck saying you will speak in this class, marched me up to the front of the room and sat me in the front row. After class I asked her why she picked on me. She was a tiny thing and I was already taller but she pulled

herself up, looked me straight in the eye and said, "Son, you have real talent and you're wasting it."

The teachers mentioned by these interviewees represented a variety of pedagogical approaches and different content areas. For example, some interviewees mentioned professors who taught upper-division literature, civilization and social science courses in the language whereas others talked primarily about the teachers who taught them in the early stages of language acquisition. The experiences they described varied from highly structured grammar-based instruction to more loosely structured "communicative" approaches. It is also significant that many interviewees spontaneously indicated how critically important it was to have teachers who spoke the language as their mother tongue. It is therefore paradoxical to note that some of these same interviewees could not remember or did not know for sure if the language teachers they described as exemplary actually were native speakers of the language. For example, one interviewee said that students who didn't have native speakers as language teachers "were deprived in a way." However when pressed for details concerning the French teacher she had described so positively, she admitted that she didn't know if she "was really French or not."

Whereas positive language memories were tied primarily to people and encompassed different classroom approaches, negative experiences were attributed directly to "bad" pedagogy. Four of the twelve interviewees had predominantly negative classroom experiences with language study. The names of intimidating, inept or indifferent language teachers were either obfuscated or forgotten. The pedagogic damage they did was not. In her recent memoir *French Lessons,* Alice Kaplan (1993) recounts her personal experience learning and teaching French in a variety of contexts in this country and abroad. She describes the language classroom as "the rawest pedagogic situation I have ever been in. A place where content means almost nothing and power, desire, and provocation almost everything" (p. 128). While this view of the classroom is not one which most language teachers would accept or perhaps even acknowledge, it resonates powerfully with some of the experiences related by the interviewees in this sample.

Congressman Farr vividly recalls the "awful" ambiance of the high school Latin class his mother insisted he take in order to improve his writing in English. He described that Latin class as a counterpoint to the many encouraging interdisciplinary experiments in pedagogy currently being undertaken in California schools to improve teacher effectiveness and student performance.[1] Congressman Farr linked his poor performance and discomfort in Latin class to outdated pedagogy and the abuse of power which Kaplan suggests language teachers can sometimes fall prey to.

> The teacher who taught me Latin had to have been educated in the 18th century. He was there with a ruler, I mean he was just vicious, a mean person and you were afraid to fail. . . . It was an uncomfortable room to go into. Unfortunately, my experience with German [in college] was not much better. Neither was stimulating or very good.

Senator Paul Simon describes himself as an example of "the deficiencies in language teaching in this country rather than the strengths." His unsatisfactory experience in a college German class is linked less to power than to pedagogy. The life had been wrung out of the German he attempted to master; he neither excelled in nor appreciated the sterile, almost exclusively grammar-based approach adopted in that course.

> It was like a language being spoken on the moon. It had nothing to do with the culture of the country. Oh, we learned some poems and things like that so there was a little bit of insight into culture but there was no consistent tie-in, no relationship to reality.

Some of the interviewees expressed the disillusionment and frustration they felt when they tested what they thought they knew in an authentic cultural setting with native speakers and failed. Jeff Munks, the Director of Marketing and Sales of AT&T Language Line and recent Visiting Fellow at the National Foreign Language Center in Washington, recalls the first real test of his Spanish after arriving in Madrid, Spain. Munks had entered the military and been stationed there largely on the strength of the four years of Spanish recorded on his high school transcript.

> When I got off the plane in Madrid I went up to the first Spaniard I met, asked for directions to the rest room, got them and walked off thinking, "I do speak Spanish." But I soon realized that I could say only four other things. I could ask for directions to the library, buy bread and butter, say hello to a woman named Isabel, and tell you my name. It was like an ocean of cold water in the face. It hadn't taken. It hadn't worked. It wasn't like math or history or, you name the subject area. I knew nothing. Nothing. I had vocabulary, that's all. And it was very limited at that.

Munks and some of the other interviewees attributed their failure in mastering high school language to the absence of a sufficiently developed "use-based" teaching approach as well as well-defined, realistic goals. Munks blamed the reigning teaching paradigm of that time (the mid to late 1960s), the ALM or Audio Lingual Method for its Skinnerian behaviorism, its emphasis on strict memorization and drill and its avoidance of autonomous language expression. He also remembers being struck by the glaring absence of rigorous performance standards in language classrooms especially compared to his other "academic" subjects. It is interesting to note that some interviewees who described their foreign language study as demanding nevertheless believed it could not compare in difficulty with core subjects such as history and math. Listen again to Jeff Munks:

> What struck me time and time again, if this had been a math or econ class and I was sitting there and listening to the kinds of responses that were not accurate, not effective, these people around me would fail. But what's happening around me is they're being told "Keep working on it" or "You're comin' along." I began to see that the whole notion of objective measures of performance, success, attainment or what have you did not exist. The only place they existed was when you put pen to paper . . . and that happened rarely. And was not the primary basis for evaluation. In fact, I think the number one driver that affected your grade was attendance and attitude.

Many will argue that both ALM and predominantly grammar-based methods have been largely abandoned for approaches which provide more balanced amounts of structure and practice with the goal of achieving measurable levels of language proficiency. Similarly, in many language departments civilization and linguistic tracks are now more fully developed than they were some years ago. Yet some of the descriptions of recent language experiences given by interviewees suggest that older paradigms may persist longer and in more settings than we think.

One interviewee is an author who has researched second language acquisition theory and written extensively on bilingual education. He had studied French from 1963–68 over a period spanning high school and one year in college. He also took a semester of Anglo Saxon as a college freshman in 1968. After a hiatus of over 20 years, he decided to begin language study again because he felt his research demanded that he experience it personally. He chose Spanish because he considers it to be the most useful language of study in this country. He contrasted the "uselessness" of the grammar-based instruction he received in 1992 in a night school Spanish course in Washington with the immersion, proficiency-based approach he experienced at a private language school in Mexico in the same year.

> I enrolled in a night school course in Spanish [in 1992] but I was very disappointed with it because, one, it was very large (20) and also, the

teacher didn't really know what she was doing. She had us doing a lot of translating. We would go around the room and each person would translate a sentence and it seemed pretty useless. It was supposed to be an intermediate course and I was not hearing much Spanish. She was conducting the course in English, so I dropped out.

All of the interviewees worked hard to achieve some functional proficiency, earning a healthy respect for the effort and time required to attain competence in a language other than their mother tongue. A common thread which ran through all the interviews was the description of a set of personalized learning strategies which they pursued (and continue to pursue) as admitted "lifelong" students of language. At various points in the process these interviewees all recognized and acted on the need to "take charge of the process" and to develop an individualized approach for internalizing linguistic structures and enhancing cultural competence. Making the language their own meant incorporating it more fully into the quotidian rhythms of their lives.

Congressman Farr explained that "it [foreign language] is not something you just go to and do two hours a week and walk away from." While preparing to go to a Spanish-speaking country with the Peace Corps he sought out Spanish language and culture outside of the classroom in a variety of contexts: on Spanish television and radio programs and in the movies, markets and restaurants. He insists that in spite of the demands of his congressional schedule he still makes time to "keep up with and use his Spanish." Congressman Oberstar remembers that during an intensive summer immersion course in French he attended at Laval University in Canada, he spent his free evenings and weekends seeking out and introducing himself to the native speakers he ran into on the street. He kept a notebook in which he recorded everything that was new linguistically and culturally. Similarly, Karen Moody, Vice-President of Deutsche Grammophon Records in New York, remembers that in college she and several other interested students met on their own three times a week to practice speaking French. Jeff Munks was so distressed at his inability to communicate when he arrived in Spain that he immediately moved out of his American quarters into an apartment complex in the city of Saragossa where there were no Americans. For two years he immersed himself in the life of his local community developing close ties with a number of neighbors. He learned Spanish by asking neighbors into his home, inviting himself into theirs and "spending long evenings over a brandy just struggling."

## The Payoff

Interviewees identified a number of both direct and indirect rewards to be gleaned from their language learning experience. While the ability to communicate orally in the language with native speakers was mentioned often it was by no means the only benefit cited by interviewees. As noted above, all but one of the interviewees do work which has a pronounced international dimension. Their skill in a foreign language afforded them important practical benefits such as using the language for work as well as symbolic recognition and cultural capital which could be usefully displayed with other elites and subordinates.

Interviewees could all point to practical, on-the-job benefits of having skill in another language regardless of the actual level of functional proficiency they had attained. They cited a range of different linguistic tasks they could perform which enhanced public relations, established a more collegial work ambiance, improved performance of their work and/or directly advanced the interests and effectiveness of the institutions or businesses which they represent. These tasks varied greatly and included the ability to greet and welcome international guests, to participate in informal conversations with foreign colleagues or visitors, to communicate on some substantive professional issues with foreign interlocutors, to participate fully in high level verbal or written negotiations or debates in another language, and to provide emergency interpretation in conflict or crisis situations where a language barrier exists.

In addition to this practical linguistic ability, many interviewees also mentioned a number of cognitive skills such as classification, comparison, logic, enhanced interpretative skill and so forth which could be broadly applied across disciplines and professions. These include the close attention to detail demanded in all language skills, the discipline and tenacity required for adolescent or adult learners of another language to do the "grunt" work of memorizing and internalizing grammar rules and vocabulary, and the close interpretative readings of text demanded in upper-level literature courses. These skills all translate well into a range of professions from high-level diplomacy to the politics of office managership. Congressman Oberstar has been an enthusiast of language study all his life and speaks French and Creole fluently. He believes that the pragmatics of the language learning experience produce good work habits. For that reason he prefers to recruit congressional office staff who have studied other languages.

In addition to developing and using functional proficiency in another language, interviewees also mentioned a more intangible benefit which they considered equally important: a heightened awareness of cultural difference. In the case of these interviewees, this new awareness led to a fascination with exploring other cultural universes. Good language teachers, the ones they remembered by name, "open other worlds" to their students. Although it may seem a worn metaphor, the "open window" recurred again and again to describe the access to culture which their language study provided. What Susan Stamberg found so intriguing about her French class was that:

> It was the first encounter with another culture . . . I mean the grammar was hard, all of that, but what was most fascinating was the notion that there were people in the world communicating in another tongue . . . that changing the way you moved your mouth and arranged it would change the way you communicated and [it] opened these worlds to you.

For Karen Moody, it was recognizing that those "worlds" were peopled by cultural beings with entirely different interpretive frames for ordering and speaking about their lives. In her experience these insights occurred in the context of a French literature course taught by an Iranian professor of French at Northern Illinois University:

> She had an intense love of literature and passed it on. I remember how amazing it was reading Camus with her. Her understanding of Arab society made the symbols and the cultural references stand out so clearly.

The new or heightened awareness of cultural difference opened their eyes to the imperative of achieving some credible level of cultural competence. This meant attempting to adjust their focus and to see the world through a different cultural lens. It implied a responsibility to exhibit both sensitivity to and tolerance for the differences encompassed within this alternate world view. Interviewees provided altruistic rationales and also cited the tactical or economic advantages to be gained from such expertise.

When Jeff Munks returned from Spain he began a career as a police officer in San Jose, California. That experience provided "dramatic evidence of the value of having communicative and cultural competence in Spanish." His proficiency in Spanish was a vital resource for his department in facilitating communication, defusing tension and building good will with the resident Hispanic community. In contrast, Munks described the anger, frustration and helplessness he felt at the reaction of local residents, including the ethnically diverse and well-educated officers on the San Jose police force, to the arrival of a large Vietnamese population in the late 1970s. Overwhelmed by large numbers of immigrants with whom they could not communicate, local attitudes revealed cultural resentments, xenophobic stereotyping and gross misunderstanding of the new arrivals. Munks related a particularly painful incident which illustrates why, in his view, cultural competence is as important as linguistic fluency. He uses himself as an example to illustrate the damage that can be done when two groups come together without the benefit of shared linguistic or cultural referents to guide them.

> I'm working alone, the middle of the night, and the radio comes alive and says, "7143 respond to 12 Center St. apt. #16, unknown circumstances, language barrier." So I'm by myself driving into a difficult area [Vietnamese neighborhood], I don't know if I'm going into a barking dog or a man with a gun. So I did the same thing my brother and sister officers were doing in all 27 states with high target populations of new immigrants or refugees. And this is coming from a guy who loves people and . . . was committed to trying to help. So I drive up, and I'd be frightened 'cause I wanna go home, ya know? . . . and I would knock on the front door and back off into the bushes and then pull my gun out, and when the door opened two frightened eyes would be looking out, and I'd say "step outside," until they got the message. I'd holster my gun, I'd search them for weapons, then I'd escort them through the threshold of the home. . . . Not a good way to start a contact. Welcome to America. And invariably who's the only English speaker in the home? A child. And so, knowing nothing about the culture, I'd look at the kid and ask who called. Not knowing that I had just stepped on the established order of the household by not addressing father first. So father, offended and embarrassed in front of his own family, is required to respond in kind and I get nothing.

This last experience was the catalyst which prompted him to create a system providing immediate telephone interpretation for those with short-term emergency needs like police officers and surgeons and long-term interests like businesspeople targeting specific ethnic markets here and abroad. Munks also developed a computer program to help US border patrol officers avoid serious cultural and linguistic blunders in dealing with a variety of foreign nationals.

Enhanced cultural competence can provide a valuable competitive edge in domains as varied as research, business, and diplomacy. Laurence Wylie relates an incident which took place when he was conducting fieldwork and archival research in rural France. He needed access to the archives of the local *châtelains*. He had been told that the archives had all burned during the 1792–1795 Vendée rebellion but wanted to verify the truth of that story in person. When he arrived for an interview at the pre-arranged time, the lady of the manor greeted him. Without knowing why, he spontaneously kissed her hand, a gesture he had previously found difficult to take seriously. Wylie noticed an immediate softening in her manner, was invited to tea and given access to family papers which dated back as far as the 16th century (Wylie & Bégué, 1970, p. 113).

Several other stories deserve to be told since they provide examples of interviewees enacting their cultural competence in strategic high level arenas. A strong recurrent theme in the interviews with the Americans in the sample was the intense satisfaction they felt at demonstrating intercultural skills and thus contradicting received wisdom about "tongue-tied Americans." For example, when one of the interviewees received his first posting to China with the US Foreign Commercial Service, he had impressive educational credentials (an MBA from the Monterey Institute of International Studies) but little professional experience. When a colleague became ill and had to return to the United States, this interviewee's knowledge of Mandarin Chinese got him the job in spite of his inexperience. He remembers the "joy" of being able to use his Chinese on official ceremonial occasions as a United States representative and of reaping the benefits it afforded.

> You would go to a joint venture opening. You would say, "We congratulate this chemical fiber company on this successful venture and on its opening." And usually you have somebody from the German consulate and the French consulate, you know, it's the same group, and you could see how the country representatives who were able to do it in Chinese got a much better reception from the audience. You would say, "I apologize I had to bother you all and have you listen to my poor Chinese." They laugh and that really opens up the people to you.

Congressman Oberstar relates an incident which illustrates the complex nexus of language and place in a shifting geopolitical order. In 1987, Oberstar was designated to represent the United States Congress at a meeting of the European parliament in Strasbourg. This meeting occurred after the air strike ordered by the Reagan administration against Libya, and Oberstar had the difficult task of explaining the US rationale for an action seen as highly unpopular by some European nations. Oberstar addressed the members of the parliament in French. After saying a few introductory sentences, he paused for a moment and the members, who had assumed that a short speech was all he could manage in French, applauded. However, Oberstar continued in French for ten more minutes and the tense ambiance in the hemicycle dissolved and was replaced with a palpable sense of astonishment. When he finally concluded, the members stood up, and in a rare show of unanimity, applauded enthusiastically. A British parliament member who spoke after Oberstar conveyed the mood in the chamber when he said, "Mr. President, I wish the ministers could have been here to hear this American speaking a European language so flawlessly."

The sub-text of the speech delivered by the British parliament member suggests the enduring power of certain received notions concerning Americans' inability or unwillingness to learn other languages and hints at traits Americans in Europe are said to display, including a lack of "culture" and blatant ethnocentrism. For Americans whose work involves considerable interaction with foreigners, the knowledge of certain geopolitically correct languages confers or reinforces elite status. As one interviewee put it, "it gives a certain sophistication." It is a skill which can be used to identify those in the same social class as well as to differentiate those in other class milieux. In arranging for these interviews I had sent out letters describing the project on Georgetown stationery which indicated my position as a professor of French civilization. When I arrived at the office of Congressman Oberstar, I was taken aback when he greeted me in French in the presence of his staff. I happily responded in kind, but as we settled in I fully expected him to switch back to English. We were, after all, both Americans attempting to get at a more complete understanding of the role of language in an American context. His insistence on speaking French throughout the entire interview, his obvious pride in having maintained perfect fluency in the language, as well as the political and cultural capital he has earned in this country and abroad for his mastery of French, reveal important class-based factors in the choice of what languages are "best" to study.

## Motivations

A recent ethnographic study of the study of English in three private Puerto Rican high schools introduces the dimension of class and ideology into the questions of student motivation and expectation with respect to language learning (Torruellas, 1990). This study departs from the traditional focus on the role of English as an instrument of Americanization and reveals the mastery of English to be a very important form of cultural capital for Puerto Rican elites. The goal of attending college in the United States is identified as a significant factor in the reproduction of elite status and an important signifier of distinction and differentiation among middle and upper classes. The data which emerged from these interviews also reveal class-based expectations to be a strong motive in the choice of what languages to study. According to the interviewee from

Argentina, María, English was a form of considerable cultural capital in middle and upper middle class milieux, whereas for American elites French, and to a lesser extent German and Latin, conferred or consolidated distinction.

Interviewees' commentary about what languages not to study was also interesting. It revealed status anxieties, cultural bias and the complex links between "dominant" languages and global geopolitical realities. Robinson's (1988, pp. 78–81) study of a Spanish program at Stanford examines the motivations behind the choice of Spanish. Her data refute commonly held perceptions about why people take languages and the positive attitudes said to develop about the target culture and people as a result of language study. An interview she conducted with a student she had judged to be one of the "best" in the classroom based on his attentiveness, preparedness, attitude and fluency revealed, instead, his disinterest in and negative attitude toward Spanish-speaking peoples from Latin America (versus Spain). He took Spanish because it was "easy" and avoided contact with Spanish-speaking students in his high school in Texas categorizing them with African Americans as "nonwhites." The following vignettes will help to illustrate some of the above.

When María was asked why she chose to study English in Argentina she laughed saying, "I really didn't choose to study English, I was *subjected* to English since I can remember. When I was four I was sent to an English kindergarten back in Argentina and later I went to a British primary school." María described how she enrolled in a well-known public high school for languages where she studied English and French. Although she emphasized the high quality of both the teachers and the school curriculum, the classes were too large to permit sufficient speaking or writing practice. To develop proficiency in those areas she engaged private tutors in both English and French. They helped her to prepare for standardized exams in English and French (given by Cambridge and the Alliance Française respectively) and to obtain important official certification of her language skill. María immersed herself in English high and popular culture in order to become fluent. She read everything from Shakespeare to the Brontës, watched English and American movies and transcribed the lyrics to popular Beatles' songs. After graduating from high school María decided to pursue a career as an interpreter, and got a university degree in translation. Disillusioned with the low pay and anxious to gain direct experience in an English-speaking culture, she accepted a position as an International Fellow at a prestigious private liberal arts college in New England. She studied and taught there for two years before pursuing a graduate degree in international relations at a university in Washington, DC. María subsequently accepted a position in a private educational foundation in the capital and is currently a senior analyst in charge of the international fellowship program.

María explained that middle- and upper-middle-class families in Argentina urge their children to put considerable time and effort into the study of English. María's mother was adamant about giving her "a head start in English from an early age" because of the opportunities it would provide later in life. These class-based expectations related to English are embedded in complex historical circumstances involving colonial domination, postcolonial economic development patterns characterized by both the polarization of rich, core nations and poor, peripheral ones as well as domestic political instability and repression in Argentina. María explained:

> At home we know we live in the periphery and we know we don't speak the language of the, of the empire. I hate to sound like this but we know that we need to acquire English and we always looked toward Europe, England or France. Well, England, after the Falklands [War] forget it but now it's the US and it's still English so that, at least in my social strata, it's a necessity. You need some tools and one of those tools is English if you want to move places. In Argentina it's a good thing, you know, knowing this language, you are culturally better. . . . I mean speaking English, for instance, makes you a cooler person. Because you are from a higher social status. I mean that's what they think. It's a class thing. It's also important to understand when I was growing up, we're talking about the time of the military repression—1973 to the 1980s—so there was a total rejection of national things and people focus on how wonderful foreign things are.

It is interesting to note that when asked to explain why they began language study, American interviewees also indicated that in reality they had very little or no choice. Foreign language was one of a number of courses required in the academic tracks of public high schools or in the general curriculum of private preparatory schools. Anyone planning to go to college needed a language. However, the choice of and attitudes concerning what specific languages to study reveal the dimensions of class, ethnicity and ideology. All but two of the interviewees chose French, German or Latin (often acting on the advice or example of their parents, not guidance counselors) as the best way to prepare for college and life. These choices reveal a sorting by class and family background as much as by career aspiration. One interviewee who did his undergraduate work at a prestigious Ivy League university explained that he studied French because it was the only modern language offered at his high school. He paused and then added:

> But I think I would have chosen French anyway because my mother had studied French, and she had given me the impression that French was a high status language, more than German or Spanish.

When asked to explain how that particular impression was conveyed to him he replied that he couldn't recall exactly but continued:

> I visited Europe with my parents when I was fairly young, at 8 and 11, and I remember deciding at the time that I wanted to learn French. Perhaps it was because my experiences in France were favorable but also because I got this idea that it was a literary high culture type language.

He studied French throughout high school and for one year in college. Not impressed with the French department at that university he stopped studying French. After a hiatus of over 20 years he began language study again this time in Spanish largely because it dovetailed with his professional research interest in bilingualism in the US.

Another interviewee, a senior government official who took French in high school, recalls the rationale for her choice:

> I started studying a language in the late 1950s in 10th grade. It was required to have two years of a foreign language as part of the college prep curriculum. Our choices were Latin, French, and Spanish. I was a bit worried about the reputation of how hard Latin was and I wanted to study a living language. Spanish had the reputation of being easy and what all the dumber kids studied. I was one of the top students so I took French.

These interviewees suggest that their choice of studying French in high school or earlier was "natural" or "logical" given who they were, where they came from, and what they expected to accomplish. On the other hand, the decision to learn French for Karen Moody represented a departure from her family and class background. As noted above, Karen holds a Master's degree in French literature, speaks Italian, is studying German, has lived, studied, and/or worked in Europe for extended periods over the past 20 years, and, although based in New York, she frequently travels to Europe as Vice-President of an international company. When asked what inspired her to choose French she responded that it was the sound. She loved the way it sounded. Later in the interview she added that French represented "sophistication"; it offered her the possibility "to get out of the south side of Chicago." In the ethnic, working-class, Catholic neighborhoods of the south side people were defined by and identified with their parish. In hers, there were predominantly Dutch, Italians, Lithuanians, and Poles. Moody's father worked at International Harvester and although he had a white-collar job, her uncles and cousins all did blue-collar work in construction or manufacturing.

There was no expectation that girls should have a college education. Indeed it was assumed that they would finish high school, get married and start a family. Moody resisted "kicking and screaming" when her mother insisted that she pursue practical subjects like typing and short hand in high school. By working for a year after graduation and taking the academic courses like biology that she had missed, she was able to begin her undergraduate coursework. One of her first decisions was to declare her major in French. It is a decision which she never regretted and a skill she actively maintains, most recently as she works with French artists on the Deutsche Grammophon label who perform regularly in New York.

Moody remembered the very first time at age seven that she encountered French. She and a friend got hold of a phrase book while on a tour of an historic district. As they tried wrapping their mouths around the strange sounds and matching them to the pictures she became enthralled. It is interesting to note that this incident occurred not too long after Moody refused to continue speaking Polish with her maternal grandparents who lived in an apartment one flight up from her parents and knew no English.

Although still very close to her family, Moody's life has taken a different course from theirs. Yet in reflecting back on her childhood she wondered if the genesis of her fascination with other languages and cultures is not to be found in the ethnic and cultural diversity of the south side neighborhood where she lived. Languages other than English were an integral part of her youth, Polish on her mother's side, Dutch on her father's. Nevertheless, the decision she made to pursue lessons in French, Italian, and German, but not in Polish, was a strategic one. The social and cultural capital conferred by these languages in the New York world of music and the arts both confirm and legitimate the executive position she currently holds.

I conclude this section on motivation by relating the experience of an interviewee who chose to study Spanish in high school, and end with a final experience related by María. Chris chose to double major in political science/international relations and Spanish in college. He studied Spanish in Mexico, traveled extensively in Central America and served with the Peace Corps in the Dominican Republic where he fell in love with and married a Dominican woman. He was influenced in his choice of what language to begin in high school by his father, who majored in anthropology and had a strong interest in Mesoamerican culture. Yet when asked what kinds of people study foreign language and why he replied:

> I think Spanish is looked at as a, like, a blue-collar language. Because it is a language where we have a huge immigrant population which is not looked upon in a positive light often. I think French is looked upon as a refined language, a white-collar language, an upper-class language.

It is interesting to note that Chris is now comfortably settled in his civil service career. Just a few months ago he and his Dominican wife began to take a French class together.

María's reception in this country and her experience suggests that for many Anglo-Americans Spanish represents a pejorative conflation of low class, little status and the wrong kind of ethnicity. These representations also served to emphasize her status as an outsider. The labels her colleagues at the foundation chose to describe her, although politically correct, still had the effect of categorizing and isolating her on the basis of both ethnicity and language. María related her experience as a native Spanish speaker:

> For Americans I am an Hispanic, that's what they call me! I don't identify with that group because to me Hispanics are the first American descendants of native Spanish speakers from Spain, Central, South America or wherever. They [Spanish-speaking immigrants] have different issues than I do. So when you grow up in a country that discriminates against you because of your ethnic background, your self-esteem is much lower. I think that someone like myself coming from a country where I was part of a certain milieu, I come with a higher self-esteem. In fact, when I first got here and saw how little people here know about the rest of the world, I often felt superior to Americans. Maybe I'm discriminated against but I don't feel it.

As María remembered her arrival in New England she also recalled that the Americans she met saw her as "exotic." (It is interesting that the international economist who has dual German-American nationality used this same word, "exotic," to describe Americans' reaction to his polyglot background.) When I asked María why she thought so and if her colleagues at the foundation view her in the same way, she said:

> Oh yes, even here at the Foundation. I'm the only Latin American manager, Hispanic manager I should say. . . . They have other foreign nationals but nobody at this level. Sometimes they want to include me in videos, proof that we are multicultural. So in a way I'm exotic, which is

really interesting because I never thought of myself as exotic until I came
to this country. I think of myself as white, as Caucasian, but Americans
call me a "woman of color."

María paused and laughed, extending her forearm to show me the color
of her skin, adding "I'm pretty dark right now actually. I'm usually
whiter than this." She grew serious again and said, "It's funny how they
play with your identity. If you don't have your own identity well-estab-
lished or know who you are, it kind of messes you up."

## Views of Language Teachers and Language Teaching

In her memoir on language teaching and learning, Kaplan (1993)
summarizes the common plight of language teachers in America when
she describes them as "badly paid, little recognized and much ma-
ligned." This last segment of the chapter explores how interviewees view
the place and importance of both the discipline and its educators. Did
interviewees see language teachers as marginalized and, if so, how did
they explain this marginality? What were their prescriptions for improving or maintaining the status of foreign language teachers and for making
language study more relevant, efficient and valued?

It is significant that all but one of the interviewees (a journalist) either
implicitly or explicitly identified language teachers as marginalized with
respect to their colleagues in core, "academic" disciplines like math,
history, and economics. The reasons they gave fall into two broad categories: our history as a nation of immigrants and deepseated cultural
ambivalence toward teacher/intellectuals in general as well as the pursuit
of "elitist," "impractical" academic pursuits like language study.

First, interviewees link negative attitudes concerning the study of
languages other than English to our history as a polyglot nation of immigrants. In the United States, learning English has been and remains
a critical element in the construction of both national identity and community. In the past, the consolidation of the American nation state followed the nineteenth century model of a socially homogeneous, territo-
rially bounded entity. The assumptions undergirding that model made
assimilation a national imperative. In our historical context the ideology
of the melting pot was coercive and absolute; linguistic diversity represented not a promise but a threat (Rosaldo, 1994). As Senator Paul Simon
put it:

It [low status of foreign language study] is part of our culture. If you're

> a second generation Italian or Pole you're proud of speaking English and
> proud of saying you don't speak Italian or Polish. You want to identify
> with the US, you want to be American. There is something very good
> about that but there is also a negative aspect and the result is a negative
> perspective on foreign languages had permeated our society.

This analysis reflects the experiences of the interviewees who came to
this country as immigrants or who lived in ethnic neighborhoods in
American cities. As we saw earlier, at the age of five Karen Moody
flatly refused to speak Polish any more with her mother's parents. Similarly, Deputy Secretary of Education Madeleine Kunin came to the
United States from Switzerland at the age of 6 and remembers how much
she wanted to learn English and "to be an American."

These ambivalent and contradictory attitudes concerning language as
an instrument of citizenship and language as an instrument of social
distinction beg an interesting question. In a recent article, anthropologist
Renato Rosaldo wonders why we say that five-year-old children are at
risk if they speak a language other than English but 21-year-old mono-
lingual Americans enrolled in university language courses are becoming
cultured? (1994, p. 403) A number of interviewees identified this
"schizophrenic mentality" on the part of Americans. One noted that
learning a language in school is looked at as a high status educational
pursuit if you're an English speaker. People who take language in school
and actually display little proficiency are given high marks whereas people who represent linguistic minorities are just expected to learn English.
Among the latter group bilingualism is not a high status condition. Another interviewee concurred noting that bilingualism in this country is
coded "immigrant" and correspondingly not accorded much respect.
Munks pointed out that our choice of how to talk about languages other
than English reveals a deepseated cultural bias. "We call languages other
than English foreign and foreign carries with it negative connotations
like subordinate, alien, different, not as good."

Yet in spite of the common American perception that language is "a
finite good" operating according to "a hydraulic model" where gains in
one language mean losses in another (Rosaldo, 1994, p. 403) these interviews do sound a positive note. While immigrants and second- or
third-generation Americans may reject the language of their parents
and/or grandparents in the rush to claim citizenship, this does not mean
that they will avoid the study of other languages. For example, Karen
Moody rejected Polish but has made the study of other languages an
ongoing part of her life. Deputy Secretary Kunin mastered English but

"got back in touch with a part of [her] past" when she took an upper-level German literature class in college.

Interviewees attribute the marginalization of foreign languages in the United States to a second reason: mainstream American cultural attitudes which devalue time, effort and money spent on useless academic courses of study and the people paid to teach them. All of these interviewees make a strong critique of the "arrogance" of American elites in many domains including education, business and government who dismiss language as an unnecessary intellectual frill. Jeff Munks calls this mentality "a classic American paradigm unique to us that says we can go successfully from birth to death comfortable and safe within the confines of American English and culture." According to this paradigm, Americans don't take languages seriously because they don't need them. Karen Moody suggests that American indifference to the rest of the world is grounded in the "unending bounty" of our nation. It also reveals certain cultural traits such as the utilitarian individualism and isolationism which Tocqueville saw as defining features of the American character when he traveled in this country in the 1830s (1969). Moody explained that "in this country [the attitude has always been] might makes right. So we really don't need to know anything about anybody. It's because we've always had so much, so many natural resources. We want to stand alone. We don't want to be dependent on anybody."

In the early 19th century, Tocqueville saw the isolation to which Americans are prone as a danger to political freedom and nascent democratic institutions. In the late 20th century, interviewees view American insularity as a direct threat to the nation's economic power and place in a new world order. On the domestic front we squander the vast linguistic resources already here in the 40 million residents whose primary language is something other than English. Internationally we surrender critical diplomatic initiatives and economic opportunities to nations willing to learn other languages and cultures.

Yet the prescriptions interviewees offered reveal that they too exhibit an enduring American preoccupation with pragmatism and favor a persistent utilitarian tradition in American education that mandates that students need skills only directly related to work (Herron, 1982, pp. 445–447). Getting a Ph.D. in French literature was fine if you wanted to teach, otherwise "it makes no sense at all." Most interviewees urged students interested in languages other than English to combine them with core disciplines or professional training like engineering, business administration, international economics, marketing and so forth. They were also adamant that the teaching of lower level language courses should reflect a strong use-based orientation. The "bottom line" should be for students to leave our classrooms with some credible level of functional proficiency in their chosen language. They also urged teachers to carefully consider pedagogies which could realistically accomplish these goals. Senator Simon reminded us that Thomas Jefferson was the first to introduce the idea of a language house at the University of Virginia and suggested that this tradition be revived or maintained because of its simulation of a true immersion experience.

Interviewees also suggested that foreign language educators could work to change their image through their "passion" and enthusiasm for their discipline. They could also aggressively market the discipline and act as "missionaries" in their communities by spreading the "word." They criticized language teachers for not taking more initiative, for not making their colleagues and critics within and beyond the academy understand what it is they do and why it is important. At the same time, these same interviewees also implied that nothing could be done about the low status of language teachers until attitudes toward teachers and education in general change. Interviewees agreed that many Americans are strongly anti-intellectual and suspect that teaching at the university level, especially in the humanities, is not really work at all.[2] A recent personal experience brought this attitude home to me. This summer we moved to a new home in suburban Maryland to lessen my daily commute to Washington. At a neighborhood block party held a few weeks after the move I remember introducing myself as a professor. One of our new neighbors is a scientist who works at a prestigious university in Baltimore and he pressed me for details. When I answered he looked me directly in the eye and asked sarcastically, "So tell me, how many actual contact hours do you have per week?"

Many interviewees suggested that pejorative attitudes toward education are reflected in the scarce resources we commit to our schools and colleges. Senator Simon put the situation into perspective when he said:

> We just have to do more with education in this country, period. In 1949, we spent 9% of our federal budget on education and today we spend 2%. We haven't awakened to the needs of 1994. For instance, you go to school in Japan 243 days a year, in Germany 240 days a year and in this country 180 days a year. Why? Why the theory is so our kids can go out and harvest the crops. The world has changed, but we haven't changed, and if we're going to be competitive, if we're going to give future generations an increased quality of life and improved standard of living, we're going to have to adapt to a world that is very different.

# Part II: The Midwest

Mark Knowles, University of Oregon

## Introduction

A majority of Knowles's Midwest respondents was from Milwaukee, with two living in Chicago. The site of the interviews may not be insignificant, given Milwaukee's fairly unique cultural, linguistic, and historical experience. With a strong wave of early, socially diverse Germans arriving to the shores of Lake Michigan and the banks of the Milwaukee River in the 1840s, immigration there, according to Conzen (1976) reflected experiences that do "not coincide neatly with the standard wisdom on immigrant accommodation and assimilation in nineteenth century America" (p. 6). Rather than characterizing Milwaukee's Germans with the classic immigrant ghetto model[3], Conzen describes the Milwaukee of the 19th century as "a preeminently German city" where "spatial congregation and economic, political, and cultural participation" encouraged "painless adjustment and good living conditions for many but which also encouraged the postponement of assimilation" (p. 7).

Today, the German influence is almost invisible, and perhaps plays only a role in a form of nostalgic identity politics. Glimpses of the once-powerful *Deutschtum* can be found in the Old Third Street district where sausages can still be ordered in German, or where one can eat in one of the nation's most reputable German restaurants. Linguistic diversity in Milwaukee is now more apparent on the South Side where Puerto Rican and Mexican immigrants often reside, or where recent immigrants from Poland join a large traditional Polish American neighborhood.

But despite the shift away from German to English and to other, more newly arrived languages, it is perhaps not by accident that the city was a pioneer in immersion education in the foreign language field, nor that the Escuela Fratny—near the 19th-century German working-class neighborhood of German-language publisher Frederik Fratny—has been cited as a premier example of community controlled, bilingual, whole-language schools in the US (Goodman, Bridges Bird, & Goodman, 1991). The other site for two of the interviews was Chicago, the most important economic and administrative center in the entire Midwest, long the nation's second city, and a traditional destination for mass migrations from Europe, Central America, and Asia. Because much of the turn of the century immigration to Chicago originated in Germany, its own historical context has similarities to Milwaukee. However, because of its high popularity as a place of settlement from several nations and places, it would be difficult to say that Chicago was dominated by any one particular ethnic group, as Milwaukee was.

If the German influence is today invisible in Milwaukee, it's legacy still resides in the minds of the people who live there. When I went to Congressman Tom Barrett's office, I noted that he had chosen to locate in the immense old Germania building where Milwaukee's largest of twenty different German-language newspapers had resided. During another interview with an African American newspaper editor, I learned how one group of 19th century Black Americans learned to speak German as they integrated into the Caucasian dominated Wisconsin village where they settled.

This study may help shed light on the issue of how regional differences affect attitudes toward foreign language study. At the time of this report's completion, I was no longer living in the Midwest, but in a part of the country that has become the new destination of choice for immigrants to America—the West Coast. Ironically, however, an election debate was raging about immigration, ethnicity, and language that mirrored another election fight 100 years earlier in Wisconsin. In that election, enormous controversy was created over Republican support of a nativist platform called the Bennett Law, part of whose effect would have singled out German-speaking children by requiring that reading, writing and arithmetic be taught in English in all public and private schools (Ulrich, 1980).

Not long after the November elections, I attended a talk (Basham, 1994) about a study documenting the struggles of the native peoples of Alaska to maintain the existence of their threatened languages. Preliminary reports from the study indicate that the new users of those languages are often those people who have had some early lifehood experience with a native language speaker. In my own research (Knowles, 1993–1994), I found early lifehood experiences were also a predictor of success in learning another language. There is growing evidence that we should extend this pattern further and ask if a region's or a city's linguistic past may also affect language learning choices and outcomes.

As language teaching professionals, it can oftentimes be frustrating to deal with what can seem to be the mysterious nature and consequences of student attitudes and motivation. While we may be beginning to understand the social grounding of human behavior and decision making, it is hoped that this research, which ties Washington, DC, to the Midwest through comparison and contrast, may shed some light on how a sense of identity and place plays a role in formal language learning.

## Experiences

Just as in Terrio's Washington, DC, sample, participants in the Midwest sample experienced language study in a variety of settings. All the respondents had some formal study of at least one language in the US, four of the nine had some formal study abroad, and seven were able to apply their linguistic skills for varying lengths of time in a speech community of the respective language. As in the Washington, DC, sample, some of these experiences were viewed more positively than others, but the Midwest participants tended to direct negative comments mainly against themselves—such as for not having been sufficiently attentive to the opportunity given them when they were young—rather than against the instruction. Perhaps because of this willingness to assume some responsibility for initial lack of success, many of the individuals in this group seemed remarkably open to giving foreign language study a second chance.

Some respondents did call into question the pedagogy of their foreign language classes. Lance Keppel, a chemist in Chicago, was perhaps the most ambivalent on this matter, since he had had what he called "painful" experiences in junior high, but has since returned to what he feels is successful language study.

Not including Keppel, five of the nine Midwest respondents were predominantly positive about their language classes. Often, as in the Washington, DC, sample, this positive impression was directly related to the personality and teaching style of their teachers. Since some of the respondents actually majored in their respective languages, the memorable classes were often at different levels and stages in their linguistic development. For example, Clint Nicholson, a former Classics major who is now an international lawyer, did not find his high school modern language classes particularly exciting, but did have fond memories of his high school Latin teacher and was very enthusiastic about the teaching from an Ivy League scholar he had in an undergraduate Latin course.

Another respondent, who later became a teacher and scholar of Islam and Oriental languages, spoke highly of his first French teacher. Now working for a major Midwestern private foundation, Michael Roscoe had this to say about his earliest foreign language experience:

> I had a very good French teacher, actually. Not by current standards, but by mine. What I mean by that is that she was very much inclined to a lot of exercises, in particular rote, I mean what I remember from 7th and 9th grade was writing out French vocabulary words 100 times each, every night, and the net consequences of that for me, actually is that, you know, a lot of French stuck with me, even though it had one downside, of course. We didn't really learn to speak French under that old system.

Interestingly, while Roscoe liked the more "rigorous" style of this teacher, and was willing to judge what he learned in French class as valuable, even if not completely usable, he was not so forgiving with respect to Hebrew, the other foreign language required in his junior high school. Roscoe told me that particularly because of the kinds of vocabulary taught in his Hebrew class, there was little relevance of this language to the lives of 20th century school children:

> I think the first text in Hebrew I had to read—because this was the way things were done in this particular school—was where we started with the Bible. But we read Leviticus, which happens to be a long catalog of all the sacrifices that high priests do which involves words, terms of activities which are, to put it mildly, not common. So you developed an odd vocabulary, which is, if the issue is being able to speak the language or form, you come to it at a rather odd angle, I would say.

Lack of relevance was only one factor in Michael Roscoe's inability to feel motivated to learn Hebrew; it may have been the core problem for Ron Sutherland with respect to his early French experience. Sutherland, an engineer at a major sport vehicle manufacturer, claims he had a teacher "who would just as soon hang me out the window." This was in part because, already as a teenager, Sutherland was deeply involved with social activism; the more concerned he became with the burning issues of the 1960s, such as the war and Civil Rights, the less interest he seemed to have in schooling. Or at least in foreign language study. For Sutherland, the entire experience "was really sterile." Assessing his own progress over that time, Sutherland had something to say that resembles an all-too-familiar refrain for language teachers:

> I don't think I can speak two words of French after three years of studying it. I was not a very good student in high school. I was not motivated to learn a language at that point. It was simply a task to get through.

The relevance (or irrelevance) of the content of foreign language courses was a salient theme for both Roscoe and Sutherland. For Ruth Mifflin, director of a theater in the Midwest, it was the tightly focused structure of an honors class that finally enabled her "breakthrough" in French. Mifflin recalls how she was floundering in an undergraduate French program after being placed in classes that were above her level. But then she was able to take an honors seminar in which the works of only three Twentieth Century writers were studied.

> In any case, I had a seminar in Sartre, Giraudoux, and Camus. And the honors seminars at that particular college—you took two seminars rather than four courses in your junior and senior years—so you went into enormous depth, so I literally read everything they had written. And you know, I crossed that line into real comprehension at last, and interest.

Two other Midwest respondents were impressed by their classes because of the way their teachers presented either the material or themselves. Linda Rainwater, an editor at a major medical journal in Chicago, was particularly impressed by her first French teacher's flair and style:

> I do remember my first French teacher though, I mean, vividly, because she was the first—I went to Wayne State in my first years, then I transferred to the University of Chicago—but during those years I remembered her because she was so unlike everyone else in Detroit and at Wayne State. She wore marvelous hats, as I recall, and had a very, a very relaxed manner. She seemed to be just very flexible, very comfortable with herself, and somehow not as rigid or as teacherly as the rest of them seemed. And I do remember the hats and the soft clothing, and I found that very appealing, so I suppose that added a little romance to studying French.

Scott Ahart, an administrator of his city's ballet company, fondly remembered his high school foreign language teacher not so much for her clothing, but for her sense of humor and constant drive to do whatever she could—no matter how unusual—to make her students connect with Latin. Ahart recalled two particularly memorable incidents:

> The instructor was a nun and we thought she was crazy. She was a little bit off her—a little bit, she was a lot—off her rocker, which is a good instructor. She really was creative in her instruction. For example, one day we walked into the classroom. All the lights were off. And she had black drapes on the blackboard. She had a casket drawn on the blackboard, and candles on her desk, lit. And it was a moratorium, it was practice with, you know to learn *moratorium,* the endings. The whole theme was death and funerals and during that class time we had to pick up those words. Another experience, during the winter . . . she would turn the desks facing the window, which is totally reversed of the way it normally is. Normally we were facing the blackboard with the windows behind us. She would turn the desks facing the windows and we would watch the snow fall down and pick up some words on snow.

The variety of experiences represented in these few glimpses echoes several of the findings from the Washington, DC, sample. First, that memories of teachers are what learners tend to recall first about their language learning experiences. And, second, that opinions about what makes teaching practices good or bad are often contradictory. Another similarity between the experiences of individuals in the two samples is that for those who went on to develop real language proficiency, language learning was not limited to the classroom, but rather was spread over a variety of different contexts, both formal and informal, and usually over several different periods of time in each individual's life.

For example, after graduating from Swarthmore with a minor in French literature, Ruth Mifflin hadn't used the language at all when she decided some twenty years later to take a trip to France. In order to retrieve her French skills, she chose to read "with a great sense of release . . . easy stuff" such as popular magazines and mysteries:

> And this was the era when the popular press began to be filled for the first time with well, what would women do if they were alone, and how women can be alone, and if you are a divorcée what you could do. I was reading, I suppose it was *Elle*, but it was a French magazine I got in Chicago. I'm on the train. I'm reading about a French-written article by a female reporter who has traveled to Rome, she's newly divorced, and she cried all the way there in the train, and I thought, "I'm retrieving my French for this? This is what I've got to read about?"

Mifflin eventually returned to reading literature, including Proust's *À la recherche du temps perdu* in its entirety. Later, during her visit to Paris, she tried her hand at translating. It was because of that chance decision that Mifflin was able to reestablish a use of French that has blossomed into the translation part of her current professional work for both her theater company and other companies in the Midwest.

A similar trajectory through both formal and out-of-classroom experiences, as well as alternation between extensive fallow periods and intense use was true for Linda Rainwater. In college, she embodied many a language teacher's ideal student: one who delighted in meticulously reading and rereading homework assignments, underlining unknown words or sentences that she liked or wanted to remember. She spent almost eight years working in Europe, but then had a long hiatus of no foreign language use back in the US before she noticed "this French activity" happening in the neighborhood between her home and her office. Since the Alliance Française was offering evening classes, Rainwater became a student again, eager "to make sure that I could go to France soon," and curious to find out if the classroom environment was different from that of her college days, when she had concentrated mostly on her reading abilities and not on her "pronunciation."

Several of the participants talked about the important contribution of informal or "out-of-classroom" learning experiences to their development of conversational abilities. This was the case for Rainwater, who found that spending time in France added this new dimension to the literacy skills she had developed in college. For Scott Ahart, whose formal language schooling included a strong emphasis on oral skills, the out-of-classroom link was one he found particularly valuable. Ahart had taken an intensive formal course in Mexico City, and then in Barcelona he joined a Berlitz class and later a course at the American University of Barcelona. Nevertheless, he credits much of his language ability to his interactions with people in his work as a dancer and through the day-to-day routines of going to the grocery store and doing errands while living in a Spanish-speaking milieu. For Scott, autodidactic book learning was also part of his strategy for learning Spanish:

> I did study it—outside the American College of Barcelona I already had my book, you know probably three different books in Spanish. There's one time even after that—probably in early '81 or '82—I was in between shows, and I'd have my book doing exercises and phrases and verbs, and I'd have the answers at the back of the book so I was self-learning the language. And then, through that, again working with the Spanish people, Castillian or Catalan or whatever, helped out a lot.

Ironically, the only member of the Midwest sample who currently speaks a foreign language on the job (in this case, Spanish and Portuguese) is Clint Nicholson, who studied Classical languages in school. Nicholson attributes his abilities in these two languages to immersion experiences required by his employer. Hired out of Georgetown as an international lawyer, Nicholson was sent from the Midwest to Mexico for almost a year and after that to Brazil for the exclusive reason of learning Spanish and Portuguese.

For Ron Sutherland, the engineer who had such a hard time finding "the point" of the French and Spanish he studied in school, the discovery that such languages are actually spoken by real people marked the turning point. Sutherland told me that much of his interest in Spanish came from experiences that were not afforded to him until after high school, such as living in Uptown, a Hispanic neighborhood in Chicago where "everything was in Spanish—the signs were in Spanish, the movies were in Spanish, the groceries were in Spanish, and you didn't hear English on the street." Also significant for explaining his new interest in Spanish is having family members marry native Spanish speakers so that "Spanish is becoming a second language in my family." As this next comment shows, Sutherland's decision to give Spanish another try does not come without some resentment toward his high school curriculum, which he feels neglected to establish the connection between Spanish and the immediate world around students' lives:

> I just had no idea that that [Spanish-speaking neighborhoods] existed anywhere in the US That led to even more anger, because I hadn't seen any of that while growing up. Anger at having been isolated, not at anyone in particular, I was just a product like anyone else of a lot of different experiences, but I was really, I was angry that I had been so isolated and so naive about the world for so long.

> . . . . As soon as I began seeing those things, the whole world began to make more sense to me and to think that I had gone all the way through high school with like a bubble around me without any understanding of the world around me, the only experience I had was my home life and the world that the education facilities opened up for me through books and history and I haven't really thought about this, but I think the picture I came away with out of my educational experience in high school was very, very different from the picture I have now of the world, and I think that's a big mistake. And that led to a lot of frustration for me, and a couple of years out in the world, I began to get a sense of how I fit in and what were things you could do and the role you could play in the world with your life.

## The Payoff

Learning a foreign language was associated with a variety of positive outcomes, some very concrete and pragmatic and others less tangible. Certainly several interviewees expressed the opinion that foreign language study could help provide a more solid base of grammatical understanding of one's own language. One of the more interesting comments in this regard was from Matthew Chambers, editor of an African American newspaper. Chambers agreed that learning a foreign language could make one more appreciative of one's own native language, but he also considered the broader impact on awareness of ethnic identity:

> The whole concept of Kwansa, etc., is Swahili. Kwansa is Swahili. I'm on the board of the Arambee Community School, and that's a Swahili term. I think Swahili has become the unofficial third language of African Americans. Not that many of us are fluent in it, but many of us pick up words, which we add to our second language which is spoken Black English, but anyway, I found it useful. It taught me a lot about African [languages] and languages in general. And it taught me a lot, it helped me with another course I took, and it also helped with something that you

consider a foreign language, called Black English, taught by [teacher's name]. I do remember that one—and it dealt with the words which have survived 300 years, 400 years. And for example, there's no "t" sound in most African languages. There may be some now because of colonialism. But that is . . . why we hear Black people say "dis" and "dat" instead of "this" and "that," and you'll find that in Swahili, there is no "t" sound. And you can feel and sense a lot of our history . . . in studies of Swahili and you can see the connection. You understand a lot more about Black people living in America by taking Swahili. It opens your mind to a lot of information.

Also important in Chambers's view was that although he was not sure that in his particular city it would be as valuable as elsewhere, he did think that the study of Spanish was important for finding work in the public arena and for bridge-building among ethnic communities in the US, a topic on which he elaborated at length:

We talk about establishing rapport, and it would benefit Black Americans to learn some Native American terms. Somebody mentioned recently about the rapport between the Black community and the Hispanic community. That's not entirely true, because "Hispanic" includes a lot of groups which I would not necessarily say are friendly with the Black community. In most urban areas of the country, you'll always find Puerto Ricans living in the central city. Directly to the east, you'll find Puerto Ricans, and they'll merge in with the Black community and they'll be able to be friends with the Black community. Mexicans normally will live in European communities. Rarely, if ever, will you find Mexicans in Black communities. Cubans are the same way, so I don't think that we are building any bridges in terms of Cubans and some Central Americans. I don't see this multicultural community that people keep talking about. I think that we are probably worse off today than we have been in some time. It probably has to do with the economy.

This very pragmatic view of linguistic and cultural knowledge as useful tools is one that was heard from several of the Midwest interviewees, and is one of the reasons that Spanish was so often recommended as the "best" second language to study. This reasoning, recalls Congressman Tom Barrett, is what prompted him to study Spanish:

I actually had a history teacher in my freshman year in high school, who talked about Spanish becoming a very important language in the world economy, and because of our cultural ties with Central and South America, and that had an influence on me. That's why I chose Spanish.

Ruth Mifflin knows French, Japanese, and Russian. She translates French plays into English, has lived in Japan and worked in Russia. Nevertheless, this is what she had to say about America's linguistic future:

I also think, and some day I want to do this, *I think every American ought to learn Spanish* [emphasis hers]. I think we have to learn Spanish, I don't think we're going to become necessarily a bilingual country, but . . . it is clearer than ever that it is one continent and most of it speaks Spanish. And increasingly the Latino populations as they are coming into the US have refused—I mean they're not coming across the water, they are just coming a little north—refuse to not use their own language. So in some ways I regret to have learned French and not Spanish.

There were others in the sample who viewed learning about other cultures as a deeply transforming experience, reminiscent of the "conversions" and "border experiences" Kramsch (1993) describes. For Linda Rainwater, for example, other cultural experiences are possible only if one is willing and has a "drive to get out of this [American] culture." Michael Roscoe, the former scholar of Islam, had this to say about people he knew who were successful language learners:

They were forced to learn the language, but having been forced to learn the language, they became enthusiasts of language and more and more interested in the people who spoke that language, or the literature written in that language and that made a tremendous impact on them, because it sort of put them in, it gave them a second life or second world or second home. It seems to me that it can be—it is perhaps one of the nicest effects of learning a second language—is that one develops these second homes in which one can at least partially move and partially feel at home even if it is never entirely on its own. I feel that way to some degree about French.

Several of the Midwesterners also view their foreign language skills as valuable "cultural capital" such as Terrio described earlier in this chapter. As with the participants in the Washington, DC, sample, perception of this benefit was particularly marked among those who had studied French. Keppel, for example, told me that his happiness with the sense of accomplishment in French is reinforced by the aesthetic pleasure he derives from the sounds and structures of French. Furthermore, as avid cyclists and wine collectors, he and his wife have plans to tour France by bicycle, where they hope to visit small villages, stopping at vineyards along the way. For Ruth Mifflin, knowledge of another language has become the *sine qua non* of understanding the playwright's world and point of view. In Mifflin's view, such sensitivity has, for example, given her theater company insights on the "Russian psyche" and has provided "quite a different window on Chekhov." For Mifflin, the foreign language abilities of her company have given it a distinctive edge in a highly competitive theater market: "We've become intensely aware that cultural differences are carried in the language, that's where they lie, really, and if you have any sense of it, you'll have a better handle on what's happening."

As the poetry editor for a medical journal, Linda Rainwater views her connection to France—a country that "is still a place with a point of view"—as an important part of her professional persona. As a young intellectual, Rainwater rejected the "deadly dull" Detroit of the 1950s in favor of "anything that was outside of America or outside of Detroit." Rainwater recalls that she and other Americans of her generation were drawn to Europe where the Existentialists brought a revolutionary feeling to the café society. Moreover, the "literateness" of France also had its pull:

> How much the French enjoy using their language, almost with a certain expertise. The sense of pleasure in the precision, and the attentiveness to language. We kind of level out our language and the French don't do that. . . . I've always had that [a certain Frenchness]. My mother was Austrian-born. I have that bi-cultural feeling, that some Americans have. To me it [unquestioned loyalty to everything American] has always been a rather questionable proposition.

Congressman Barrett also spoke of foreign language knowledge as providing cultural capital. Barrett told me that his predecessor in the House was Jim Moody, who learned six languages as a child and has maintained them all. According to Barrett, Moody could connect to voters because of his ability to interact with them in their own native tongues.

All the Midwesterners recognized the pragmatic value of language study for enhancing one's ability to communicate with others, even though not all members of this group had actually found themselves in a position to make use of foreign language skills on the job. Within the Midwest sample four respondents claimed to have used their language skills for job-related tasks, and of these currently two were still doing so.

Whereas few of the Midwesterners likened the completion of their secondary school language requirements to major endurance tests, a number of those interviewed were disappointed to find that they could do so little with what they had learned in the classroom. However, at least one felt that his brief classroom exposure had given him a remarkably good beginning. During trips to Mexico, Congressman Barrett found that although his two years of college Spanish were "not enough to make you fluent, it was nice to at least converse or at least to be able to get some information and give some information."

One salient difference between the two samples concerns their views on the economic impact of language learning. Despite some lip service to the contrary, the Midwesterners rarely, if ever, were convinced that foreign language study would actually return measurable economic benefits. The most enthusiastic person on this side of the question was Scott Ahart. But while he may have learned Spanish as he was earning his living in Spain, and his language abilities may have helped earn him contracts throughout the world, that does not mean he would see language abilities as doing that for everyone. Even Clint Nicholson would not be sure that foreign language study would give anyone a competitive edge in a highly-coveted job opportunity. When I asked Nicholson if his Classics background had anything to do with his getting the job he has, he told me that international lawyers are hired on their legal abilities, not on their linguistic ones. Furthermore, he claimed that a firm that wants a lawyer with good language abilities will look for a graduate with a strong law school record and then train him or her in the language that best fits the firm's needs—in most cases by sending the individual to a country where the language is used. In fact, concluded Nicholson, it is not the good language learners, but the "sailing champions or the triathletes" that are more predictably successful international lawyers.

Michael Roscoe was equally blunt about the irrelevance of foreign language skills for "ordinary people" in the business world. Citing the fact that specially trained translators will always be available for those who need them, he points out that this is in fact the tactic of one major telecommunications company:

> They have a bank of hundreds, thousands of translators. If you want to call Kazakstan and speak Kazak but you don't speak it, you call up and they've got some person who speaks Kazak and they put you on the line and handle it that way . . . for all I know, there will be various other advances in technology . . . [that] will reduce the . . . occasional need for languages in a sort of business use.

In this Midwest sample, then, it appears that cases connecting foreign language skills to career benefits are infrequent compared to areas such as Washington, DC, which are characterized by more international activity. The cultural and linguistic isolation that Ron Sutherland felt in his hometown of Cincinnati may still not be unusual at all for many people in Midwest metropolitan areas.[4] Such isolation contributes to and continually reinforces the notion that learning other languages is both unnecessary and impractical, a fact that a number of the Midwest participants were quick to recognize. Listen to Ruth Mifflin:

> We haven't learned foreign languages well, because we lived in a world for a generation perhaps, or a generation and a half, where we didn't need to. We were very large, the world had not gotten small, we were extraordinarily powerful . . . and it seemed unnecessary. . . . I think it isn't that

they [Americans] can't or don't [learn foreign language well], I think that they didn't . . . know they needed it.

Lack of direct, tangible payoffs notwithstanding, a number of the Midwestern participants in this study spoke of the deep, personal satisfaction involved in accomplishing something that had earlier eluded them. Such is the case of Lance Keppel, who "failed miserably" in junior high Spanish, had recently taken up French and was feeling very buoyant about it.

It's hard for me [to say what are the payoffs of foreign language learning], because I hated it as a child, so if I remember how it was for me as a child, the simplest answer to that question would be pain. Actually with mathematics as well. As far as an adult, the satisfaction of learning something that you've not done before that's difficult. For me, personally, it's the satisfaction of achieving something that I heretofore felt [was] unachievable. So I couldn't do it before and I can now—I think it's fun.

## Views on Language Teaching

The prescriptions the Midwest respondents offered to the foreign language profession were as diverse as their experiences. While some were hard pressed to imagine how foreign language teachers could improve upon what they are doing now—particularly because they had not observed a foreign language class for so long—others were able to give their point of view with very little hesitation.

Many of these opinions can be classified in the "critical period" (Lenneberg, 1967) vein. "You need to get them [students] when they are young," was a common refrain. "If they were exposed to it at a young age, they'd be just as good at foreign languages as any European. They're just not," was how Lance Keppel explained the American reputation for not being good language learners.

Congressman Barrett, who pointed to the strides made in the immersion schools of his congressional district, had this to say:

I think it has to be more aggressive and try to get more younger people. I think it's a feeder system and if you don't get younger people to get interested in it, it's going to be more and more difficult, so I certainly would work with as young a population as I could.

Ron Sutherland also felt that getting people from an early age was important, although he thought that simply giving children foreign language classes was not enough. Instead, an approach that would whet the appetite toward other cultures would be more efficacious:

Go for the kids, go for them as early as you can. I think [it's necessary] to really turn away from just language programs and really do a, tie the language to the culture and focus on creating people who want to study foreign languages and foreign countries by getting the young kids excited about it. I don't think there's anything you can do with the curriculum if no one's going to sign up for the courses. It's not going to be any better, but once you have people knocking on the door, I think any number of [methods of ] teaching languages will work. To me it's a question of tying it to a real need and something which will enrich your life.

At the other end of the spectrum were recommendations to make foreign language study more accessible to adults, whose job and family responsibilities often make it difficult for them to enroll in classes that follow a conventional structure.

Despite the positive attitudes towards foreign language instruction for both younger and older people, there were those who nevertheless cautioned that foreign language study may not be for everybody. Lance Keppel, for one, did not endorse a foreign language requirement for every youngster:

From a practical perspective, foreign language in America is superfluous. Without going out of my way, I find it so difficult to find people to converse with in French. I have to make a very concerted effort to do that. I'm trying. I have friends who do speak French and [I] make it a point to try to do so. From a practical perspective, there isn't a need, which is why in many schools, foreign languages have been dropped over the last twenty to twenty-five years. As far as an opinion, should they? I don't have an opinion on whether they should or not.

Michael Roscoe, whose own children are learning French, was philosophically in favor of a foreign language requirement for all Americans, but, like Keppel, concluded that on the practical side there are bigger issues that should take precedence over foreign language study:

We never knew before [studying a foreign language] that English has nouns and verbs and so forth. That is very useful. So there might be that kind of advantage, but it does seem to be that their most immediate problem in American education does not have to do with the fact that American students do not learn foreign languages. Their most immediate problem is their own [language]. So it seems to me that one would have to look at it from that point of view.

Matthew Chambers told me that one could argue that foreign languages are irrelevant to the death-defying lifestyles young people in his readership's neighborhoods are adopting, but he feels such an argument is not completely persuasive:

Well, you could say that about anything. What is the relationship of chemistry to what's happening on the streets unless you just want to mix better drugs? I think if you had this foundation [of foreign language skills], you are least likely to be killed. If you could get that thirst for knowledge.

Although Chambers sees a lot of potential for foreign language learning, his prescription at this point would be to follow W.E.B. Du Bois's precepts and offer foreign language instruction to "any kid that is in what is called the talented ten. . . . Today it may be the talented 20, they are the ones who go to college. I would expand it into what could be the talented 35 today."

Like their counterparts in the Washington, DC, sample, participants in the Midwest sample recognized that all academic subjects are not created equal. For many Americans, English, science and mathematics are "core"; foreign languages, on the other hand, are often perceived as a superfluous "frill." Since foreign languages can be seen as a subject reserved for only certain groups within the general American population, this leaves the discipline vulnerable to charges of elitism. On the other hand, at least one Midwesterner rejected the notion that teachers should become "missionaries" out to convert others to the value of foreign language study with their "passion" for the subject. Ruth Mifflin went so far as to decry this attitude, saying foreign language teachers needed to reject the role of "spiritual flame keepers" of language study and instead make the connection between foreign language study and access to other forms of knowledge the burning issue.

Overall, on the subject of language teaching, perhaps the one particularly salient note common to both samples was advocacy of a use-based approach, that is, an approach that would enable learners to develop useable skills. At the same time, there seemed to be a recognition that the true benefits of foreign language study may not be directly connected to achieving either economic or strategic needs. In his 1980 book, *The Tongue-Tied American,* Senator Paul Simon, another Midwesterner, used an anecdote to convey this same message. When a foreign language teacher was asked, Simon recounts, why young people in rural areas who rarely leave their home towns should learn a foreign language, she replied that it was precisely for that reason (p. 76).

It is significant, therefore, that the recommendation to teach useable skills was often accompanied by reminders of the need to enable learners to become culturally competent as well. For Michael Roscoe, there is serious value in "entering into someone's way of life" through the study of that person's language and culture, even if one never "wind[s] up in another country."

> One can try to learn about other places in a serious fashion. To do that means to try to really enter into the spirit and history and culture of other people. The best way to do that is to take one particular thing. Find out

about France, or China, or Japan, or whatever it is and [have students] really dedicate themselves to really see what it's like to grow another skin and see what it's like to live in another skin. I mean . . . it's not really going to be another person, ultimately, but—for the most part, there are a few people who wind up in another country and wind up going native, but by and large, that is not going to happen—but it's the closest one is going to come to really entering into someone's way of life. And the only way to really do that is to learn another language. Because the language both expresses and records the life and vitality of another people. If foreign language people really want to get some business and perform a public service I think that is the way they should go.

Ron Sutherland is briefer, but his point is essentially the same:

In general, I think, we need to start with a broader brush on language, integrate it with culture and history, give people the idea of the world around them to get people interested in it, and from that give them different paths to different ways of thinking.

# Conclusions

The data from two samples have been analyzed in order to gain a better understanding of how people in a range of professions outside academia view foreign language study and foreign language learning. Additionally, we wanted to compare the attitudes, experiences, and motivations of Midwesterners with those of Easterners in important metropolitan centers. A brief summary of the similarities linking the two samples will be followed by points on which they diverge.

The most striking commonality in both samples involves the contradictions which emerge in the description of respondents' experiences learning foreign language and the attitudes they currently hold about foreign language. For example, a majority of the adult respondents in both samples recognize the value and importance of foreign language study despite the fact that as young people many of them had disappointing, frustrating, or, in a few cases, even horrific experiences in a foreign language classroom. In addition, a number of respondents criticized their foreign language classes for not having a sufficiently developed "use-based" teaching approach. At the same time, the positive experiences related by some of these same respondents were not tied to any particular pedagogical approach. Indeed, those who had good experiences and positive memories either could not remember any specifics regarding the foreign language pedagogy used or reported a range of pedagogical methods from grammar-based to proficiency-oriented. Respondents in both samples claimed to be strong advocates of beginning foreign language education with young children, yet there was no general consensus favoring the establishment of a language requirement at this level.

In both samples favorable impressions of foreign language study were strongly linked to particular teachers and involved highly personalized criteria like teaching style and individual presentation. However, what these educators provided is not clear. Were they exemplars as teachers, as speakers of a foreign tongue, or as both? Were they important mentors who appeared at propitious moments in the educational trajectories of inquisitive young learners? Is it possible that through their persons they allowed students to connect a static, theoretical discipline with a living, ongoing communicative endeavor? Did these teachers embody, at least in part, essentialized, exoticized notions of French, German, or Spanish "others" in an otherwise largely homogeneous American educational landscape? Perhaps this explains what so intrigued Susan Stamberg about a French teacher "who was unlike anyone" she ever knew. It may also help us to understand why Linda Rainwater was drawn to the distinctive personal style of her teacher marked by "marvelous hats and soft clothing."

It is also significant that respondents in both samples who described themselves as serious students of foreign languages developed a series of eclectic and personalized learning strategies. In every case, committed language learners related how they took the initiative to individualize their learning, expanding it beyond the formal classroom and linking it to a myriad of situations which involved or simulated real-life. The fact that different pedagogical approaches appealed to respondents and that they organized their own learning in highly individualized ways begs important questions with regard to curricular design (see below).

In addition to a number of similarities, there were also significant differences which emerged in the two samples. Respondents in the Washington sample who had had bad experiences in the foreign language classroom blamed inappropriate pedagogy whereas Midwesterners blamed themselves. Midwesterners generally did not consider foreign language teachers to be marginalized within the teaching profession in contrast to individuals in the Washington sample who overwhelmingly saw them as marginalized but attributed this to a larger problem of

American anti-intellectualism. Moreover, Eastern elites were very vocal in their criticism of what they perceived to be mainstream American biases against intellectualism and cosmopolitanism. Although they were critical of a persistent utilitarian tradition in American education their own prescriptions for young American students reflect the very mainstream attitudes they seemed to reject. Midwesterners' discourse also expressed a critique of these biases but it surfaced differently as a rejection of "home" values and local practices. Foreign language was the idiom through which some educated Midwesterners made a critique of America's heartland. This critique found expression in their attraction to and identification with European high culture and a community of intellectual peers. Both were defined in opposition to the "deadly dull" Detroit of the 1950s or the ethnically marked south side neighborhoods of Chicago. The appeal of "foreignness," the search for "sophistication" or a "literate point of view" reflect what some Midwesterners sought in the study of other languages. Yet only certain languages qualified in this search. It is interesting to note that a majority in both groups considered French, Latin and, to a lesser extent, German to be languages with significant cultural capital. It is therefore paradoxical to note that in the Midwest most respondents agreed that Spanish is the "best" language to study despite their consensus that it conferred little apparent cultural capital. In contrast, those in the Washington sample recognized French, Latin and German as the most "important" languages and studied them.

The summary of the data presented in both samples reveals, among other things, that certain underlying social attitudes and cultural practices are shared by Americans regardless of where they live. This preliminary investigation of learner attitudes outside academia centers on and begins to address a significant lacuna in the current research on second language acquisition. Over the past twenty years one of the most salient areas of investigation has been in the area of communicative language teaching. A defining principle of research in this area has been a shift in the focus from teacher to learner. Despite renewed attention to learner attitudes, motivations and the requirements of a learner-centered classroom, the area of social attitudes has rarely been the object of in-depth investigation.

Stern has argued that "the success of language teaching is dependent upon major forces in the society, such as the role, or perception, of language in that society" (1983, p. 426). More recently, Berns (1990) has maintained that close attention must be paid to the way human linguistic behavior is linked to a given social structure. According to her, this is important because attitudes about language affect the way languages are taught. For example, if a society views foreign language learning in a given context as developing a kind of social behavior as opposed to developing mental discipline, then different curricular approaches are likely to be encouraged in the classroom as a result. Similarly, Kennedy (1988) argues that efforts to redesign curricula must privilege cultural factors rather than institutional ones.

Our data corroborate this scholarship and other work which identify motivation as a primary factor in the success or failure of language learners (Gardner & Lambert, 1972; Gardner, 1985; Gardner & Clément, 1990). The information gleaned from both these samples indicates that motivation is closely linked to social attitudes in a given cultural context. For example, in Argentina prevalent social attitudes made English a highly desirable political good for children like María from upper-middle-class milieux whereas for white American professionals from the same social class French and German were recognized as languages of cultural capital. Our samples do not explore the attitudes of minorities in the United States. However, the importance of studying Swahili for well-educated African Americans like Matthew Chambers is fascinating and demands further study.

Our samples show that respondents understood at an early age that language study was connected to important life and career choices. They also learned from their parents, relatives, educators and/or elites outside the family that certain languages were important cultural goods which could be used as a device to facilitate social mobility or to maintain and consolidate current class status. Our data further show that as adults they have continued to make decisions for themselves and for their children which reflect these attitudes. It is significant that Chris studied Spanish in college but took up French lessons in Washington as an established professional. Despite Lance Keppel's painful experience in a foreign language classroom, as an adult he is very enthusiastic about a number of up-scale "leisure" pursuits which include learning French, wine connoisseurship, and cycling.

What are the implications of these findings for both future research and curricular design? They confirm the claims of Stern (1983) and Berns (1990) concerning the centrality of social attitudes and demonstrate that these are embedded in a complex, continually changing sociocultural matrix. Moreover, these data suggest that a much more systematic investigation of social attitudes in various, local contexts is needed. At the same time they raise the question of whether a set of uniform, organizing principles in curricular design is workable. One of the authors recently attended a local conference organized to redress the perceived decline in the number of French students at the university level. There were few high school teachers in attendance, no members of the community, no current or former learners of French. Clearly the conference organizers felt that curriculum work was an academic pursuit best left to "experts." The findings of this study imply otherwise: in order to decide what approaches within and beyond the classroom will be the most effective, "experts" must actively collaborate with many different sources.[5]

Finally, we conclude by reminding our readers of the quintessential Midwesterner, Mark Twain, and his experiences abroad. Despite a series of misfired attempts at communication in a number of contexts including sightseeing, shopping and Parisian barber shops, Twain and his fellows persisted in their attempts to make themselves understood in a foreign tongue. Understanding the motivations driving that persistence should inform our best efforts to teach our students how better to succeed.

# Notes

[1]Congressman Farr described some of the features of a new California State University which include a requirement that every graduating senior will have studied foreign language in an immersion language house setting for a semester. He added that satisfactory completion of the language requirement will be defined in terms of a rating of the student's functional proficiency.

[2]Virtually all of these interviewees see themselves as intellectuals by virtue of their education as well as their career and leisure pursuits. At the same time, all but three spontaneously identified anti-intellectualism and anti-cosmopolitanism as pervasive cultural attitudes among Americans (see Lamont, 1992).

[3]The ghetto model postulates that members gradually move to more attractive neighborhoods.

[4]Recent figures released by the Joint National Committee for Languages (JNCL Fact Sheet, 1994) do not necessarily bear out any correlation between a region's amount of international contact and foreign language enrollments in primary and secondary classes. In Wisconsin, 2.4% of the total elementary enrollment and 41.9% of the secondary enrollment were taking foreign languages. The figures for Maryland were virtually the same: 2.3% and 42.3% figures for those respective categories. Two other midwestern states showed even higher foreign language enrollments than Wisconsin. Iowa and Nebraska had respective figures of 13.9% and 4.5% for elementary foreign language enrollments and 50.6% and 66% in secondary enrollments. Unfortunately, enrollment percentages were not available for Washington, DC.

[5]For other relevant statements about the investigation of community values as a part of curriculum design, see Ashworth (1985), Dubin & Olshtain (1986), Richterich & Chancerel (1977) and Yalden (1987).

# References

Ashworth, M. (1985). *Beyond methodology: Second language teaching and the community.* Cambridge: Cambridge University Press.

Basham, C. (1994, November). *Language revitalization: Academic and community perspectives.* Paper presented at the "Language, Culture, and Society" Discussion Series, Department of Linguistics, University of Oregon, Eugene, OR.

Berns, M. (1990). *Contexts of competence: Social and cultural considerations in communicative language teaching.* New York: Plenum Press.

Bourdieu, P. (1984). *Distinction: A social critique of the judgement of taste.* (R. Nice, Trans.). Cambridge, MA: Harvard University Press.

Conzen, K. (1976). *Immigrant Milwaukee.* Cambridge, MA: Harvard University Press.

Dubin, F. & Olshtain, E. (1986). *Course design.* Cambridge: Cambridge University Press.

Gardner, R.C. (1985). *Social psychology and second language learning.* London: Edward Arnold.

———, & Clément, R. (1990). Social psychological perspectives on second language acquisition. In H. Giles and W. P. Robinson, (Eds.), *Handbook of language and social psychology.* Chichester, Eng.: John Wiley & Sons.

Gardner, R.C., & Lambert, W. (1972). *Attitudes and motivations in second-language learning.* Rowley, MA: Newbury House.

Giddens, A. (1973). *The class structure of the advanced societies.* New York: Harper and Row.

Goodman, K.S., Bridges Bird, L., & Goodman, Y.M. (Eds.) (1991). *The whole language catalogue.* Santa Rosa, CA: American School Publishers.

Herron, C. (1982). Who should study a foreign language? The myth of elitism. *Foreign Language Annals, 15,* 441–449.

JNCL Fact Sheet: Languages. (1994, November). *A.A.T.F. National Bulletin,* p. 5.

Kaplan, A.Y. (1993). *French lessons.* Chicago: University of Chicago Press.

Knowles, M. (1994). Self-directed curriculum renewal: A process analysis in one university French department. (Doctoral dissertation, University of Illinois, Urbana, 1993). *Dissertation Abstracts International, 54,* 4080A.

Kramsch, C. (1993). *Context and culture in language teaching.* Oxford: Oxford University Press.

Kunin, M. (1994). *Living a political life.* New York: Alfred A. Knopf.

Lamont, M. (1992). *Money, morals, and manners.* Chicago: University of Chicago Press.

Lenneberg, E. (1967). *Biological foundations of language.* New York: John Wiley.

Marcus, G. (Ed.). (1983). *Elites.* Albuquerque: University of New Mexico Press.

Richterich, R. & Chancerel, J.L. (1977). *L'identification des besoins des adultes apprenant une langue étrangère.* Conseil de L'Europe: Hatier.

Rosaldo, R. (1994). Cultural citizenship and educational democracy. *Cultural Anthropology, 9,* 402–411.

Robinson, G.N. (1988). *Crosscultural understanding.* New York: Prentice Hall.

Simon, P. (1981) *The tongue-tied American.* New York: Continuum.

Stern, H.H. (1983). *Fundamental concepts of language teaching.* Oxford: Oxford University Press.

de Tocqueville, A. (1969). *Democracy in America* (G. Lawrence, Trans.) (J.P. Mayer, Ed.) New York: Doubleday.

Torruellas, R.M. (1990). Learning English in three private schools in Puerto Rico: Issues of class, identity and ideology (Doctoral dissertation, New York University, 1990). *Dissertation Abstracts International, 51,* 1290.

Twain, M. (Samuel L. Clemens). (1895). *The innocents abroad or The new pilgrim's progress.* Boston: Joseph Knight Company.

Ulrich, R.J. (1980). *The Bennett Law of 1889.* New York: Arno Press.

Wylie, L., & Bégué, A. (1970). *Les Français.* Englewood Cliffs, N.J.: Prentice Hall.

Yalden, J. (1987). *Principles of course design for language teaching.* Cambridge: Cambridge University Press.

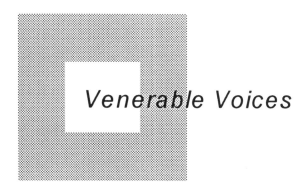

# Venerable Voices

Dolly Jesusita Young

*The University of Tennessee*

Mary Kimball

*Pacific University*

## Introduction

Our nation's long neglect of minorities whose skin is dark is perhaps only a little worse than our neglect of another minority whose hair is white.
—Lyndon B. Johnson

In many other cultures, age is associated with experience and wisdom and, for this reason, holds prestige and honor. In this country, the "minority whose hair is white" finds that our youth-obsessed culture often neglects the wisdom of those whose perceptions of the present and insights into the future have been gleaned from the past. With the twenty-first century in sight, we look forward with anticipation to how the future will unfold. Glimpses into the past would be helpful, for how can we know where we are going if we do not know where we have been? Evelyn Brega, a well-respected high school teacher of French with 37 years' classroom experience and a history of active involvement in the foreign language profession, describes the role that "venerable voices" can play:

> I would like to simply make a plea. It is almost a crime how we are not utilizing the wonderful resource that is available by ignoring people sixty

and over. It is so foolish and it is a dinosaur mentality. Why is it that in education we constantly make the same mistakes over and over again? Why can't we learn from experience? Well, we certainly cannot learn from it if we don't listen to those who have had it.

Our belief in the links among history, the person, and the profession leads us to look for the evolution of professional development in the personal lives of individuals. Our purpose in doing so is to contribute to the reconceptualization of educational research "so as to assure that the teacher's voice is heard, heard loudly, heard articulately" (Goodson, 1992, p. 10). The voices in this chapter represent a small sample of the many venerable voices in our profession, individuals who through decades of hard work, immeasurable enthusiasm, and unrelenting dedication have contributed significantly to the nature and evolution of foreign language education in this country. In this chapter, fourteen eminent leaders from the field of foreign language and culture education—a brief synopsis of each person's career appears in Appendix D—invite us to hear their voices on a variety of issues related to learning and teaching. In addition, we are permitted glimpses into their lives, personalities, professional histories and experiences.

# Methodology

## Acknowledging our Lenses

> The story of our research endeavour must be located within a genealogy of context.
> —Ivor Goodson

In qualitative research, it is important to know the researcher's background and biases because the data are necessarily filtered through them. Coe (1991) has pointed out that it is important that researchers-as-authors indicate their positioning in relation to the research process. Indeed, the unique research backgrounds of the co-investigators of this chapter exercised a profound effect on its development. A qualitative researcher with strong convictions regarding the power of life history *methodology* as a tool to provide insights into educators, Kimball approached her interviewees from the perspective of seeing the connections between each teacher's personal life and his or her professional persona.[1] Kimball conducted her interviews—most of which are quite lengthy—in

person; in addition to obtaining reactions to the specific issues we identified, she encouraged digressive exploration of life memories and experiences. The theory behind life history methodology profoundly influenced the way she approached and conducted the interviews and the
way she interpreted the data that were gathered. Young was interested
in gathering data regarding specific issues in foreign language education
today. She conducted her interviews by telephone to increase the number
of interviewee voices and in this way to obtain an increased diversity of
perspectives. Her interviews were shorter than Kimball's and were based
on a tighter question/answer format. The two of us both aimed at the
same goal, but we saw the data through different lenses.

Richardson (1992) cautions that investigators should also acknowledge the social similarities and differences between themselves and their
research subjects because these enter into and shape the researchers'
concept of "knowledge" in any research venture. It is important to be
aware of the agents or filters through which the voices for this chapter
have been heard.

The two of us share lifelong interests in understanding people through
hearing their stories. Young has devoted much of her professional career
to listening to the voices of language learners and scholars as they discuss
issues related to language anxiety, foreign language reading, and language textbooks. Her use of quantitative and qualitative research has
offered insights into second language acquisition gained by listening
carefully to students and teachers alike. Kimball's professional formation builds on a background of anthropology and includes the teaching
of French, German, and multicultural approaches to learning in levels
spanning middle school to the university, with a particular interest in the
teaching of culture. As a qualitative researcher, Kimball advocates the
use of video as a research tool which can effectively strengthen life
histories by contributing to "thick description" (Geertz, 1973) through
non-verbal data. Her dissertation (Kimball, in progress) is, in fact, a
critical life history of Laurence Wylie. Life history methods, she believes, seem best able to give both substantive and methodological support to studying teachers' lives through "stories of action within a theory
of context" (Goodson, 1992, p. ix).[2]

The differences in format for the interviews yielded differences in
the interview data. Eight interviews were conducted by telephone and
audiotaped; six were conducted in person, one of these was audiotaped,
and the other five were videotaped. This information is summarized

briefly below.

| Interview Formats | | |
|---|---|---|
| *Person Interviewed* | *Interviewed by* | *Capture Format* |
| German Brée | Young | telephone, audiotaped |
| Evelyn Brega | Kimball | in person, videotaped |
| John Carroll | Young | telephone, audiotaped |
| Kenneth Chastain | Young | telephone, audiotaped |
| Stephen Freeman | Barnes-Karol[a] | in person, audiotaped |
| Frank Grittner | Young | telephone, audiotaped |
| Eleanor Jorden | Kline[b] | in person, videotaped |
| Constance Knop | Young | telephone, audiotaped |
| Wilga Rivers | Kimball | in person, videotaped |
| Eleanor Sandstrom | Kimball | in person, videotaped |
| Earl Stevick | Young | telephone, audiotaped |
| Mary Thompson | Kimball | in person, videotaped |
| Albert Valdman | Young | telephone, audiotaped |
| Laurence Wylie | Kimball | in person, videotaped |

[a]Gwendolyn Barnes-Karol, author of Chapter 2 in this volume, conducted this interview.
[b]Rebecca Kline, author of the Introduction to this volume, conducted this interview while Kimball videotaped.

The length of the interviews varied, with the telephone interviews tending to last from 1 to 1½ hours and the face-to-face interviews ranging from 1½ to 3½ hours. As mentioned earlier, the telephone interviews tended to be issues oriented whereas the interviews conducted in person were longer and in addition to exploring issues lent themselves to sharing life stories. Furthermore, while setting up the video equipment, an "after tea" rapport was established between the interviewer and the interviewee. The gesture of offering tea has also been recognized by Measor (1992, p. 216), who noted that she was served tea in the best family china by all the retired teachers she interviewed. Thus the abundance of shared stories in the face-to-face interviews may be due primarily to the increased ease of establishing rapport in person. In this research, none of the persons interviewed appeared daunted by the fact that the interviews were being audio or videotaped. As our research evolved, we realized how well our different "lenses" complemented each other, and the synergy between the two has made for a richer, and more profound product than the two individual parts. This is perhaps most visibly apparent in the unique structure of this chapter itself, which combines a thematic organization based around the major issues that emerged from the interviews, with in-depth portraits of a number of the participants created from excerpts from the interviews. These portraits are intended to give readers more of the sense of the person behind the point of view.

## Procedure

We conducted the interviews between April and November of 1994. We contacted each individual first by mail in a letter explaining this project. A follow-up phone call allowed us to arrange the dates and times for the interviews. Many of the interview questions were the same as those included in the other interviews (see Appendix A). Given the special character of this group, and the motivation to elicit life history data, a number of the interview questions were particular to this chapter only. For example, we asked participants to suggest future directions in foreign language education, to speculate on what they would be most apprehensive about and what they would be most looking forward to if they were to begin their careers over, and to describe a typical day in one of their own classes. The entire list of special questions is included as Appendix E.

The answers to these questions would themselves comprise a book. For the purposes of this volume, therefore, we identified three primary themes to frame the chapter: (1) How is learning a foreign language different from learning other subjects? (2) What is it that people "get" out of learning a foreign language? and, (3) What does it mean to be a language teacher today? We selected the issues which we thought foreign language teachers would find most relevant to their lives today, issues which we also believed connected to other overarching issues in the field of foreign language education.

## Participants: Profile and Portrait

### *Profile*

The objective of this study was to interview distinguished elders of the field. Within that pool, we had planned to interview a sample balanced for gender, language, level, geographic location, and ethnicity. Ultimately, we had to accept less heterogeneity than we had sought with respect to ethnicity, language and level. Nonetheless, participants in the study represent a wide variety of backgrounds: foreign language teachers, foreign language professors, curriculum specialists, linguists, a representative from anthropology and the social sciences, an educational psychologist, and a psycholinguist. As a group, they represent classroom teaching experiences at all levels, from university to high school to elementary school. Several describe experiences from the Second World War, and all speak at least two languages other than English. They have pioneered new fields of study, opened avenues for new areas of research, and dedicated their lives to passionate promotion of the teaching and learning of foreign languages and cultures. Their nationalities include American, Australian, Canadian, French, and Swiss.

### *Portraits*

We seek to learn from those people whose experience and contributions we respect. We are curious to understand their perspective because we learn most effectively when we can relate to what we are encountering. We used excerpts from the videotaped interviews to develop personal "portraits" of some of the participants. We hope that these portraits will enable readers to gain a richer sense of the person behind the dedicated professional. The wise and often humorous perspectives they offer us about the place and role of the foreign language teacher today are derived from their unique personalities as well as from their own personal experiences as learners and teachers and from the historical moments in which they have lived.

We hope that through these portraits and other parts of the interviews you will capture glimpses of Eleanor Jorden's sense of humor, Eleanor Sandstrom's compassion and concern for her students, Stephen Freeman's dedication to Middlebury, Germaine Brée's humility, and John Carroll's enthusiasm for research. We hope you will hear through Wilga Rivers's own voice the connection between her real world experiences and the development of pedagogical principles, the insights into teacher training offered by Constance Knop, the love of teaching young people voiced by Frank Grittner. We hope we have captured for you the innovative maverick in Laurence Wylie, who pioneered the development of teaching French civilization in a world dominated at the time by teaching French literature, the pragmatist in Evelyn Brega, the inspirer in Mary Thompson, the bluntness and Copernican perspective of Earl Stevick, the precision of Albert Valdman, and the gentle reflector and philosopher in Kenneth Chastain.

# Themes

## How Is Learning a Foreign Language Different from Learning Other Subjects?

> One's speech is part of one's self. —Earl Stevick

In reflecting on the question about how learning a foreign language might be different from learning other subjects, Earl Stevick identified the fundamental issue in typically direct fashion:

> One's speech is part of one's self. One's ability to interpret or remember history or to do mathematical gymnastics and so forth is a skill, but it's not part of one's self. This is particularly true with pronunciation. I think there's a strong social element to skill or lack of skill in pronunciation, although I certainly wouldn't claim that that's all there is to it.

The connection between language and self was particularly important to Wilga Rivers, too, whose comments echo the subtle and not-so-subtle messages that reverberated throughout many of the interviews.

> I've had experience with other subjects, and learning a language is very different from the other subjects because you are putting people in a very vulnerable situation, you are asking them to reveal themselves in a way which is very threatening because when they don't know the language very well and they don't have the means to express themselves, they are unsure of what kind of expression they are giving and they feel threatened. They feel they're making a fool of themselves and they probably are. . . . They feel, you know, people, their peers might laugh at them. . . . The classroom atmosphere must be an atmosphere of acceptance and mutual respect

. . . where students know how to appreciate other students, teachers appreciate students, and students appreciate the teacher. When you've got that kind of relaxed atmosphere, then students can try to reveal themselves through another language in a genuine kind of way.

Recalling an experience with one of her students, Evelyn Brega relates a delightful story that exemplifies how the "self" can change in a foreign language class.

I was very pleased over the years to notice that many students, not many, but a number of students with disabilities—for example they stuttered, they stammered badly—when they were speaking a foreign language they did not stutter. Now that in itself is a clue. It gives you a great deal of information about other things. Now why didn't they stutter in a foreign language? I had one boy who could hardly get a sentence out, but when he spoke French he sounded like Charles deGaulle, he was terrific. It was because he was able to get out of himself and assume the role of another person. That was something that gave me a lot of pleasure to see that the teaching of a foreign language and perhaps what I was able to do helped that person.

All of the individuals interviewed maintained that language learning is fundamentally different from other learning experiences. Learning science, for example, is about science, and learning history is about history, but learning language, they told us again and again, is not really about language. Ken Chastain talked about the difference in the following way. "I think it

# Mary Thompson

Around 1945, Theodore ("Tug") Andersson, who was in charge of the MAT program at Yale, put on a series of French lectures on Saturday mornings. I think almost every French teacher in Connecticut must have attended. There was this huge outpouring of interest because nothing had happened before, you know, for a long time. That's where the idea of the Northeast Conference came from. And he started it. The first one ever was held at Yale.

Then about 1950 Tug Andersson asked if anyone had any interest in foreign language teaching in the elementary school. My superintendent in Fairfield, who was a Middlebury graduate and a French minor, thought it would be a great idea to start it in Fairfield. So I wrote a proposal for three classes, two French and one Spanish. Joyce Green, a terrific teacher and a great person, volunteered to teach a third-grade class in French. I'm sure there are a lot of people in the Northeast Conference, older ones, who remember her. I didn't know anything about elementary school, so I visited five or six third grades to get the feeling of the classroom. We started it and it was the most terrific success you can ever imagine. We immediately began to get telephone calls and letters and can we come visit and you know there was hardly a day that one of us didn't have a visitor. Of course Tug Andersson was keeping his eye on this like crazy, and he arranged a meeting of language teachers in Connecticut that was held at Fairfield so that Joyce Green did the demonstration class with the third grade that she was using, and everybody was all excited, and the whole town wanted language put in every third grade. Where were we gonna get the teachers? We increased the program as much as we could. Sometimes I had to lend my car to our college graduate teachers so that they could commute between schools to teach. I could teach my class, and then she could pick up my car and go teach her class. I got teachers from Tug Andersson's MAT program at Yale. The only way we could hire new teachers was for elementary positions. One time I know that Tug Andersson gave a student—Sandy—the money to go to New Haven State Teacher's College to start getting some credits toward elementary education so that I could hire her to teach third grade. I really hired Sandy to teach French. She really didn't know much about third grade at all. Her principal was not in favor of her performance at all, especially when Sandy went to the principal at Christmas and said that she'd finished the arithmetic book. He told her to do it over again. She was a fantastic French teacher, and we had all kinds of problems like that. Soon after, Greenwich started a program, then Lexington. (Evelyn Brega taught in the elementary program in Lexington.) Quite a few other programs started. We didn't talk to each other particularly.

Tug Andersson was very much a

[learning a foreign language] is newer and more different," he says, "and therefore can offer greater insights into yourself, your own language and your own culture. I don't think any other one subject can do so many things."

If, indeed, the experience of learning a foreign language is unique among learning experiences, we as teachers may need to be sensitized to our role in this experience. If the learner's self is more exposed, and more susceptible to change, then we as teachers have more capacity to affect the "self" of language learners. If the teacher is authoritarian and intimidating, the learner is particularly vulnerable to harm, as this personal experience recounted by Rivers underscores. The young Rivers had been asked to provide an oral *explication de texte* in French class; what happened next has stayed vividly in her memory years after the event.

I was totally nervous. And there was this hall totally full of these people who, as long as people keep their mouth shut, always look as though they know more than you do. So Mr. A said OK and I got up and I started my *explication* of a section from Racine and Mr. A had not been taught modern pedagogical principles. And every time I opened my mouth, he jumped down my throat. Either it was mispronunciation of a vowel, or it was a misuse of a word, or it was the wrong intonation, or it was something. So after about three or four minutes of constant interruption, I just burst into stormy tears in front of the whole assembly. I just burst into those hysterical tears where the more people tap you on the shoulder, the more you cry. And I just bellowed there, and the professor was extremely embarrassed, and he tried to get me to calm down, and of course I couldn't. Finally I pulled myself together, and he said, "I won't say another word." Which is the best thing he ever did. Then I got through the whole thing quite nicely you see.

Among the "modern pedagogical principles" missing from Mr. A's repertoire were surely techniques for putting students at ease, and creating a non-threatening classroom atmosphere. Interestingly, in the same way that language *learning* is not just about language, the very best language teachers seem to recognize that language *teaching* is not just about language either. No one was more aware of this than Eleanor Sandstrom.

I tried to make it easier for the students to catch on. I tried to get them to reach for meaning. You have a lot of objective things that they could see and touch and handle and smell like flowers and colors. You know there's an awful lot just around you if you look for it. I'll tell you what foreign language teachers shouldn't do and that's to simply conjugate verbs. I just felt that had to go. Education should be loved, it should be creative. And I think it's important to create situations such as meeting a friend, having a problem of some kind, to be able to talk it out privately with another student. I think that's the way they learn, and they don't feel afraid of making a error.

part of the MLA at that point, and Ken Mildenberger. The MLA decided that instead of having everyone write his own program that we ought to pull this together somehow. I think Nelson Brooks was the Chairman of the first committee that the MLA appointed to write a guide for French in the third grade, and I was asked to be on the committee. We didn't really have any guidelines about what we were doing. We weren't teaching grammar-translation. '57 they sent Sputnik up, and my Director of Secondary Ed asked me if I would be his Assistant if he moved to Glastonbury as Superintendent. With Math and Science programs starting in Washington, I was asked to head a department for elementary school language, but I said I had just arrived in Glastonbury and couldn't leave.

In the Northeast Conference we had this rebellious group of people from Connecticut who were asking questions of some of the fathers of the profession in all the great universities. Look at the College Board exam! Look at how it is! Who wants to prepare for that kind of test? What does it have to do with language teaching? We plotted all kinds of things, and we had a whole agenda for the Northeast Conference. I can remember they had some publishers on the stage. I remember asking all the representatives to name one book that put listening and speaking skills first. They named a college text which was coming close; it was the best thing they had. The consensus seemed to be that you couldn't change language teaching unless you changed the textbook materials because teachers had a tendency to view the textbook as curriculum, to just open the book, turn the pages, and follow it. So, after foreign languages were added to the Science & Math proposal in Congress, they needed someone to head the language effort. They wanted us to write materials and then do a pilot program in Washington, to pick up some people and do some units and send them out to anyone who asked for them. When we had completed a year of curriculum for five languages, Bill Parker and Ken Mildenberger sent out bids to the publishing companies. Never got so much attention in my life while all these publishers were trying to get this contract to publish the work and change language teaching. The government really wanted them promoted, so the publishers had to present their proposals for publishing and advertising. Our books put listening and speaking in their proper position.

While most of the participants in our sample argued that learning a foreign language was a unique experience for students, Sandstrom and others also spoke about language learning from the perspective of the teacher, pointing out that the complex and diverse background necessary to teach foreign languages successfully sets the discipline apart from other subject areas. Listen again to Stevick:

Language teaching is not a subspecialty of food and nutrition. It's not a sub-specialty of history. I think these have something to contribute, but I think Pit Corder, the one person who stood up for the idea that language teaching is not a subspecialty, is not merely applied linguistics, although linguistics can be applied to it, but so can many other things, including interpersonal psychology and sociology. To me, [what is] terribly important is the interpersonal stuff, which is related peripherally to cognition, but you can find lots of cognitive studies which ignore it. So there's the interpersonal stuff, there's the cognition, there's the linguistic structure, there's the concern for social interests. There are all these things that impinge on the language teacher.

For many people, it seems logical that the individual most likely to have what it takes to teach a foreign language would be a native speaker. Albert Valdman reminds us why such a conclusion is simplistic:

Language learning and the use of language is a skill. And it has knowledge. So you have two factors. It is also for that reason that you can't take the average native speaker, because the native speaker has the skill, but the native speaker does not have the knowledge. You ask a native speaker a question about structure, they will be able to deal with it. You ask them a question about culture, they are not engaged in introspection to be able to analyze the culture. Furthermore, their horizons may be limited. For example, in the case of the French, you can't expect [just] any French speaker to know about the culture of Louisiana, about Africa.

In fact, any teacher today that deals with beginning and intermediate French needs to have some knowledge of a culture beyond France. We can't expect this from native speakers. You can't ask someone from Quebec to be able to have knowledge of the culture in France. That's a set of knowledge. In this regard, you could say that there is a parallel between foreign languages and the other content areas. However, in addition language is a skill, and there is a certain technique in imparting a skill that obviously you would not find in imparting mathematics. Mathematics is not a skill. It is a set of knowledge. If you teach chemistry, you have to know enough chemistry to be able to field questions, to be able to explain concepts. Now in foreign languages I think the error that we make is at the college level we entrust language instruction to students who just have a BA and do not have the knowledge base, do not have enough experience in pedagogy to be able to impart skill. So they're deficient in that regard. If you take distinguished professors in linguistics and literature, and you put them before a first-year class, with the type of knowledge they have, it may be that some of them will not have the general knowledge of culture or the ability to analyze the language that is required. If you are a linguist, you may not have been exposed to enough culture. If you're a liteature specialist, you don't know how to answer questions, you simply know it. If you're not a native speaker, you've used the language long enough so that you've forgotten the problems you have had. So all this means that what we need in language instruction, we need to have instructors who have a high level of competence in the language, native competence, we need to have instructors with enough training in how to analyze the language, who know enough about language acquisition and some of the problems of why people have difficulties. That errors are natural, and that students make errors, and make them over and over again. It's not because they're stupid. Then of course you need knowledge about the culture.

Recognition of the different kinds of knowledge and skill that must come together for succesful language teaching—particularly when the target language is vastly different from the native language—led Eleanor Jorden to design her now-famous team-teaching model. In this model, two instructors work as a team: one teacher comes from the native culture and the other from the target culture. In this way, learners always have access to a model of the target language and culture (the native speaker) and to a master teacher (the non-native speaker) who shares their same cultural and linguistic background and can help the learners move successfully from familiar to new ground.

# What Is it That People "Get" out of Language Learning?

> If you study enough language, it changes your philosophy, because learning about people with different values forces you to question the values you've been brought up with.
> —Laurence Wylie

While people responded with a variety of answers, two dominant strands emerged. On the one hand, the experience of learning another language was associated with personal, internal change: it affects values, perspectives, and points of view, opens one's mind and expands one's horizons. On the other hand, language learning was connected with a series of external changes, more pragmatic and "real world" attainments: enhanced language and communication skills, and resulting access to jobs and to knowledge in a variety of content areas.

Laurence Wylie, for example, talked about the profound internal change in his life that stemmed from learning a foreign language:

When I went to college, people told me that since I wanted to go into the Foreign Service I had to learn French. After my first year of college French at Indiana, I decided that I would go to France my junior year. But the teachers said I didn't have enough French to go with either of the two foreign study groups that existed at the time, Delaware and Smith. My sophomore year I doubled up on French courses so I learned enough to get into the third year abroad. In the 18th century course that I took, we read everything of Voltaire that we could in one semester. That was when I got a completely new version

## Eleanor Jorden

There is the myth that the best way to learn a language is to go to the country. The best way to learn a language is to get a really, really good course and start out in *this* country, if you're an American. Get a good foundation and then go to the country. You must go to the country eventually. But if you go at the beginning, certainly for Japanese, you'll get into all kinds of problems. There's been some very interesting research recently in connection with Russian. It's been going on for years and years. And what they're finding is that the only, the *only* students who make real progress when they go to Russia are those who go in with a very solid knowledge of the structure, how the language works and so on, and then they make tremendous progress. The other ones go on and develop what we usually call abominable fluency, which is a terrible disease.

When I was at Bryn Mawr, a very sharp dean asked me what it was I liked about language. I looked her in the eye and said grammar and she and vision of religion. So the professor and Voltaire were the end of my childhood dreams of possibly becoming a Methodist preacher like my father. If you study enough language, it changes your philosophy, because learning about people with different values forces you to question the values you've been brought up with. That was terribly important to me. It really changed my whole outlook on life.

Similarly, Constance Knop found that language learning had added "another dimension" to the way she views life.

I think it's made me a much better communicator. I think it offered me not only the knowledge of words, but the idea of looking at points of views in different ways, because of the different cultural insights that come. It is a combination of language and culture that a concept or a term or an experience has so many ways of looking at it, neither of which is exclusive of the other. It just gives another added dimension to how you perceive experiences. I think it's made me more open minded. That is, *not* thinking that there is just one way to say or do or believe something, but opening my eyes and seeing that there are millions of ways of experiencing life through language, through people, through experiences.

Frank Grittner takes the students' perspective in his response to this question and highlights cognitive or intellectual benefits that motivate some students: for them, a foreign language is a tool, something fun to use and enjoy.

The kids develop a feeling for how languages work and some insights

said, "Huh?" So she said what you want is linguistics! During one of the courses I later took to learn a new language, we drilled and drilled on phonology because the professor was a phonological specialist. I don't know how many hours we spent on the verb "to belch" because it was the only one that had a particular vowel in final position. I was too docile to raise my hand and say, "If it's the only one and it means belch, is it worth worrying about?" Of course today that's the only thing I can say in that language, "My maternal grandmother belches." My only languages at that point had been Sanskrit, Latin, Greek, Gothic, Old Saxon, Old Norse, so I wasn't conversing in anything else.

Later on, I worked under this [man], my mentor, the man to whom I owe everything, Professor Bernard Block, who is a fabulous linguist. We worked on a textbook, the only one then that was linguistically based. But I got over to Japan and realized that the most frequently used expressions that I was just hearing around me all the time were nowhere in that book. Nowhere in that book. Because you would never get at that. Never get at that through any kind of Western thought. I also realized that dictionaries don't work. Because I went over to Japan on a freighter, and the captain knew that I was working frantically on Japanese. We came into Yokohama harbor, and he called me and said, "C'mon up on the bridge. The Japanese pilot is coming and you'll have your first chance to speak to a Japanese in Japanese." I thought, "Oh, my

Lord, what's the word for pilot?" So I checked my dictionary and I got this long complicated compound. So I went up on the bridge and this very pleasant looking man got on, you know, and he was bowing at everybody, so I gulped and went up to him, and I came out with this thing, and I said it again. Of course they were using the English borrowing, and this thing that I had found must have been Magi period or something. So anyway I thought, dictionaries, oh dictionaries. It was just a constant learning experience. The first thing I wanted to do when I stepped off that boat was to start writing another textbook, because you just had to know more about the culture. More about how people work together.

Then I set up the Foreign Service Institute's school for diplomats, and it was very interesting to have the experience of teaching Japanese to Americans while in Japan, and that also convinced me that you have to live at home. Everything came at them so suddenly and with no organization, no ordering, no system to it. It was terribly confusing. And then the other problem I always had was, how are you going to keep them in the tape lab once they've seen the Ginza? I mean they wanted to be out all the time. Floating around and they were not at the level where they could really understand what they were hearing or the implications of it. They didn't know whether they were picking up polite speech, or direct-style speech, or feminine speech, or what they were picking up. So I realized

into the culture. I don't think they have to go so far as to want to be a part of that culture. That helps with motivation, but I think just the fun of seeing how the language works, using it and experiencing it as a communicative vehicle. Seeing kids do that was, I think, the most satisfying.

Chastain underscores and further develops the value of language learning from the students' perspective:

I don't know if you've ever read it or not. There's a poem, "The Chambered Nautilus," and it describes the nautilus, which is a shell-like creature like a snail. The whole idea behind the poem is that we grow in ever-widening and ever-increasing circles. We're always in a sense stepping beyond the known into the unknown, or we should be as we're learning. Of course, if we're not learning then we're not doing that. But I think this is the great potential of languages, often not realized, but the great potential is just to open people's eyes, students' eyes, students' minds, and help them see beyond themselves, beyond their own language, beyond their own culture into something new and different and exciting, maybe better, maybe not as good, maybe there's no judgment to it at all. It's just a different way of doing things. That's the good part. I've always insisted to the students here that you don't really understand your own language 'til you study another one. You don't really understand your own culture 'til you've seen another one. That's good for you. That's one of the excitements of students who come back from a semester abroad. They feel as if they're so much broader as an individual, so much greater inside in culture and life and language. With me, language has been a continuous interest and stimulation and challenge. It's just a way to grow beyond yourself and beyond your own language and your own culture.

With a lifetime as language learners and teachers, these individuals often speak of language learning in philosophical terms, as the above examples show. But they are mindful of the practical benefits of language study as well. For example, to John Carroll, learning a foreign language meant gaining access to knowledge he wanted and needed for his own professional development.

> It made it possible for me to access all kinds of knowledge I was interested in. When I was in college, I majored in the classics, Latin and Greek. Of course, quite a bit of scholarship in the classics was in German. I perfected my knowledge of German to the extent that I believe I had a better reading knowledge of German. My early studies of language have stood me in very good stead ever since. . . . I remember that Edward Sapir said in college what I should do is make sure that I learned to read as many foreign languages as I could, particularly French and German, because a lot of the scholarship in linguistics was at that time conducted in French or German. I even learned Russian somewhat. . . . I've always been an exponent of learning foreign language for scholars.

Chastain also recognized the many economic and career motivations for learning a foreign language in this country.

> It may be avocational, it may be vocational. Certainly it can be a good avocation all the way from reading to movies to short-wave radio to travel.

then for someone to come over into Japan where everything is going to go through an English filter, it's hopeless. The assumptions that we make based on our native language are just tremendous. Somebody has compared this to computer wiring. You can get all kinds of software but you can never change the wiring of the computer. The initial wiring is there. As a native American, I can live in Japan, and I can become very Japanized, and people can say she's just like a Japanese, but I'm still seeing things as an American. I still have all the American filters.

Methodologies? We used TPR the first day, for one thing only, and that is to teach classroom expressions. I saw a demonstration of TPR by Asher with a Japanese scholar sitting next to me, and the whole demonstration on the film was in Japanese, the first work Asher did was in Japanese. The Japanese scholar said, "Oh, it's a little like training dogs." I'll never forget that, it was so incredible in terms of reality. In Japanese, imperatives are confrontational, so you would never sit there saying, "Stand up, sit down." In Community Language Learning, you tell the teacher what you want to say. Now how does the student know culturally what he would want to say? And the Silent Way. I've never understood the rods. This is no way to learn language, there is no attention paid to culture whatsoever. So I have to say that none of these methods has really appealed to me. What we do [in my classes] is we memorize short dialogues. We work in lots of substitution within them, but the dialogues are very definitely contextualized, and we use video showing the dialogues acted out by native speakers, with all the proper context around them. We insist right from the beginning that it be authentic language. I don't like substitution drills like, "Is that a clock? No, it's a desk." Now figure that one out. Even coming out of a moving van, they would not look alike. We do drills in class that we call application drills, with enough visual aids in the room so that we can always, always refer to those. Everything is made as realistic as possible. We're very wary of role playing until the student can actually handle the role and we never have free conversation. I mean, what do you mean by free conversation? A student just comes in and says, you know, let's have free conversation? What are you going to learn from this? And with Japanese, unless it's a situation they know how to cover, the worst thing in the world would be for them to start practicing. In free conversation, there usually is nothing leading anywhere, it's not a learning exercise. It's something the students can do outside, but in terms of class, we are always thinking, what is the student learning this hour?

As I said earlier, you just can't separate language from its culture. For example, the Japanese treatment of guests which is, you know, nothing is too good. And just being so solicitous. They are never going to tell you when you've made a mistake. And

It can certainly be good in the vocational arena: international business. Finally, it is publicly recognized that we are no longer the dominant economic force in the world, we're one of the economic powerhouses but certainly not the most powerful or the only one anymore, and we have to compete in the international trade. . . . I had a student this semester who wants to be a doctor, but he wants to work in an area in the US where there are a lot of Spanish-speaking people. He wants to be a doctor to those people. Maybe people who want to go to graduate school, and they want Spanish as part of that. As the opportunities grow, the number of students will increase. A lot of students major in Spanish and say "I want to go ahead using my Spanish. How can I do that?" You go to law school, and how do you continue using your Spanish? Or you go work at a bank in New York City. How do you continue using your Spanish, or French? I think some are able to do it, and some of them are not. If they're not, then of course if they don't use their language, they forget it. But as these jobs increase, and as there is increasing contact with Spanish-speaking businesses and the Spanish-speaking world, an increase in the number of students who are interested will increase. . . . As Latin America develops economically, then the number of jobs will increase.

Germaine Brée echoes Chastain's thoughts when she notes that successful cooperative international ventures depend not only on the financial resources one brings to the enterprise, but—and in her view, this is just as important—on one's social capital as well.

I can think of no better social capital

than to be able to speak your partner's language. You have to be able to speak the language of the people you want to create an economic partnership with. It's going to be important, to say nothing of the fact that traveling is getting more and more intense from country to country. There will be a lot of jobs open involved with that exchange.

These two strands of thought on what one "gets" out of the experience of learning another language, which we have here called internal and external, were not offered in opposition to one another. Rather, they often overlapped and intertwined. For example, Grittner points out that acquiring cross-cultural awareness and sensitivity can represent tangible benefits to students.

they're not going to be open about telling you what you should do or anything like that, and so you can go on and on and on making these horrible mistakes, and that's why it's so important to have this base native here who has been in Japan.

My favorite story? OK: trip to Japan. I was going to a conference, staying at a hotel, I had just arrived, and I was terribly jet-lagged. I was really, you know, almost seeing cross-eyed, I'd been traveling about 24 hours. And in the hotel on the desk it said if you want to be awakened in the morning you can dial these numbers and you don't have to call the front desk or anything. So I followed the directions very carefully and I went to bed. Early in the morning, I heard this noise, the phone, and I sat up in bed. I knew something was ringing, but I didn't know where, you know, with the jet leg, but then I reached for the phone, and this voice said in English, "Your hour has come."

I've talked to some of our Wisconsin business leaders of various big industries. They said, "We don't necessarily want highly fluent, perfect translators and that kind of thing. But we do need people to go into a country with the sensitivity that Anglo-American culture is not the only one and not the last word necessary in cultures. Those people who have some kind of foreign language experience are more useful to us, not for their specific skills, but for their general attitudes."

And Valdman, like Carroll, acknowledges an external value to learning a foreign language, but also considers the cultural insights it affords.

As a professional, I've found it useful to be able to know a variety of languages so that I can communicate with colleagues in other countries with whom I do not share a language. For example, I've used German to communicate with a Russian scholar. . . . I think that obviously it's an aid to communication. It gives you insights into a culture that is very different from Western culture. Without that experience I would not know that people do different things, solve problems differently in this world, have different systems of belief.

Without question, the insights gained from the study of another culture were deemed to be the most valuable consequence of language learning. Eleanor Jorden's belief that one needs to be grounded in the target language and target culture *before* going abroad resonated throughout her interview. She comically recalls a cultural misunderstanding she experienced in Japan early in her career.

> The Japanese love to ask for criticism of themselves, of their system, of the country. And the worst thing in the world you can do is answer this with anything negative. And I knew this intellectually. I'd heard this, and then I visited this English class in a high school, a junior high school, and it was really, it was such a sad class because the material was just awful, and they were practicing this "have you once been to Germany, have you twice been to Germany," you know. I mean this kind of thing. And so I came out, and they brought me into the principal's office, and they said, "How is the class?" "Oh it was very good, it was very nice." "No, what did you really think of the English that was going on?" "Oh it was fine." "No, really, we want really to know what you thought of it." Well, you know at that stage, you think well if you really . . . So, I said, "I was concerned about the English that was being taught. The actual English. Not the method, the professors, the teachers here. . . ." There was dead silence after that, and a minute later I found that the teacher was called to the telephone, and she never came back, and the principal disappeared, and there I was. Ended up sitting there, and so then someone came in and said the class this afternoon that you are going to visit isn't going to meet and walked out. And I thought, "Oh my land, I've done it. I've really done it." Well, it was a school where you took your shoes off when you entered the building. I couldn't even remember where my shoes were. So I was wandering around the hallways, and I kept thinking, "What am I gonna do? What am I gonna do?" And finally this little boy, so cute, he came up. I guess he could tell, and he said "Is there anything I can do?" Thank God . . . and I said, "The truth of the matter is I don't know where my shoes are." So he took me down, I got my shoes and went out. I just wanted to die on the spot.

The teacher whose class was cancelled that day sought out Eleanor Jorden later for advice; she came to view Jorden as her mentor and still maintains contact with her.

Stephen Freeman saw far-reaching positive implications to developing cultural sensitivities in language learners.

> The construction of an attitude, which will promote understanding of foreign people, can be done in a language class . . . it terribly needs to be done because perhaps that will help out in the long run in constructing peace around the world.

What is it, then, that people "get" out of learning a foreign language? In this section, we hear these highly respected voices remind us of the kernel of what we in the foreign language profession are about: learning skills, learning facts and knowledge; sensitizing learners to other cultures, other ways of viewing the world; and learning about ourselves.

While we may acknowledge these multiple benefits of language learning, several of the venerable voices suggested that we need to publicize these advantages much more compellingly than we have in the past. This is particularly important since, as Stevick points out, for many people the decision to study a foreign language is often motivated by a very different kind of need—passing or completing a requirement — and the experience may be neither pleasant nor successful:

> Remembering back on times when I've run into people at parties or something and they've found out what line of work I was in, I think the thing that a lot of people get out of it is discouragement. "Well, I was never any good at languages." That kind of thing. . . . They immediately become self-conscious, and they refer to their own past inadequacies.

Chastain contends that the profession must both promote the value of language learning with students, and also deliver on the promises that we make:

> I think the role of the profession is to continue to put this before the public and put this before their students. I don't think we do it enough with our students. One thing we should do at least once a year is to say "Why study a foreign language?" and go through all this litany of things we believe in but that often we don't communicate with our students. The other thing over which we do have a lot of control, of course, is the type of course we teach. If we can teach students something about the culture of the country of the language and if we can teach them in such a way so that when they leave our classes, whether it's after two years or

## Laurence Wylie

I remember I used to get up very early in the morning when my father got up to work on his sermons. Poor guy, trying to work on his sermons and had this little 2 or 3 or 4 year-old asking for a lot more attention than he was prepared to give me. So what he did to keep me busy was to pull down an old first-year Greek book to teach me the Greek alphabet. So before I knew the English alphabet, I knew the alphabet began with alpha, beta, gamma, delta, and so on.

When it came time to study languages, I had to decide which I was going to study. French of course was the most highly rated, but was nothing I would lay claim to because it was only for the elite, top class, Episcopalian families. The Baptists and the football players studied Spanish 'cause that was supposedly easiest. Since I was a preacher's son, I took Latin. When I was about 12, I read the autobiography of Washington Irving and read that he had been Ambassador to Spain. I decided I would like to do that. That meant I had to learn Spanish, so I began to study on my own from a Spanish grammar somebody had left around our house. Then I found out that the major French teacher in my high school knew Spanish, and he was terribly nice, sympathetic. So I would try to do a Spanish lesson every night and then I would come in first thing in the morning, and he would use a half-hour of his time to go over the exercises that I had done.

What really got me interested in civilization was a course on the United States I took with André Siegfried at the Ecole de Sciences Politiques my junior year in France. Through him, I got a whole new idea of my own country and my own civilization. I 'member him talking about how capitalism had evolved, using the popular advertisement, "Reach for a lucky instead of a sweet," to show the competition between tobacco and candy. "Competition between producers of different products was a new kind of competition we should look at," Siegfried said. Siegfried's course showed me how other people look at our culture. Later, when I was teaching at Haverford, I was able to start a French Civilization course for graduate students who were at Haverford in 1943 as relief workers for the Quakers. I got Henri Peyre to come speak on life in France and there were other French refugees around that could be brought in to give lectures. One of the dormitories was turned into a French house that my wife and I were in charge of. By 1945, I managed to make French Civilization a regular course at Haverford. Then in 1959 McGeorge Bundy, then Dean of Harvard College, asked me if I would be interested in filling Harvard's new Chair of French Civilization. I had a degree in Romance languages and

three years of four years or six years, that they can communicate at a certain level. Then I think their feelings will be so positive about themselves and what they've been able to accomplish about the subject matter that we won't have to worry about the rest of it. The worst thing we can do is try to create enthusiasm if we're really not delivering.

The issue of accountability in teaching was an important one for members of this group, particularly with respect to culture. In Rivers's words, "We can handle the language, it's the culture that trips us." Several individuals expressed concern and frustration over what they perceived as widespread neglect of culturally oriented instruction or experiences in most foreign language classes. Others were deeply worried by the fact that many prospective teachers lack significant cultural knowledge and experience. The following comment by Valdman reflects the concern over the status of cultural instruction in foreign language classes. First, he defines culture as "a set of sensitivities and knowledges." He goes on to say,

It is paradoxical that culture is still very neglected in language instruction. People think it's something that you add on. What is basic is the knowledge of grammar and vocabulary and then after that, you learn culture. Whereas in fact in the real world, in terms of people who need to interact with foreigners on their own turf, it is the culture that is more important than the language itself.

By this, Valdman specifically refers

to countries with cultures vastly different from ours. He explains:

> I know this because my son is in international banking and has offices where the personnel need the local language to transact business. But he's told me that more than the language—it happens he is also bilingual—it's the knowledge of the culture, and it's the knowledge of a specific business culture that you need to acquire. For example, when you have a business lunch, at what time do you switch to the business at hand? This is done differently in different cultures, and it is that type of knowledge that is more important than the language itself.

Chastain attributes some of our failures in the teaching of culture to the manner in which it is conveyed in foreign language textbooks.

> I think culture is never going to be a basic component in the program as long as it's put in sort of little boxes in the book later on in the chapter which say "You should know that Spanish-speaking people eat dinner at 9:00" or something like that. It needs to be inherent in all the readings and all the activities that they do.

Among these interviewees, enhanced cultural awareness and understanding was the number one benefit of language study. Still, the views voiced here reflect a concept of culture that is difficult to define and perhaps even more difficult to teach. For example, Jorden and Valdman view culture as being woven into the interac-

had published a book on a nineteenth-century French critic. I had then studied anthropology and had just written a widely accepted study of a French village, published by the Harvard Press and glaringly present in all the bookstore windows of Harvard Square. Harvard had just created a new department, Social Relations, to bring together professors from anthropology, psychology, and sociology, professors who concentrated on the study of contemporary humans. So there I was, and because of the visits to Haverford by Clyde Kluckhohn and other new members of Social Relations, these Harvard professors knew me and would be willing to admit to their ranks a man who had a degree in Romance languages but who was interested in living people. So Bundy appointed David Reisman, Erik Erikson, David McClelland, and me. I was given an appointment in the social relations department with the understanding that I would teach a seminar on the social structure of a French village and a big, general course on French life.[3]

I ended up at Harvard teaching in the realm of social relations as the result of my struggle with what I had wanted to do with my French. I had been torn between the life I felt that I should lead and the life of people who have a doctorate in French language and literature. It seemed to me that there was something much more I would like to be able to teach about France. I wanted to be able to talk about how the French are really different. My Americans had such a poor understanding of France. When Ashley Montagu talked at Haverford about the new developments in the teaching of social sciences and above all about the studies that had been made of how people grew up in different places in a different way, I thought, "Now, *there's* something that really interests me." I made an appointment with Ashley Montagu, and then I went to Penn and told the anthropologist who did village studies, Irving Hallowell, there that I would like to make a study of France and what people are like in France, a study that would be similar to what Margaret Mead and Ruth Benedict were doing. So I arranged my classes at Haverford, which is something you can do at a small school, and I went to his course on village studies three times a week for three years. This gave me a whole new idea about the life I could lead. I dedicated my book, *Village in the Vaucluse* to Hallowell. Later, when I began applying for grants to send my Harvard students to France to study the village of Chanzeaux, it was difficult because grant-giving operations were divided by field, and people had trouble categorizing my work since it overlapped different fields. Here I had a doctorate in Romance language and literature and I wanted to do a study of a village in France. Well, what is this person trying to do? I mean he's not a sociologist. He's not an anthropologist. He's a French teacher. So I had a very hard time because each field saw my work as venturing out of its domain and into theirs.

tions between different peoples. Chastain, Grittner, Wylie, and Knop talk about culture as a phenomenon that one experiences only through the study of foreign languages and peoples. Significantly, if the quality of language textbooks is a guide, neither of these two views of culture make their way very often into the language class, where instruction still resembles the "little boxes" approach decried by Chastain. Consider this case: A recent survey (Young, in progress) of cultural instruction in 10 current editions of introductory Spanish texts indicates that culture is overwhelmingly treated as factual information, generally conveyed in the form of readings, in English or Spanish, that occur at least once in each textbook chapter. Typical cultural topics include: Hispanic universities, last names, Hispanic holidays, shopping, food, bullfighting, sports, housing, relationships, professional women, greetings, clothes, education, work and play, indigenous groups, the concept of time, Hispanics in the United States, gestures, the family, music, transportation, and famous people and places in Spanish-speaking countries.[4]

In the last ten years, cultural information has become more visible and is conveyed more frequently in language classes, but it still tends to be "item-like" in character, something that can be listed like vocabulary and verb tenses. Culture as valued by the individuals in this chapter seems to have little to do with the culture treated by language textbooks today. One has to wonder, therefore, to what extent we are giving learners access to the most prized internal consequence of language learning. In fact, this disparity highlights the paradox about cultural instruction that challenges the profession: we know that culture can be learned, witness reports from learners who have returned from study abroad programs (Milleret, 1991), but we must question whether such "insights" can be successfully taught in a language class. For several of the individuals we interviewed, the answer is to insist that learners have access not to cultural information, but to cultural experiences. Knop has worked to train future language teachers for thirty years. She comments on the other concern often expressed, the scarcity of cultural experiences that prospective teachers have.

> Many of the people that come into teacher education or teacher training don't have a strong enough background in the language and culture and haven't had the immersion experiences that I think are really crucial and that we now require as entry experience. Many of the students have not been outside their own culture or have not had very many experiences and opportunities to use the language for real purposes.

Knop and others offered study-abroad programs as a partial solution for both students and teachers. Grittner believed so strongly in the benefits of study abroad for teachers that, as state

# Eleanor Sandstrom

Ellis College, a school for fatherless girls on the Main Line, decided to invite me to come help their students just after I graduated from Hunter College, where I had majored in Spanish and minored in German because you couldn't major in two Romance languages. I think I was like the girls' mother. I didn't baby them but I didn't abuse them in any way. They knew what they were learning. The girls were scared, so you had to provide the incentive. Very quickly, they were doing a show at the Academy of Music. A few years ago we had a reunion, and the girls came up and grabbed me from behind, squeezed my breath away, and hugged me from the front. Really, it was fabulous. And one of the girls is now a librarian in one of the schools in Philadelphia. She comes over, and we talk.

I tried to make it easier for the students to catch on. I tried to get them to reach for meaning. You have a lot of objective things that they could see and touch and handle and smell like flowers and colors. You know there's an awful lot just around you if you look for it. I'll tell you what foreign language teachers shouldn't do and that's to conjugate verbs. I just felt that had to go. Education should be loved, it should be creative. And I think it's important to create situations such as meeting a friend, having a problem of some kind, to be able to talk it out privately with another student. I think that's the way they learn, and they don't feel afraid of making an error.

I didn't think education should be punitive. You have to have a teacher who knows how to instill confidence, who doesn't mock them, who doesn't insult them and make fun of them. There are some teachers that just about bite your head off if you make a grammatical error or you use the wrong noun or whatever. You can't just put a child or an adolescent or even a grown person before you and humiliate that person, which a lot of teachers seem to like to do. You are not supposed to take whatever hurts you inside out on the students. You're supposed to be inspiring and helping them. You yourself are different from day to day. One day you have a good day and one day you know it's a bad day. You just can't demand from children what you yourself can't control. Just explain patiently, not humiliating them if they don't know something. You can sense when the students begin to trust you. It comes across and it's very important to not obliterate that kind of sensitivity. Have them try to understand but don't shout at them. I've been subjected to that kind of stuff when I was in school. Where your head was practically blown off because you didn't get the right answer. I don't believe in humiliating anybody who is learning anything. That's very important to me.

I think that what's important is to have a commitment to help students learn. You have to show true interest, to be concerned enough to find out if a stu-

foreign language supervisor, he worked to establish a state-required study-abroad experience for foreign language teachers in Wisconsin.

The disturbing paradox of trying to teach what may not be teachable, plus the multi-faceted nature of the skills, knowledge, and experiences that language teachers must bring to their task explains why teaching a foreign language may be one of the greatest challenges facing a teacher. We have evidence to suggest that foreign language learning may also be the most significant experience a learner can have. We asked the fourteen individuals to recall what influenced their decision to study a foreign language or to recount who influenced them most when they started their careers. Eleven of the 14 described either a methods teacher, a language teacher, or a professor. For example, John Carroll talked about his Greek teacher; Earl Stevick, his Latin teacher; Ken Chastain and Mary Thompson, particular methods teachers; and Stephen Freeman and Albert Valdman, a college professor. Freeman recalls Harvard professor André Morize:

[He had] a tremendous impact on me not only as a teacher, he was the guiding light in my doctoral thesis. . . . He evidently liked me, and I certainly liked him, and that is why when he needed somebody to come up to Middlebury, President Paul D. Moody had asked him to get the French school on the right track, he asked me if I'd come up. . . . He was a wonderful guide.

Wylie reports that his first French language professor, Antoinette Billant, interested him in the French and in France, mostly because her class was a lot of fun and she had a wonderful sense of humor. Wylie also cited his 18th-century literature professor, Lander MacClintock, as "one of the smartest men I have ever met," because he taught him to question his own beliefs. Valdman spoke of Pierre Delattre, recalling that "he was my mentor, my counsel at the beginning of my career. Also, I think he was a very inspirational teacher, full of energy. . . . He's the one that told me that he felt I had a good ear for discriminating sounds." Rivers names her methods teacher, W. H. Frederick, as the most influential person in her career. Describing him as "active" and "exciting," she recalled that "he taught me that you can do anything in the classroom as long as you don't feel embarrassed."

dent is upset about something even though you don't want to probe too much. You kind of try to draw the student out to find out how she could be helped. I think kids accept that, and they don't feel demeaned. If you're involved with education, you have to want to help people. Just explain patiently. Have them try to understand, but don't shout at them. The teacher must not be sarcastic, not humiliate them. Both students and teachers need to share a common interest and try to help each other.

I started programs when people came to me for help. I created the Adult Evening School for Cultural Studies for neighborhood working- class people in the vicinity of Broad and Olney in Philadelphia who wanted to take courses other than just the drill press and typing courses that were normally offered. We taught music, art, and language, including Polish, Russian, Ukrainian, Japanese, and Chinese, as well as Spanish, French, and Italian. It was incredible. The first night almost 1000 people showed up. There were more than twenty-five different languages taught at night and on Saturday mornings. Students at my school practiced the language with meaningful conversation.

In recalling their own experiences as learners and teachers, as well as those of their students, the individuals interviewed in this chapter were firm in their view that we as language teachers are called upon to be more than teachers of a specified body of knowledge or a defined area of skills. At the same time, they also remind us of why, in a profession full of challenges, teachers persevere. In other words, of what we as teachers "get" out of language teaching. When asked to identify her most valuable contribution to the field of foreign language education,

Germaine Brée responds

> Well, I look around and I see some of my students. For example Elaine
> Marks, who was president of the MLA and who did her thesis under my
> direction, is a wonderful example of what a professor can look at and say,
> "it worked."

Perhaps, then, the reward in teaching a foreign language results from
the enthusiasm and success of our students, and the countless occasions
when we can say to ourselves, "it worked."

## What Does it Mean to Be a
## Foreign Language Teacher Today?

> We have one foot in the old world and the other in the new
> world and are trying to cross over to that new world and it's
> exciting. It's also dangerous, but it's exciting.
> —Evelyn Brega

In order to more fully appreciate the data gathered from the wise and
experienced professionals interviewed, consideration needs to be given
to the historical context in which they evolved as educators. As Bogdan
(1970, p. 121) ) has pointed out, in life history research we seek to situate
the individual within "the history of his time." Ivor Goodson (1992), a
powerful advocate of the use of life history in studying teachers' careers,
cites the Popular Memory Group (1982) in stressing the importance of
historical context: "Major shifts are more likely to arise from changes in
political and theoretical preoccupation induced by contemporary social
events than from discovery of new sources or methods." In other words,
what it means to be a foreign language teacher is defined and shaped by
the social, historical and political contexts in which we find ourselves
teaching. A good example of this, described by both Wylie and Freeman,
is the effect of global political events on the development of French
language and civilization courses in the United States. Listen to Wylie:

> I don't think anybody had any idea of a course in French civilization before
> the First World War. After the war, the political and military officials in
> France realized that they had a problem on their hands. Here were a mil-
> lion young Americans set loose in France, and you didn't have a whole
> fleet of airplanes to take them back, only a certain number of boats. In
> order to keep the young men interested and out of mischief, they decided
> to offer a course to help them learn to observe this phenomenon of French
> civilization. The course was free to any American soldiers who wanted to
> take it. A professor at the Sorbonne named Guignebert developed the
> course, and then other universities in France developed similar courses.

Then, about 1919, Columbia and Harvard started courses in French civilization. A lot of the soldiers got interested in France and in French. In studying the history of the French department at Harvard, I found an astounding fact that around 1922 the French major, the Romance language major, was the third largest in the university. André Morize gave his course at Harvard on French civilization and then started the Middlebury summer course on French civilization, which he asked Stephen Freeman to head. When I went back to France as cultural attaché in 1962, there were about sixty foreign study groups.

Freeman connects the development of foreign study groups to the needs of American soldiers in France at the end of World War II:

The American Army had sent over hundreds of thousands of students to Europe, and they couldn't repatriate them all of a sudden. They didn't have the ships and they didn't have the materiel to get them all back here right away. So in order to keep them busy in France, the government asked me to be the head of a liberal arts program there. I'd teach vocabulary in the French class at 8:00 in the morning, and the next morning at 8:00 the students would come back and teach me the language that the girls on the beach had taught them that afternoon. I got the idea that young people at the college age could adapt very well and get a great deal of profit out of an experience of studying in France. By the summer of '49, we had started a Middlebury program with the University of Paris. In 1952, we tried to establish a similar program with the University of Madrid, but Franco refused to let us have any control of university courses, so we organized a university with our own professors. After establishing programs in Germany and Italy, we tried to start one in Moscow, but no way. We had to wait until after the whole regiment changed before we started one there. I've been connected with Middlebury for fifty years, from 1925 to 1975, a period of many political changes throughout the world.

Historical context provided the spark for Stevick's personal interest in foreign languages as well. He recalls that during the Depression there were coupons that could be redeemed for discounts. "It was the soap," he recalls. "The directions were printed in numerous languages. I'd try to dope that out. I'd try to figure out what words meant what in which language."

In Chapter 5 ("The View from the Center") of this volume, Senator Paul Simon points out that the world has changed and cautions that we must adapt. The people we interviewed for this chapter recognized the truth of this assertion and spoke with great compassion of today's teachers, who face challenges hardly contemplated in their time. Grittner describes today as a different era. He talks about the consequences of societal changes that have radically altered the language teaching context.

I never worried about any kid carrying a gun to school when I was teaching. *Now,* these kinds of cultural attitudes spill over into the public school. It didn't when I went out teaching before. I read . . . the popular press and see in some of the schools I've visited that there is a deterioration of the willingness on the part of the students to study. That world concerns me. . . . I don't know how I would deal with some of those problems now. When I was teaching in the '50s and '60s, I thought the attitudes of students were [that] it felt like a very safe, supportive environment, and I think most of the kids felt that way.

Knop points out that the clientele in the foreign language class is very different today than it was in the past, and that as a consequence, the teacher's role is changing as well.

Most of the classes that I visit now are open to all students. I mean students of all backgrounds, motivations, and abilities, [classes] that have a fair number of learning disabled or emotionally disabled students . . . and it's not easy. . . . And teachers are having to spend a fair amount of time being psychologists and guidance counselors, and being a teacher is almost something that comes after you try to settle some of these other issues.

Brée's observations were particularly poignant:

Sometimes I'm very sorry for the teachers, because everybody seems to round up on the teachers. The students come in, they are undisciplined, and the teachers can't do everything, can't do all the teaching they need to do. You can't both discipline and teach them to get involved in your class. I sympathize a lot with the teachers. I think there are more good teachers in America than anybody realizes.

If in some respects—for example, with respect to culture—pedagogical materials have seemed to evolve more slowly than is desirable, in another area individuals noted that change has taken place with stunning, and sometimes confusing, rapidity. Rivers marvels at the great changes brought about by advances in instructional technol-

## Evelyn Brega

We are in a unique position to branch out more, to anticipate the future toward a world curricula, to help students understand better the impact of cultures and world peace; we should have a better background in the religions in the world, the various ways different cultures look at things. We desperately need a world curriculum to prepare our students for the next century. Foreign languages will play a big role in that. Underdevelopment is a state of mind; culture determines the development of nations. Countries that hold back the women are generally the underdeveloped countries, wasting 51% of the population.

I don't think that people realize that when anything is cut in the field of foreign languages, it's because we haven't been able to sell it, and I think we need people who can sell it just as you sell a product. You have to make it indispensable to education; it has to be so important that they wouldn't think of dropping it. We could learn a lot from the business community.

ogy, while at the same time reiterating her belief that, in education, technology is always subordinate to the personal interaction between teacher and learner.

The interesting thing is things are so different. We had, no, we didn't even have gramophone records. We had no video. I mean when the magnetic tape came in the 1940s, we thought this was a miracle. We read about it in the paper how this marvelous thing was being invented that you could put sound on tape. First time I heard a record with authentic French speech was when I was in the second to last year of high school, and we had this French teacher who tried to get us to listen to this record and to pronounce French with the correct intonation, and we just got the giggles. . . . People these days don't know how lucky they are. They've got tape supports. They've got video supports. They've got film. They've got satellite broadcasts. So I think . . . if I went back into the classroom I would be intimidated by knowing how to use all these things because I can manage very well with me and the kids but with all these other things intervening [I'm not so sure]. I thing it's extremely important for people to realize, however, that the real teaching goes on in the personal relationship and that this can be drowned with too much external things. All of this can be a great help and can be used again in relationship to the course but it can't be the whole course. You have to have the opportunity for people to try to communicate in person because if they try to communicate with a tape or a program or a computer, that computer isn't going to temp the wind to the shore. In other words, we see the person hesitating, we give them longer. We repeat, we rephrase

We're inclined to consider that a little beneath us, but we're wrong. Put on international evenings, dinners, or a gala of some sort. May I suggest that in doing so that all the Gros Légumes are there? You get them to come by making them part of the program, to introduce a guest speaker or to present an award. If you just use a little imagination, you can get them to come to your meeting. All you have to do is say to them to please come early enough so that they can partake of the wonderful refreshments and the champagne and the belly dancers. You may get a little antagonism from the other departments but never mind, the important thing is to get them there.

Occasionally you do get a teacher very frankly who is what I, excuse me, but my only way of describing this teacher is a constipated basset hound. And if you have too many in a department you're really in trouble. Basset hounds are darling, but if you have to look at them all day long every period, it can be very stressful. Keep that sparkle, and don't ever become a constipated basset hound. I would say that I think one of the best ways in the world to help teachers improve themselves is for them to visit one another. Visit, visit, visit. And visit at all levels, including the elementary. You'll find that there you will observe the best methodology in the world because they have to use it in order to reach the little ones. Take that methodology and adapt it to any level all the way through college.

A teacher that can teach several languages is much better, because you have a wider scope, more ideas, and you understand the formation of language better. Go into several languages and that makes for an interesting person, a more exciting person.

I'm a great believer in using the classroom. When reading Proust, bring in some madeleines when discussing the scene where he's recalling his childhood. Where they mention garlic in Daudet, put some garlic in the room. If nothing else, it will wake them up. Throw in a bit of a shark every day or a surprise. Find something to celebrate, such as Louis XIV's birthday. There's nothing wrong with serving a little food, a little pastry. There's nothing wrong with having a little music. All this fitting into the lesson. That's the joy about teaching because it allows you to really use imagination which if you don't have as a teacher you should get it. Have the students come into the room to music. Have them leave reciting a poem together. Poetry is wonderful.

because we see that scared look in the eye, and so we're able to bring things out of people in a way that machines can't.

In the same breath, Rivers talks about the necessity of change in education and of keeping abreast of changes.

[I] look back to my early days and things are continually developing and changing. And we have to be there and be ready to keep on continually keeping in step and looking at our own expertise and what we can provide in relationship to whatever the direction of the time is. Just the same as we had to do when the big push came in multimedia and all that. . . . We had to have those people, Capretz and VanPatten, who were willing to get in there and devote many, many hours of very solid, hardly rewarded, work in order to push us ahead in this new area and seize the opportunity. What the next one around the corner will be, we don't know, but we have to be ready and willing to continually adapt and readapt. That's what education is.

Some individuals noted that changes in the curriculum have created both new challenges and new opportunities for language teaching. Knop describes how the growing interest in content-based teaching encourages foreign language teachers to become knowledgeable in content areas other than their own.

I feel we need to be looking more and more at how we can tie foreign language study into more authentic materials, more cross-disciplinary kinds of materials, materials that are there to be learned from, not just to be studied as a separate language.

Often individuals emphasized the value of their role as language teachers in contributing to the development of a future society, tolerant of many cultures and sensitive to the needs of different human communities, both within and beyond our borders. Brega said it in the following way.

We desperately need to prepare our students for the next century. I think that foreign languages will play a big role in that. And, we need to do more to study various cultural aspects and religions of the world and so on. What I'm thinking of is a world approach toward certain subjects.

# Implications

The world of the foreign language learner and the foreign language classroom teacher is different today. These interviews make abundantly clear that if teachers are ever to respond adequately to the challenges that face them, the nature and quality of teacher preparation must be recognized and addressed. Study abroad and immersion programs would go a long way, as suggested by several individuals in this chapter, in offering teachers and learners the linguistic skills and sensitivities toward other cultures that are absolutely necessary in language learning. Mandated immersion experiences, such as the program implemented in Wisconsin, could guarantee that all prospective foreign language teachers obtain this experience. We may need, however, to rethink ways to make study abroad programs more accessible to teachers and students alike because, while grants, fellowships, and scholarships exist, few are available in relation to the number of teachers and students who would benefit from them.

We also need to disseminate information about innovative programs that offer teachers retooling and professional growth. Summer institutes, for example, can offer teachers linguistic growth, cultural insights, and a wide spectrum of methodologi-

## Wilga Rivers

Why did I study French? My father failed to get into the English navy when he was in England for six months, because he didn't know his French alphabet. My father was sixty-five when I was born and was a dear old daddy with gray hair and a gray beard when I was growing. I thought he was wonderful. I often wonder if I decided deep in my psyche, if I decided to justify, to validate my father's experience by knowing my French alphabet or whatever. Either that or *The Scarlet Pimpernel,* which we read with great enthusiasm as children. I was just determined that French was the thing I loved and that I was going to do. At the high school triangle, we were all grouped by language, and there were too many in the French group, so they asked some of the French group to move over to Latin or German. I hid behind the other kids because I didn't want to be taken out of the French group.

Later in high school, we had an oral interview as part of our exam. I was sixteen and very anxious to do well. My father had died. I needed a scholarship to go to the university. There was no way I could go otherwise. And what did they ask me? They asked me whether I would prefer to die by the rope, a gun, or poison! And I thought in my innocence that the university professors testing me wanted a serious answer. Instead of thinking in French, here I was trying to work out an absolutely incredible answer, when I didn't want to die at all. At my stage of life, it was so absurd. When I taught high school classes later to go to these exams, I trained my students to respond to a question like that by smiling sweetly and saying, "Well, I really don't want to die at all. Because next year, I'm going to Europe." And then the professor would immediately say, "Oh, you are going to Europe, where are you going?" "To France." "And what are you going to see in France?" "Oh, well, I'm dying to see the Tour Eiffel," and then they come out with their prepared spiel. See, so you have to train them how to handle these things. If you are trying to put your ideas together in another language, you've got cognitive overload, you've got the thought content, the development of the thought, the expression of the thought, the syntax, the vocabulary, the phonology, the intonation, you've got the whole thing, and if people keep stopping and correcting you, you can't continue, it's impossible.

I think the most liberating experience I had was in my first teaching experience, perhaps a month into my teaching. I was teaching 8th-grade English,

cal approaches often hard to obtain during the school year, particularly for teachers who primarily teach beginning and intermediate levels of the target language.

We must as a profession recognize that advances in technology are changing the texture of foreign language learning. We need to rethink teacher training to include the increasing variety of software that can help language learners, such as the writing programs for the development of writing, i.e., *Daedalus*, *Système-D*, and *Atajo*.[5] Universities and school districts should acquire personnel with expertise in computer-assisted learning to help lead the profession into the next century of language learning.

In addition, teacher training, whether through methods courses, summer institutes, practicums, or in-service workshops, needs to acknowledge the dynamics of the language learning experience and consider affective and cognitive aspects of language learning. As often expressed by the venerable voices we heard here, learning a foreign language is not merely developing language skills. Language learning is intricately tied to an individual's concept of self and identity, both of which are shaped by that individual's culture.

Interestingly, a central message that emerges from these interviews is the view that language learning is not exclusively one thing or another. It cannot be dissected and compartmentalized or easily understood or explained. It is dynamic, as dynamic as individuals are themselves. It is civilization, linguistics, culture, sociology, psychology, and so forth. Perhaps in the 21st century new ways of looking at language learning will advance, some rooted in the thoughts of individuals whose wise and thoughtful perspectives have been tempered by years of experience.

## Conclusions

We began this chapter with a quote from Lyndon Baines Johnson that condemns our society's neglect of a whole group of people with a wealth of experience, hindsight, and wisdom to offer. Rather than ignore one of the richest resources that we have—our most experienced, highly achieved, and widely acclaimed foreign language teachers and specialists—we asked their opinions, asked them to tell us their stories, and we listened. We heard them express their perspectives on a range of topics. We heard them talk about the importance of teaching culture and recognizing learner needs. We heard them voice their thoughts on the changes that have brought about both concern and hope. And, we heard them give witness to the significance of their experiences and their mentors.

The teachers and scholars we interviewed for this chapter taught hundreds of serious language students who will in turn contribute to the personal and professional development of other students of foreign languages. And the cycle gets repeated. And, if the cycle is repeated enough times, perhaps we will meet the challenge of our decade and the new century to come and help to create a society of multicultural, bilingual, and insightful citizens who see the world as a place for all.

> and something came up in the reading that I didn't know. One of the girls asked the meaning of the word, "kale." It was a kind of cabbage we didn't have in Australia, my family certainly didn't eat it, and I never heard of it. I can remember to this day, my asking myself, "What am I gonna do? Here I've got these kids that I'm trying to impress, and I don't know." I had to decide then and there whether to bluff or to say straight out, "I'm sorry, I don't know." I decided to say, "I'm sorry, I don't know. We'll look it up and find out by tomorrow." I consider that to be one of the most liberating experiences of my whole teaching career, because that liberated me from the need to know everything and be the great authority, and to realize that learning is a cooperative experience and that we're learning together.

Part of the allure of gathering stories in an effort to learn from the experiences of others is the impact that such an experience has on the researcher. As Gorelick (1991) observes, "The researcher is transformed in the process of research—influenced and taught by her respondent-participants as she influences them. Theory and practice emerge from their interaction" (p. 469). As researchers, we feel privileged to report our transformation. Personally, we are inspired by the dedication demonstrated in the life work of our participants. Professionally, we find ourselves incorporating their wisdom and citing their ideas both within the classroom and among colleagues when discussing current issues in our profession. We would like to publicly express our profound gratitude to our venerable respondents. Laurence Wylie reminded us once that this group of people might better be called "vulnerables" instead of "venerables," given the challenges they face in our culture due to their age. This may be true, but, as Evelyn Brega's words also remind us, their spirit and their example stand out as powerful models for us all.

> Retirement is a thing of the past, and I would encourage everyone in the Northeast Conference to read Betty Freidan's book on the fountain of age. And Kenneth Goldbright's article on what he calls the "still syndrome." When people come up to him and they say to him, "you're still writing and you're still speaking, you're still doing that." 'Course he's still doing it.

# Notes

[1]Lincoln and Guba (1985) write of the need for the emic perspectives of research participants; that is, the perspective looking from the inside out. One way to capture this inside perspective is to conduct interviews with research participants seeking to connect their lives to their careers. Faraday and Plummer (1979, pp. 773–795) see life history as an excellent tool for generating concepts and ideas "both at the local and situational level and on a historical structural level and within the same field and in relationship to other fields." Thus, life history methodology is particularly appropriate for investigating foreign language education today through the voices of its participants, even when actual life histories are not being conducted.

[2]Stories provide a sense of meaning and belonging to our lives. They "attach us to others and to our own histories by providing a tapestry rich with threads of time, place, character, and even advice on what we might do with our lives" (Witherell and Noddings, 1991, p. 1). According to Connelly and Clandinin (1990), stories are collaborative. The stories we write are "mutually constructed stories created out of the lives of both the researcher and the participant" (p. 12).

[3]These words come from an unpublished manuscript, "How I Became a Professor at Harvard," which Laurence Wylie shared with Kimball during interviews for her dissertation on him.

[4]An examination of most of the ACTFL 1994 presentations or workshops about culture echo variations of these same topics.

[5]*Atajo* (Boston: Heinle and Heinle, 1994) is written by Frank Dominguez, James S. Noblitt, and Willem J. A. Pet; *Système-D* (Boston: Heinle & Heinle, 1993) is written by James S. Noblitt, Willem J. A. Pet, and Donald Solá (see Virginia Scott, 1990); *Daedalus* (Austin, TX: Daedalus Group) is an Integrated Writing Environment (see Beauvois, 1992).

# References

Beauvois, M. H. (1992). Computer-assisted classroom discussion in the foreign language classroom: Conversation in slow motion. *Foreign Language Annals, 25,* 455–463.

Bogdan, R., & Taylor, S. (1970). *Introduction to qualitative research methods.* NY: Wiley.

Coe, D. (1991). Levels of knowing in ethnographic inquiry. *International Journal of Qualitative Studies in Education, 4*(4), 313–331.

Connolly, F., & Clandinen, D. (1990). Stories of experience and narrative inquiry. *Educational Researcher, 19*(5), 2–24.

Faraday, A., & Plummer, K. (1979). Doing life histories. *Sociological Review, 27*(4), 773–793.

Geertz, C. (1973). Thick description: Toward an interpretive theory of culture. In C. Geertz (Ed.), *The interpretation of cultures* (pp. 3–30). New York: Basic Books.

Goodson, I. (1992). *Studying teachers' lives: Problems and possibilities.* New York: Teachers College Press, Columbia University.

Gorelick, S. (1991). Contradictions of feminist methodology. *Gender & Society, 5*(4), 459–477.

Kimball, M. (in progress). Breaking bounds: A critical life history of Professor Laurence Wylie, Professor of French Civilization (Diss., The Pennsylvania State University).

Lincoln, Y., & Guba, E. (1985). *Naturalistic inquiry.* Beverly Hills, CA: Sage.

Measor, L., and Sikes, P. (1992) . Visiting lives: Ethics and methodology in life history. In I. Goodson (Ed.), *Studying teachers' lives: Problems and possibilities* (pp. 209–233). New York: Teachers College Press, Columbia University.

Milleret, M. (1991). The validity of the Portuguese speaking test for use in a Summer Study Abroad Program. *Hispania, 74,* 778–787.

Popular Memory Group (1982). Popular memory: Theory, politics, method. In R. Johnson, G. McLennan, B. Schwarz, & D. Sutton (Eds.), Making histories (pp. 205–252). London: Centre for Contemporary Cultural Studies.

Richardson, L. (1992). Trash on the corner: Ethnics and technography. *Journal of Contemporary Ethnography, 21*(1), 103–119.

Scott, V. (1990). Task-oriented creative writing with Système-D. *CALICO* (March), 58–67.

Witherell, C., & Noddings, N. (1991). *Stories lives tell: Narrative and dialogue in education.* New York: Teachers College Press, Columbia University.

Wylie, L. (1994). *How I Became a Professor at Harvard.* Unpublished manuscript.

Young, D. J. (in progress). Cultural readings: Student voices, student frustrations. In D. J. Young (Ed.), *Affect in L2 learning: A practical guide to dealing with learner anxieties.* San Francisco: McGraw-Hill.

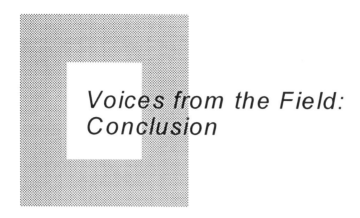

# Voices from the Field:
# Conclusion

Trisha Dvorak

*University of Michigan*

## Introduction

T he Voices from the Field project was undertaken to gather information to help foreign language professionals understand more fully the impact and significance that foreign languages have in the lives of those who study them, as well as the perceptions that people hold regarding the place and value of foreign language study in American education today. Aware of the insularity that often characterizes our discussions of such professional topics—"we tend to talk to each other rather than to 'others'" (Kline, p. xii)—this project purposely moved further afield. Researchers for this project interviewed members of six different constituencies:

- foreign language learners in traditional classroom environments
- foreign language learners in a variety of non-traditional environments
- native speakers who had studied their language in a formal, classroom environment
- teachers in disciplines other than foreign language
- individuals outside academia, representing fields such as government, private industry, the arts and journalism
- senior members of the foreign language profession, fourteen individuals who together represent more than 500 years of experience and service

The project did not expect or intend to uncover definitive answers to any of the questions investigated; rather it was hoped that it might provide a new perspective on these questions, this time from the frame of reference of those we interviewed: current and former foreign language learners. Many of these individuals now find themselves "out in the real world," and we were particularly curious to hear their perceptions of the value and impact of those learner experiences. Across the six different participant groups the researchers listened to many individual stories and viewpoints, each richly memorable and provocative. Despite the uniquely personal nature of these accounts, certain messages emerged over and over again both within and across the different groups. Some of the messages are familiar ones, while others were more surprising; some will make foreign language professionals smile with satisfaction, and others will leave them puzzling over the ironies and seeming contradictions.

All of the chapter authors advised readers that no sample was intended to be statistically representative, and that one cannot base broad generalizations on the data gathered. I repeat here those cautions, but at the same time encourage readers to explore the data themselves, listening attentively to what these voices from the field have to tell us. Unless otherwise noted, the references cited here refer to chapters in this volume.

# Listening to the Voices: A Summary of the Major Findings of the 1995 Reports

### 1.  People study a foreign language because they have to.

The answer to the first "why" question—"why did you decide to study a foreign language?"—came back across all six constituencies with few variations: the most common reason that people gave for their initial foray into foreign language study was because they were required to do so; without the trigger of a requirement, virtually all individuals said they would not have chosen to study a foreign language. The exact nature of the requirement varied slightly; more often than not, it was an academic requirement (either entrance or exit). The major exception to this pattern was voiced by the native speakers, who explained that their requirement had been framed not by schools but rather by parents, who were anxious for their children to remain connected to their heritage culture and community (Garretón).

Robinson's 1988 study has alerted the profession to the fact that learners'choices as to which language to study should not automatically suggest interest in or attraction to a particular language or even to the culture of the individuals who speak it. Like the work done by Stern (1983) and Berns (1990), the investigations in this volume highlight the connections between language study and the role of language in our culture. Three chapters (Barnes, Terrio & Knowles, Brooks) speak directly to the issue of why learners made the choices they did. They found that the first decision about which language to study was generally influenced by parents and other individuals whom the learners admired, as opposed to teachers or academic counselors, and that the decision typically reflected a variety of sociocultural attitudes about language that have been current in this country for many decades (see, for example, Chastain [1980] and McCabe [1994] for discussions of this issue). French, German and, to a lesser extent, Latin, were considered more difficult, "prestige" languages; as such, these languages tended to be viewed as important "cultural goods" (Terrio & Knowles, p. 189) which attracted those learners curious about language for intellectual and/or artistic reasons (Brooks), or for whom such a choice communicated membership in a particular social and educational group (Terrio & Knowles). Spanish was invariably viewed as the most useful (and the easiest), and was specified as the language of choice by those who were particularly motivated by pragmatic interests: ability to use the language on the job, for example, or to communicate with members of a local ethnic community. Sometimes Spanish was rejected, despite its potential usefulness, because it was associated with low-status: it was the language, for example, that "the dumber kids studied" (Terrio & Knowles, p. 164). When learners were deciding on a third or a fourth language, several of these same cultural attitudes were sometimes involved (Terrio & Knowles), but often this time the choice revealed personal connections between the learner and a particular language and/or cultural group (Barnes).

2. **Once having taken the plunge, learners invariably discovered that learning a language was a lot harder than they had thought it would be, that it took longer and that the goal of developing enough fluency to actually be able to do something in the language seemed hopelessly unachievable.**

Interestingly, young learners phrased their surprise by comparing foreign language to other school subjects: Spanish was *harder than spelling*, for example; whereas adult learners were comparing the experience to the expectation: Spanish was *harder than they thought it would be*. Why had they thought learning a foreign language would be easy? Where had such an assumption come from? Hall and Davis suggest that this belief is widely shared in the U.S.:

> The American cultural myth that learning other languages is easy and quick . . . is ubiquitous, reinforced by movies in which we see the protagonist becoming instantly bilingual after a short stay in the other culture, and by companies selling video and audio tapes purporting to make one fluent almost overnight. (p. 28)

The origin of such myths is still something of an issue. The fact that relatively few Americans have experience as language learners (not including the time spent acquiring a first language) coupled with the fact that most Americans seem to have very little awareness of the use of English—an observation made almost thirty years ago by Joshua Fishman (1966) that still seems current today—possibly contributes to their sense that language actually involves very little effort. One wonders, as well, what role the standard two-year sequence may play in suggesting that mastery is achievable in a short time frame.[1] Whatever its source, this myth contributes not only to the "sticker shock" that hits language learners as they become aware of the costs in time and energy that learning a language entails. The myth contributes as well to the unreasonably high expectations that others have for the hapless learner whose friends and relatives become concerned that she (or her teacher) may have "some deficiency or something" (Hall & Davis, p. 15) because she is not totally fluent after a year or two of study.

3. **Aspects of the language learning experience were definitely viewed as unpleasant.**

In this study, learner criticisms converged on two aspects in particular. The first relates to the kinds of form-based activities that in the learners' view seemed to dominate the early stages of language study. Agreement on this point was not universal; in fact, opinions on what constituted "good" and "bad" teaching practices were diverse and even contradictory. Although some learners (Barnes, Garretón, Terrio & Knowles, Young & Kimball) spoke of later recognizing the value of drill and practice, the majority found intense focus on form, coupled with an overly heavy reliance on the text—"the book stuff" (—Connie, Brooks, p. 127)—to be boring (Hall & Davis, Brooks), irrelevant (Terrio & Knowles, Garretón), unengaging (Barnes, Young & Kimball), or worse: "hideous" (—I: 18, Hall & Davis, p. 11), "canned" (—Isabel, Brooks, p. 125), "absurd, ridiculous" (—Kathryn, Barnes, p. 125). These learners' descriptions of their classroom experiences bear a disappointing resemblance to the kind of teaching practices that Mary Thompson had criticized forty years earlier: "teachers had a tendency to view the textbook as curriculum, to just open the book, turn the pages, and follow it" (Young & Kimball, p. 203).

Many students were impatient with a system that required them to "build up to" real language use by mastering grammar and vocabulary first; these comments are typical:

> I wanted to [learn Greek] when I was younger. I wanted to know how to speak it, but I didn't want to go through all the stuff to learn the grammar and the vocabulary. I just wanted to be able to speak the language. (—Stacy, Garretón, p. 88)

> I'd want to read texts in French—books. I didn't want to read verb forms and stuff. I just wanted to get right into it. (—Rachel, Barnes, p. 49)

The description offered to Hall and Davis by a university level Spanish student encapsulates much of the frustration and disdain voiced by these learners for an approach that seemed to them to value "picking language apart" over "using it" (—Teresa, Barnes, p. 49):

> They spend 45 minutes discussing, you know, two phrases and you have people talk about it for two minutes and then you go the next day and no one remembers any of it. It's just a nightmare . . . she would speak in Spanish for about ten minutes out of the whole class . . . I mean, pretty much if you're, if you have a pulse, you're not going to be challenged in those [classes]. (—I: 18, Hall & Davis, p. 11)

What's more, learners found that the results fell considerably short of the goal. They were disappointed and discouraged to find that either they could actually do very little with what they had worked so hard to learn, or that what they had learned seemed unrelated to real life language (Hall & Davis, Terrio & Knowles, Brooks).

The second significant complaint of the participants in this study was concerned less with the structure or content of their lessons than with the classroom atmosphere. As Wilga Rivers points out, "learning a language is very different from the other subjects because you are putting people in a very vulnerable situation, you are asking them to reveal themselves in a way which is very threatening. . . ." (Young & Kimball, p. 199). Learners recalled this feeling in words that left little room for doubt about its impact on them: "awful, uncomfortable" (—Sam Farr, Terrio & Knowles, pp. 153–154), "intimidating" (—Miné, Garretón, p. 103), "frightening, terrifying" (—Katherine, Brooks, p. 124). The project did not gather sufficient data for a comparative perspective on this point, but one has to wonder and indeed worry if learners would have used similarly "loaded" terms to describe unsatisfactory experiences in other subject areas. A brief and totally unscientific survey of a number of colleagues found terms like "boring," "dry, unsatisfying," "frustrating," "hard," and "abstract" offered in response to a request that they describe unenjoyable courses (but not foreign language) in high school or college. The contrast in emotional impact between these terms and those used to describe negative foreign language experiences is startling. If a more careful survey were to corroborate this pattern, we would have an indication that the close connection between language and self, the connection that makes language study such a uniquely personal experience for learners, may be a double-edged sword.

The good news is that, looked at in their entirety, the opinions voiced by these learners seemed an overwhelming validation of current trends in the profession, which have moved toward enabling learners to develop "real world" abilities, and at the same time have recognized the profound impact which affective factors have on the learner. The note of caution is that the difficulties which learners described were present across all age groups—that is, the people who have been in the classroom most recently have the same complaints as those who were students twenty years ago—suggesting "that older [instructional] paradigms may persist longer and in more settings than we think" (Terrio & Knowles, p. 155).

4. **Despite these and other difficulties, both current and former language learners were overwhelmingly positive about the value of foreign language study.** [2]

Their reasons clustered around three primary points. First and foremost, was their conviction that through language study they might come to an enhanced awareness of other cultures. Learning another language "opened a window" on new ways of viewing the world (Terrio & Knowles), adding a new "dimension to how you perceive experiences" (—Constance Knop, Young & Kimball, p. 206), and helping individuals to appreciate that "the American way of thinking is by no means the only way" (—I: 13, Hall & Davis, p. 21). While for some the possibility of language as a means "for bridge-building among ethnic communities in the U.S." (—Matthew Chambers, Terrio & Knowles, p. 179) seemed more a dream than a reality, others mentioned that as a result of language study, they felt they had become more open-minded and had developed a greater tolerance for others of different cultural backgrounds (Brooks, Young & Kimball). For the native speakers, the experience of learning their own language was intimately connected with a deeply personal journey toward identity and self-awareness: what does it mean to be Asian and what does it mean to be Asian American (Garretón)?

Second, many of the interviewees clearly had a lot of fun learning to use another language. Again and again, one is struck by their excitement and exuberance in exploring this new ability:

> [it was like] wow! This is so much fun. It was like I was putting pieces of a puzzle together . . . it's like an everyday challenge. Whatever we're discussing in class, if I can follow along, and when the professor calls on me to say something back, I'm like a little kid, you know, anxious to answer. (—I: 23, Hall & Davis, p. 16)

> I like learning languages. It's exciting when you do find links that pierce through several languages, it's just kind of a thrill in a way. I suppose I could use them for a purpose, but mostly it is for personal enrichment. (—Tom, Garretón, p. 91)

Earl Stevick and others among the venerable voices (Young & Kimball, pp. 199–205) assert that the central distinction between learning a language and learning anything else is the powerful connection between language and self. We saw the "dark side" of this connection in the discussion of the findings leading to point 3 above. But there is a bright side as well: learning a language often results in enhanced self-confidence and self-esteem. Learners repeatedly mentioned the intense pride they felt in being able to use another language effectively, a result as much of the sense of having accomplished a difficult task, as of being accepted by members of the target language community.

> For most of the interviewees, a tangential benefit of language study proved to be the development of self-confidence and self-esteem produced in part by their exposure to, and growing potential to develop relationships with, a variety of different people. Especially significant to these learners were the feelings of success and competence they experienced in their interactions with native speakers. One student reported how good it made him feel to speak with others in German and to be praised for his ability to communicate. Another student in high school had had the opportunity to travel to France with her family, an opportunity which turned out to be a wonderful experience. She talked about being able to connect with the French people with whom she spoke, and how good communicating with them made her feel. (Hall & Davis, p. 18)

Barnes movingly describes this experience as the sudden awareness that one has somehow ceased to be a language learner "other" and become "just another" member of the group, and that people are actually responding to what one is saying rather than to how (Barnes, pp. 62–64). In this respect, the non-native speakers found they were at a decided disadvantage. When the "target language community" was not Japanese American but Japanese; not Mexican American but Mexican, the native speakers found that the language skills which had cost them so dearly to develop—skills which from a non-native speaker would have been received with gracious and generous praise—tended never to be quite good enough. Compare these examples from Barnes and Garretón:

> The moment of triumph in my life would have been . . . while we were sitting there waiting [while on a tour], and [a woman] starting asking questions, and she said, "Oh, you speak so well, so well." And then . . . . [all the Chinese people waiting there] were all saying, "Oh, [you speak] so well." (—Gayle, Barnes, p. 62)

> . . . there were people who just got real angry if I told them I wasn't from Japan, I was from Chicago and that is why I don't understand, could you please speak slower. I would have people just "huh" and walk away and I swear it was because they didn't believe me. If my Caucasian friends said exactly the same thing, they would bend over backwards and do anything to accommodate them. (—Christine, Garretón, p. 99)

Third, regardless of their ultimate level of achievement in the language, the interviewees thought that language study made sense for pragmatic reasons: it might result in language skills that could prove useful socially, professionally or economically. For the majority of the non-native speakers, this was clearly a benefit in theory only, either because they felt that for "ordinary" Americans foreign language skills were largely irrelevant in terms of a job (Terrio & Knowles, p. 182), or because developing functional language skills proved elusive. For the relative few who stuck with it long enough to develop useable language skills, the second language represented a pathway to new knowledge, to job or career benefits (Barnes, Garretón, Terrio & Knowles, Young & Kimball), and to relationships with others that led to their being able to participate in and be accepted as part of a community (Barnes, Garretón, Young & Kimball). In addition, Americans typically found that skill in a second language also resulted in considerable recognition and prestige in the eyes of those more familiar with the tongue-tied image (Hall & Davis, Barnes, Terrio & Knowles, Young & Kimball).

**5. There was a curious and prevalent "disconnect" between the memories that individuals had of their experiences, and the value they currently attributed to language study.**

That is, individuals who recalled their own experiences in the language classroom as having been difficult, painful or worse ("worthless" is a term that one of Brooks's interviewees used, p. 135) were nonetheless firm and even enthusiastic supporters of language study. How is this possible and what are we to make of it? Some of the questions raised by this "disconnect" are not easily answerable with the current data, but at least three sources seem possible.

First, some individuals explained this change of heart as simply a natural result of "mature reflection," achieved after the passage of time allows the value of something rejected earlier to be perceived and appreciated. One of Brooks's interviewees, for example, faced with just such a contradictory pattern in her own remarks said simply that "things change with time. They smooth out" (p. 136). Barnes gives another example from Irina, for whom class exercises seemed silly. "I remember," she told Barnes, "we saw this movie from the 50s, we went through this old poetry, we did these silly exercises in class that were just like: 'Ask Rhona if she knows how to milk a cow.' It was nothing that we could relate to. . . ." But later Irina admitted that "now I'd probably be interested in the kinds of things we did then, but I think [they weren't] the kinds of things that were attractive to our interests at the time" (p. 44).

Second, the opinions that many individuals held about the value of language study tended not to derive from their classroom experiences alone, but rather arose out of a combination of experiences, both academic and personal, across an individual's life (Brooks, Terrio & Knowles). And third, individuals in western societies share a number of assumptions about what constitutes an "educated person." Foreign language is one of the areas such an individual is expected to study; as scientist Glenn Crosby (cited in Kline, p. xiii) recognized, "foreign language acquisition is necessary to be an educated, sentient person with empathy for foreign peoples and cultures." Regardless of one's own personal experiences, the "cultural capital" our society associates with foreign languages may simply make it unacceptable, or tacky at the very least, to claim that language study is perhaps not such a good thing.

Whatever the source of the gap between experience and belief, since the reasons many people have for supporting language study seem largely unrelated to the classroom experience, teachers (and textbook writers and program designers and so on) should be careful not to presume too much credit for point 4 above. Nevertheless, it is heartening to know that, despite some of our shortcomings as educators, most individuals still hold to the belief that learning another language is good for you.

6. **The interviews for this study emphasize again and again the critical importance of the teacher.**

In fact, memories of teachers are what learners tended to recall first about their experience. In chapter after chapter, teachers were constantly credited with "playing a pivotal role in motivating the interviewees to begin, to continue and to perfect their language skills. They often provided a watershed experience for the interviewees" (Terrio & Knowles, p. 152). The teacher was "one of the primary influences that [the interviewees] cited in explaining whether they liked their language classes, and upon which they based their decisions to continue studying a particular language or to continue language study beyond the required number of years" (Hall & Davis, p. 9). Among the venerable voices as well, the individual whom they identified as having the most influence on them was invariably a teacher, sometimes of language or linguistics, sometimes of literature, sometimes of pedagogy, but a teacher nonetheless.

As with language teaching methods, opinions about what qualities made a teacher "great" varied. Terrio (Terrio & Knowles, p. 153) reports, for example, that among the individuals she interviewed, "native speaker" was considered a crucial characteristic of the good teacher, but when pressed none could actually say for sure if the individuals they had previously identified as great teachers had been native speakers. Some teachers seem to have been special because they were creative and knew how to make the classes interesting and engaging, others were special because they were rigorous, demanding and passionate about their subject matter, motivating the learners to high standards, others because they had a sense of humor and were fun; some were mentors and role models as well as teachers, and for not a few learners, the foreign language teacher was memorable because he or she had flair and style and stood out as being different from other adults the learners knew.

The characteristics of poor teachers demonstrated less variety: they were described as mean or cruel (Brooks, Terrio & Knowles), some seemed unable to control their own classrooms (Garretón, Hall & Davis), whereas others were authoritarian and even tyrannical (Brooks, Terrio & Knowles, Young & Kimball); they either did not speak the foreign language much in their classes or spoke it badly (Barnes).

These data clearly establish the teacher as the critical figure for language learners; they confirm the complex and many-sided profile of the good language teacher described so affectingly by the venerable voices (Young & Kimball, pp. 201–204). The data raise some interesting questions as well. For example, it seems clear that some of the characteristics that made teachers memorable related more to cultural and personality factors than to skills or qualities that the profession has actively sought to promote. In general, how closely do the "good teacher qualities" that learners identify correspond to the qualities that tend to be prioritized in methods courses? Indeed, are most "good teacher qualities" identified by learners actually characteristics that individuals can learn or be taught? What role do cultural and personality factors play? And to what extent do these cultural traits tend to represent "exoticized notions of French, German or Spanish 'others'" (Terrio & Knowles, p. 187)? And a question that has certainly been asked before remains to some extent still unanswered in this study: to what extent, or under what conditions do learners distinguish between "effective" and "memorable" teachers, or between "ineffective" and "hateful"?

Two other factors may contribute to the complexity of defining and measuring the qualities that go into good teaching. The first was touched upon in the discussion of point 5 above: the value of certain kinds of instructional activities, and even the value of the entire experience itself, is not always immediately apparent to the learner. The perceived value

of certain teacher traits, and their impact on the learner, may also be
something that evolves and changes over time. Several of the chapters
allude to this likelihood; the following quote comes from Barnes:

> I left high school thinking that I hadn't learned all that much in Spanish
> class. I enjoyed it usually, but I didn't feel like I'd learned all that much.
> Now that I've seen Spanish taught in a number of ways and now that I've
> had to teach Spanish, I've had a chance to look back on my high school
> experience and realize how good it was. Maybe I really wasn't conversa-
> tionally proficient when I left high school at all, but I had the right kind
> of learning experiences, I had hands-on learning, it wasn't straight drill.
> Yes, we conjugated verbs on the blackboard, but we were very involved
> in our learning. We dramatized fairy tales, we did demonstration
> speeches, we taught the class how to make malts in Spanish, we did those
> things. We had a teacher who was willing to take us on trips abroad, to
> smuggle us out of the school and go for the Mexican buffet at the Holiday
> Inn, things like that. I really appreciate my high school Spanish classes
> and my Spanish teacher much more six years later than I ever did at the
> time. (—Barbara, Barnes, p. 53)

The second factor will be discussed more fully in point 8 below:
teachers are often the catalyst for the experiences that affect learners,
but they themselves are only one piece of a larger universe—the classroom or learner community—that also shapes the learner's perceptions
of the language learning experience.

7. **The data result in a more sympathetic understanding of and appreciation for the learner.**

At the same time that these interviews underscored the importance
of the instructional activities and the affective environment in the classroom, at the same time that they pointed out the central importance of
the teacher, they also reminded us that for all this, the teacher and the
classroom are actually only a small part of the whole story. The participants' voices speak of how deeply the language learning process affects
them, how difficult that process can be and how fragile they often feel.
Learning to communicate with native speakers is "up and down . . . not
only is it up and down, it goes backwards. It takes a long time and it
shatters your ego a lot" (—I: 16, Hall & Davis, p. 14). Across all of the
constituencies studied, individuals were very much aware of participating in "a long, arduous but worthwhile quest for linguistic and cultural
competence that would probably extend a lifetime" (Terrio & Knowles,
p. 152). The experience was viewed particularly poignantly by the native
speakers; for members of this group, faced with the cultural dilemma

created by their hyphenated status, language learning is a very personal journey toward self-discovery that "often involved a painful coming to grips with who they are not" (Garretón, p. 98).

Over and over again, the interviews showed that successful learners do not simply react to instruction, they take charge of it (Barnes, Garretón, Terrio & Knowles). Learners developed their own strategies and techniques, some of which look surprisingly similar to the form-focused activities that they had rejected when imposed by their classroom teachers: they read "every label, box, or scrap of paper with printing on it," and kept diaries and "notebooks of expressions and 'million dollar words' that they could practice on their own and later interject into conversations." They resourcefully eavesdropped on conversations, created their own personal dictionaries and practiced taking dictation from the radio (Barnes, p. 57). They sought out television, movies, restaurants and markets, actively looking for ways of incorporating the language into their day-to-day routines, and of making sense of their own learning (Terrio & Knowles).

Most learners, even Barnes's supercharged learners—the ones who learned three, four and five languages, who enthusiastically threw themselves into multiple types of learning environments—actually had to overcome long odds, persisting with language study, sometimes in spite of ineffective teachers ("biding their time" as Hall & Davis describe it, until they could move on to a different instructor, p. 10) and often through significant periods when learning a language was neither easy nor enjoyable for them (Hall & Davis, Barnes, Garretón, Terrio & Knowles, Brooks). Many of the learners in fact dropped in and out of language study on multiple occasions, many struggled and "did minimal work [and] thought most class activities were corny or weird [and] were not the types of classroom learners that some foreign language educators might anticipate would become the enthusiastic language learners they are now" (Barnes, p. 72). Teachers who often feel they face too many unmotivated, uninterested learners should be at least somewhat encouraged by the fact that some of these learners do go on to enjoy and be successful at language learning; at the same time, this pattern (is it really unpredictable?) should caution teachers, parents, academic advisors and guidance counselors from assuming too quickly that a learner "isn't cut out" for language study.

8.  **Whether it's developing communication skills or finding out about other cultures, from the learners' perspective, the "point" of learning another language is to establish a human connection.**

As was mentioned with relation to point 4 above, for most of the individuals interviewed, the value of learning another language was connected both to developing communication skills and to learning about other cultures. The first of these is clearly related to human interaction; this ability has its pragmatic side—"it's really handy to be able to speak the language of the country [you travel to], even if just a little bit." (—Charles, Brooks, p. 122). And being able to communicate with others is the source of a great deal of pride and enjoyment for learners:

> It [speaking Chinese] makes me feel more confident. I had one Chinese person tell me that my Chinese is better than theirs because I spoke more of the standard accent than they did. It is just a real good feeling to be able to speak Chinese and have others understand me (—I:1, Hall & Davis, p. 19)

But even more important was the interpersonal side, that is, the excitement and satisfaction they derived from being able to interact with other speakers of the language(s) they had studied, of getting to use a language "for real" (Barnes, p. 45). Within and across every chapter in this volume, their stories reveal that establishing this link with other people is the single most important factor explaining their motivation, their success and their attitudes with respect to language study.

> The participants in this study made clear time and time again that people had opened the doors to new languages and that new languages had opened the doors to new people and new friendships. More than anything else, for them, effective language learning and use were social acts that led to being part of a community. (Barnes, p. 64)

> . . . what was most fascinating was the notion that there were people in the world communicating in another tongue . . . that changing the way you moved your mouth and arranged it would change the way you communicated and [it] opened these worlds to you. (—Susan Stamberg, Terrio & Knowles, p. 158)

Many learners also spoke about their classmates as forming significant communities for them. This community was sometimes dysfunctional. For example, when students found that their enthusiasm for the material was not shared by others, they deeply "resented having to deal with classmates whose lack of interest in the language class was evident in their classroom behavior" (Hall & Davis, p. 11). At other times, the sense of community that developed among language learners proved extraordinarily powerful. Barnes describes the "bonding" that seemed to happen among many of the participants in intensive language learning contexts, LAC courses and immersion settings in particular.

> By the time the semester was ending, we were committed to each other, not to just the material we were studying, and for students who were normally very competitive, we ended up working together . . . and it didn't matter at that point who got what grade because we were all in it for the learning . . . a lot of that was based on the shared language that we'd used, and [that] shared language being a language other than our own . . . I think it made the bond stronger. (—Barbara, Barnes, p. 61)

The connection between learning other languages and learning about different cultures is mentioned by many individuals in all of the groups interviewed. However, the way many learners talked about culture suggests that for them "culture" may mean something quite different than what it means for teachers or curriculum designers or textbook authors. For the latter, teaching about "culture" seems generally to mean *conveying information* about mores, values, customs and expectations, as well as important sociohistorical data. For these language learners, culture certainly had that meaning, but for them two other notions stand out above everything else.

First, they tended not to speak of culture and language in separate breaths, but rather as constructs that are tightly interconnected and develop together: they typically "spoke of how their awareness and understanding of other cultures and viewpoints grew *alongside* their developing language abilities" (Hall & Davis, p. 20, emphasis mine).

Second, in many cases, whenever these learners talked about culture, they did so in the context of *talking to and interacting with* people (Barnes, Terrio & Knowles, Young & Kimball). For these learners, it appears that learning about culture is indeed not so much about information as it is about developing the capacity and/or getting the opportunity to get to know and interact with people from other cultures in their language. In other words, interactions with others, which themselves result from the development of functional language proficiencies, are the primary means by which students learn about another culture. The pathway, then, is not language-culture, but language-people-culture. Allan's premise (cited in Kline, p. xiv) that teaching culture is more serious work than instruction in language may be true, but it may also be impossible to get to one without the other. The comments of these learners about culture as connection to others perfectly echo those of the venerable voices, who insist that what is important is for learners to "have access not to cultural information, but to cultural experiences" (Young & Kimball, p. 216).

For the native speakers, learning their language represented a significant connection to family, and they often spoke of how learning the language gave them "new insights into parents, grandparents and themselves" (Garretón, p. 109). Interestingly, the native speakers were insistent that culture was something that really had to be experienced, but at the same time they were anxious to learn cultural "facts" in the classroom, and often criticized their classes for omitting cultural information.

## 9. Foreign languages definitely belong in American education; but do they belong in the classroom?

One of the issues that this project set out to explore was the place of foreign language study in American education. Reactions of the interviewees were decidedly mixed, representing the deeply "ambivalent and contradictory" (Terrio & Knowles, p. 168) attitudes concerning language that are found in this country. On the one hand, foreign language study was definitely viewed as important and valuable and deserving of a place within the curriculum; no one, regardless of difficulties encountered in language study, and regardless of the level of proficiency ultimately achieved, indicated that he or she regretted the experience. In addition, interviewees spoke often and loudly about the importance of beginning foreign language study as early as possible. On the other hand, most people felt that foreign languages were not as important as other academic subjects. Demonstrating what Terrio and Knowles call "the American preoccupation with pragmatism," they felt that education should prioritize skills "only directly related to work" (Terrio & Knowles, pp. 169–170), a position which inevitably led to a certain amount of skepticism with respect to foreign language study, even among those who defended it:

> From a practical perspective, foreign language in America is superfluous. Without going out of my way, I find it so difficult to find people to converse with in French. I have to make a very concerted effort to do that. I'm trying. I have friends who do speak French and [I] make it a point to try to do so. From a practical perspective, there isn't a need, which is why in many schools, foreign languages have been dropped over the last twenty to twenty-five years. (—Lance Keppel, Terrio & Knowles, p. 42)

This same view was shared by school-aged individuals, who had to prioritize how they spent their study time. Once a student has elected a major, everything else simply becomes less important. Sadly, this was also the case even among the native speakers, many of whom dropped their language classes in order to focus on "more valuable" academic subjects (Garretón). The individuals interviewed spoke of a growing awareness that the world is indeed becoming a smaller place and that knowing another language could represent a marketable skill; but at the same time, in disappointingly repetitive fashion, most people felt that for "ordinary" people, language ability was pretty useless. The primary exception to this view, and this is perhaps an interesting twist, was the notion that skill with another language could be very valuable in the schools and the local economies of particular communities *within* this country as a means to work with growing populations of non-English speakers.

The more intriguing question may not be "do foreign languages belong in the curriculum?" but, rather "do they belong in the classroom?" Here, the data create a considerably more interesting picture. At first glance, it would appear that the answer is "no." The kinds of activities that many learners are apparently still doing in language classrooms are often rejected as either not interesting or not helpful or both; in addition, the classroom is often viewed as a hopelessly slow path to success:

> I think school is one of the worst places to learn a language, because if you're getting it for a half-hour for five days a week, it's obviously going to take you a longer time than if you hear it every day (—Teresa, Barnes, p. 50)

By contrast, the kinds of activities that learners unanimously get excited about doing are those which typically happen *outside* of classrooms: getting to know and become friends with native speakers, and through this interaction, developing their language skills and learning about other cultures. However, while the experiential route is unarguably more successful for the learner, it has the disadvantage of lacking the intellectual or cognitive side that most learning must demonstrate in order to justify inclusion in an academic setting. We seem to be full circle to the question of whether or not language study belongs in the curriculum. The individuals interviewed in this project voiced an answer to the dilemma: language learning belongs exclusively neither inside nor outside the classroom. That is, the most effective context was consistently described as a combination of classroom and out-of-classroom learning.

> For those who went on to develop real language proficiency, language learning was not limited to the classroom, but rather was spread over a variety of different contexts, both formal and informal, and usually over several different periods of time in each individual's life. (Terrio & Knowles, p. 176)

As Eleanor Jorden and others (Young & Kimball) have often said, each of these two contexts—classroom and out-of-classoom—clearly contribute crucial pieces to the experience: outside the classroom, learners have the opportunity to realize, in Barnes's words, the "interpersonal dimension" of language learning and to use language "for real" in a way that profoundly changes them as individuals. Inside the classroom, learners have a chance to be both introspective and reflective:

> I really see my experience in terms of the model of experiential language learning because it was circular, cyclical. . . . I experienced the language and the culture, and then I had an opportunity to dissect it, to analyze it, to look at it in an academic light, and then continue to experience it. . . . (—Barbara, Barnes, p. 53)

The classroom context also provides the framework for intellectual activity—"access to worlds beyond personal encounters" (Barnes, pp. 65–67)—by developing foreign language literacy. The experience of one Classics student, who was interested in "interacting with other readers" is particularly suggestive in this regard:

> We had like ten adult learners . . . and we had people in there that could read Greek, a housewife, someone who had been an engineer and not taken any humanities . . . an undergrad, people from all walks of life, and it was shared between a professor that was a Greek professor and a professor that was English . . . and between the ping pong of that we went through a lot of shared inquiry. I found the shared inquiry fascinating because how the housewife saw the *Odyssey* was completely different from how I as a bachelor, someone who's always been in academics looked at it . . . and it was just beautiful to see how different people's minds were . . . and it made me realize that Homer is all things to all people. (—I: 22, Hall & Davis, p. 20)

One further observation about the complementary roles that formal and informal contexts play for language learners was suggested by learners' descriptions of the types of strategies and "tricks" they used on their own (see point 7 above). In the classroom, current methods urge greater and greater incorporation of "real life" experiences; learners, when out in the real world, seem to add back structured "classroom" exercises.

# Conclusion

This project began with a number of questions about the process and the impact of language learning, and set about gathering information on those issues by talking—and listening—to over a hundred individuals of different ages, different racial and ethnic groups, and from different regions of the country. The researchers interviewed boys and girls, and men and women representing different lifestyles and professional occupations. The results illuminate important trends and patterns regarding the way foreign language study is perceived in this country, and suggest areas for further investigation as well, among them:

- It is likely that the teacher is a critical figure in many, if not most, learning experiences; does the special nature of language ("one's speech is part of one's self") therefore mean that language teachers have a greater impact on the learner than other subject matter teachers? What are the implications for teacher development, national standards, and so forth?
- Are the criticisms that learners have of their language courses really any different from comments they might make about other courses? Language learning apparently is perceived as much harder than learners thought it would be; what impact does that realization have on their perceptions of their classes (and their teachers)? Where do their expectations come from and what are the implications for language instruction?
- How do *learners* define "culture" and what is the process by which they learn it? What is the role of interpersonal interaction? What are the implications for language program design?
- If the ideal language learning environment is a combination of classroom and out-of-classroom experiences, what modifications can be made to most academic programs to keep the intellectual and the interpersonal dimensions from being in opposition to one another?
- Language programs and language teachers do seem to be marginalized within American education; these notions are directly connected both to our sociocultural views of language as well as to typically American views of education. This has often created no-win situations for language teachers. For example, many individuals believe that language study should result in the ability to use language: "Just like I think you should be able to use math when you come out of math class, when you come out of a Spanish or a French or German class, you should be able to use it. . . ." (—Margo, Brooks, p. 136). However, courses that are seen as developing "skills"—and individuals involved in teaching such courses—typically occupy an extremely low rung on the academic ladder. What can language teachers do, then, to change the way that their colleagues and compatriots perceive them?
- If during the last fifteen years, the buzzword for language programs has been "communication," this study suggests that another powerful metaphor for teaching/learning has emerged, and that is "community." Both within and outside the classroom, becoming part of, belonging to, and participating in a community of speakers of a language structures and motivates learner progress

and development. Outside the classroom, for example, it is participation in these communities which appears to frame learner perceptions of culture; inside the classroom, we have "only glimpses," to use Hall and Davis's phrase, of what such communities are and what they do. What is the nature of the classroom and out-of-classroom communities to which learners strive to belong, and what are the consequences of participation in them? In what ways do teachers and learners separately and jointly construct classroom communities? How and why do some learner communities become dysfunctional and what can be done about that? Can the notion of community be extended to include interpretive or reader communities? How effective can this latter experience be in overcoming the logistical difficulties of putting learners in direct and frequent contact with native speakers?

Further investigation of the two questions behind this project is also in order. For example, there were groups that we did not have a chance to speak to in this first effort: administrators and other gatekeepers and school-aged learners who had abandoned language study. And there are many, many more venerables in the profession who have stories to tell us, insights to share, guidance to offer. Throughout this project we have been reminded again and again of this heretofore largely neglected resource, our "collective memory" and at times our collective conscience as well. We can think of no finer outcome to our efforts than that a path should begin forming to their doors.

In responding to one set of questions and suggesting new ones, this study has amply indicated the potential of its qualitative methodology; in addition, the project proved to be a particularly moving experience for all the researchers involved. It seems especially appropriate that such insights should have developed out of the simplest and most fundamental of language interactions: talking and listening, asking and answering questions. Like Dorothy's ruby slippers, the means to "go home," to understand our own condition, may have always been just that close to us. It is hoped that this and other qualitative research techniques can join quantitative instruments in helping the profession to observe, interpret and understand the world that language teachers and language learners jointly inhabit.

# Notes

[1]Ironically, when the 1929 Coleman Report recommended that schools standardize on the two-year sequence, it suggested that programs concentrate on grammar and reading skills, as this seemed the only reasonable goal for such a short length of study. Many foreign language educators at that time were furious with this report because they feared (justifiably, as it turned out) that this would spell the end to efforts to develop other skills in the language curriculum (McCabe, 1994). The problem today is that although the goals have expanded, the time frame has not.

[2]Keep in mind that the samples are characterized by a certain amount of self-selection in that individuals who did not feel positively about foreign language study may have declined to participate. Also, other than with the adults, we did not intentionally interview learners who had begun language study and then abandoned it.

# References

Berns, M. (1990). *Contexts of competence: Social and cultural considerations in communicative language teaching.* New York: Plenum Press.

Chastain, K. (1980). Second language study: Historical background and current status. In F.M. Grittner, (Ed.). *Learning a second language* (pp. 1–25). Seventy-ninth Yearbook of the National Society for the Study of Education. Part II. Chicago: University of Chicago Press.

Fishman, J. (1966). *Language loyalty in the United States.* The Hague: Mouton.

McCabe, M.R. (1994) Why teach a second language? A historical study of the status of second language learning in the curriculum. (Doctoral dissertation, University of Michigan). *Dissertation Abstracts International, 55/04,* p. 893.

Robinson, G. N. (1988) *Crosscultural understanding.* New York: Prentice Hall.

Stern, H.H. (1983). *Fundamental concepts of language teaching.* Oxford: Oxford University Press.

# Appendix A: Guidelines for Investigators and Interview Questions

## GUIDELINES FOR INVESTIGATORS/AUTHORS

1 The description of your chapter includes an enumeration of the categories of individuals you should try not to overlook. Based on "purposeful sampling" principles, this enumeration does not aim for representation, but rather for inclusion. At the same time, we have suggested a certain *number and distribution* of interviews, the interpretation and findings for which represent a minimum amount of data necessary for credibility. You may, of course, need to conduct more than the chosen number of interviews in order to come up with 10 or 30 where interviewees provided ample and appropriate information.

2 Since the main focus of the *Reports* is to listen to the voices of individuals recount and interpret their experiences as language learners, questions about that experience will be a common thread across all interviews in all groups. We are including herein a core interview protocol relating to this aspect. The phrasing of the questions themselves will vary according to the specific individual being interviewed, of course, and to your perceptions as each interview progresses. In addition to the Core questions on the learning experience, you will want to explore other issues with your interviewees, particularly in Groups 3–6. Included here are a sampling of such additional questions for Group 4 (Teachers). The interviews should be fairly informal or semi-structured, lasting about an hour. Please share successful questions with others. Thank you!

Some of you have conducted research that relies more on participant observation, surveys, numerical data, etc., than on ethnographic interviewing. Begging the indulgence of those with broad interviewing experience, we add here some tips for fruitful interviews (adapted from Seidman, I.E. (1991). *Interviewing as Qualitative Research*. New York: Teachers College Press, pp. 56–71):

- listen attentively and follow-up: keep track of where the interview is going, but get interviewees to elaborate;
- ask questions when you don't understand, and even sometimes when you think you do: if someone says, "FL learning is hard," don't assume you know what "hard" means;
- explore, don't probe, and avoid leading questions: this is very important in an interview where the interviewee will assume you "want" to hear certain things about FLs—let them know you don't have an agenda and need their honest feelings and opinions;
- consider asking participants to talk to you as if you were someone else: "What would you tell me if I were your FL teacher?"
- ask for stories;
- ask for concrete details;
- ask for reconstruction, not remembering: "What happened?" and not "Do you remember what happened?";
- avoid reinforcing responses by listening silently, nodding, rather than agreeing

or saying "uh-huh";

- engage in good "teacher behaviors," OPI practices, etc.: don't evaluate, be sure to tolerate some silence, don't rephrase questions unless necessary, don't repeat answers, etc.
- it is a good idea to close each interview by offering the individual an opportunity to make any additional remarks (answer any questions that he/she wished you had asked but you didn't) or comments.

3 This project has been reviewed by the Human Subjects Committee at the University of Michigan. You will need to have each interviewee (or his/her guardian, in the case of children) sign an "informed consent" document. This will be sent to you in a separate mailing. If the institution where you will conduct interviews insists that its own consent form be used, you will be responsible for attending to that requirement. Please have the interviewee sign all documents before beginning the interview. Send all consent forms to us when you have completed data gathering.

4 Finally, we are including a brief questionnaire. You may use this questionnaire if you deem it appropriate and helpful with your particular group. We have designed it to provide you with some basic "facts" about the interviewee prior to the interview, ensuring that interview time will be spent on the primary research questions and not on details ("How long have you studied Chinese?," "What grade are you in?," etc.). We understand, however, that certain interviewees may benefit from beginning with questions of a "small talk" nature.

5 We ask that, wherever possible, you record these interviews on audio- or videotape. Naturally, if such measures make you or the interviewee ill-at-ease, you should simply take notes.

6 You may engage co-researchers in this task. Indeed, we would be pleased to see graduate students in the fields of foreign language acquisition or applied linguistics included in the project. The co-researchers' names may appear as co-authors or merely acknowledged in a footnote, depending upon your perception of their level of contribution. You are, however, principal author, and are free to use the data you collect for further analysis and publication (subject to conventional requirements for acknowledgment of prior publication).

# PRE-INTERVIEW QUESTIONNAIRE

The following information will help me to get ready for our interview. I am the only person who will see your answers, and your identity will be kept confidential. You are still free to leave certain spaces blank if you wish.

Name_____ Age_____ M   F

Race/ethnic background   _____

Position or job, if applicable   _____

Company or organization   _____

Grade or year, if applicable   _____

School   _____

What languages do you know:

❖ Native (first) language   _____   Others:   _____

❖ Languages used in the home   _____

What languages have you studied:

❖ Language studied: _____

   when: _____   how long: _____   where: _____

❖ Language studied: _____

   when: _____   how long: _____   where: _____

❖ Language studied: _____

   when: _____   how long: _____   where: _____

❖ Language studied: _____

   when: _____   how long: _____   where: _____

❖ Language studied: _____

   when: _____   how long: _____   where: _____

## Interview Protocol

The ethnographic interviews conducted for the *Reports* will be based on one core protocol, with individual questions tailored for each "audience" by the respective investigators.

The following questions constitute the "core protocol" for the study. Please note these caveats:
1  The questions are organized into two groups, and appear in a loosely logical fashion within those groups, but this is not meant to imply or suggest that the interviews proceed in this order.
2  The questions suggest information that we are after in the survey; remember that the actual phrasing of each question may need to change according to the group and individual being interviewed. For groups 1 and 2 (current students), the primary focus of the interview will be the language learning experience from the perspective of the learner; additional perspectives can be added. For the other groups, we are interested both in their personal perspectives on the languge learning experience (or lack of it, if they never studied a language) as well as the exploration of other perspectives. The protocol suggests some directions for this extra exploration, but investigators are encouraged to develop this part of their interviews according to their own insights and interests.

---

PART 1. Core Questions for *All Interviews*
PART 2. Modifying the Questionnaire: Additional Suggestions for Group 4
PART 3. Core Questions for *All Interviews*

---

PART 1. Language learning from the learner's perspective: motivations, experience, impact, choices

1  Individual's prior (or current) experience as a language learner
   • what, where, when, why, for how long
   • What influenced choice to study FL: why do you think people study foreign languages; why did you?
   • What are (were) FL classes like (compared to other classes: typical activities, assignments, work load, satisfactions/challenges)
   • story about a memorable experience as a learner
   • What did you expect to get out of FL study and has it been what you expected?
   • any encounters with the FL outside the classroom context

2  Feelings/Analysis
   • How do/did you feel about the experience: class, teacher, book, other students
   • Are/were you good at language learning? Why do you think that?
   • How is/was studying a language similar to and/or different from studying

anything else?
- In general do you think that your experiences as a student — the things that you learn in school — will affect (have affected) your life in specific ways? Where do your experiences as a language learner fit? Do you think that studying x language has had or will have an effect on you in the future? (How would you be different if you hadn't studied it, how does it fit into your future.)
- What kinds of people
  ... continue (major in/have a career using) foreign languages?
  ... really should study FLs?
- Do you know anyone who (whose life/career) has been affected by studying a FL?

PART 2. Modifying the Questionnaire: Additional Suggestions for Group 4
[Non-FL Teachers]

All of the individuals interviewed are likely to have been, at one time or another, language learners. For this reason, the CORE questionnaire asks for recollections and reflections on that experience. Groups 3-4-5-6 also can be seen to represent specific constituencies with other areas of concern and/or "agendas" to share with us. After posing the questions related to language learning, each researcher is encouraged to formulate other questions to enable him/her to get at these other areas. As an example (and this is an example only!), here are some questions that might be asked of the non-FL teachers.

Language learning from the outside: place, role, value in the overall educational scene

1  Personal beliefs
   - What do you think that people "get out" of studying another language?
   - Why do you think that people study other languages? Why did (do) you?
   - What comes to mind first when you think of ...
     FL teachers       FL departments       FL majors
     FL programs       FL research
     FL classes        FL requirements
   - Consider for a moment, what the relationship — for your discipline — is between study and development of expertise and/or knowledge. Do you think that this same relationship holds true for most or all disciplines? How about for FLs? How do you think Foreign Language study is similar to or different from the study of other disciplines? Why do you think that? How do you think that the study of a FL "connects" to the study of other content areas? Where does this study "fit" into the overall educational curriculum? How do you think it should fit?
   - Have you had a memorable experience with FLs (here at your institution)?
   - Who should study a FL? What advice would you give to someone planning to study a FL (here)?

2  Analysis
   - What roles do FLs play here (at your institution)?
   - How important is FL study in the US (here at your institution)?

- People say that Americans aren't very good at languages, why do you think they say this?
- What do you think the FL profession should attempt to do in this country/in the coming years?

PART 3. One last check

Is there anything I should have asked you that I didn't? Anything you expected me to ask that I didn't? Anything you would like to add to what you've said already?

# Appendix B: Informed Consent Documents

This study involves individuals from many different regions in the United States. Its objective is to discover and understand the place of foreign languages in the educational landscape in this country, and the impact of foreign language study in the lives and experiences of individuals of different ages and from different walks of life. Quotes from the interview may be used in publications and/or presentations based on the study, but names and personal identifying information will be eliminated.

To keep an accurate record of each conversation, we would like your permission to audio tape and videotape the interview. The audio recordings will be transcribed and analyzed by the researcher. The videotapes—edited to eliminate personal names—would be included as part of presentations and discussions of this study at professional conferences.

This is to certify that I, _____, hereby agree to participate as a volunteer in this study as an authorized part of the education and research program of the University of Michigan.

The study, and my part in it have been defined and fully explained to me by _____, and I understand his/her explanation.
I have been given an opportunity to ask whatever questions I may have had and all such questions and inquiries have been answered to my satisfaction.
I understand that I am free to deny answers to specific items or questions in the interview.
I understand that any data or answers to questions will remain confidential with regard to my identity.
I further understand that I am free to withdraw my consent and terminate my participation at any time.

_____          _____
Date                                Signature

                                  _____
                                  Date of birth

I give my permission to have this interview audio taped; I understand that the audio tapes are intended to ensure accuracy of data gathering and will not be made available to anyone not directly connected with this research study.

_____          _____
Date                                Signature

I give my permission to have this interview videotaped; I understand that the videotape or excerpts from it may be included as part of presentations and discussions of the study at professional conferences, and that the tapes will be physically edited to delete any references that might enable viewers to personally identify me or others.

---------------                        ---------------

Date                                        Signature

I, the undersigned, have defined and fully explained the investigation to the above subject.

---------------                        ---------------

Date                                        Signature

This study involves individuals from many different regions in the United States. Its objective is to discover and understand the place of foreign languages in the educational landscape in this country, and the impact of foreign language study in the lives and experiences of individuals of different ages and from different walks of life. Quotes from the interview may be used in publications and presentations based on the study, but names and personal identifying information will be eliminated.

To keep an accurate record of each conversation, we would like your permission to audio tape and videotape the interview. The audio recordings will be transcribed and analyzed by the researcher. The videotapes — edited to eliminate personal names —would be included as part of presentations and discussions of this study at professional conferences.

Part I. Consent of parent or guardian

This is to certify that I, _____, hereby give permission to
    have my child participate as a volunteer in this study as an authorized part of the education
    and research program of the University of Michigan.
The study, and my child's part in it have been defined and fully explained to me by
    _____, and I understand his/her explanation.
I have been given an opportunity to ask whatever questions I may have had and all such
    questions and inquiries have been answered to my satisfaction.
I understand that I am free to deny answers to specific items or questions in the interview.
I further understand that I am free to withdraw my consent and terminate my child's
    participation at any time.
I hearby consent to the participation of _____, a minor, as a subject in
    the study described above.


_____           _____
    Date                            Signature of parent or guardian


I give my permission to have this interview audio taped; I understand that the audio tapes are intended to ensure accuracy of data gathering and will not be made available to anyone not directly connected with this research study.


_____           _____
    Date                            Signature of parent or guardian


I give my permission to have this interview videotaped; I understand that the videotape or excerpts from it may be included as part of presentations and discussions of the study at professional conferences, and that the tapes will be physically edited to delete any references that might enable viewers to personally identify my child or others.


_____           _____
    Date                            Signature of parent or guardian

Part II. Consent of minor

This is to certify that I, _____, hereby agree to participate
as a volunteer in this study as an authorized part of the education and research program
of the University of Michigan.
The study, and my part in it have been defined and fully explained to me by
_____, and I understand his/her explanation.
I have been given an opportunity to ask whatever questions I may have had and all such
questions and inquiries have been answered to my satisfaction.
I understand that I am free to deny answers to specific items or questions in the interview.
I further understand that I am free to withdraw my consent and terminate my participation
at any time.

_____                    _____
Date                                Signature of subject

                                    _____
                                    Date of birth

I give my permission to have this interview audio taped; I understand that the audio
tapes are intended to ensure accuracy of data gathering and will not be made available to
anyone not directly connected with this research study.

_____                    _____
Date                                Signature of Subject

I give my permission to have this interview videotaped; I understand that the videotape
or excerpts from it may be included as part of presentations and discussions of the study
at professional conferences, and that the tapes will be physically edited to delete any
references that might enable viewers to personally identify me or others.

_____                    _____
Date                                Signature of Subject

I, the undersigned, have defined and fully explained the investigation to the above
subject.

_____                    _____
Date                                Investigator's Signature

**VOICES FROM THE FIELD**　　　　　　PROJECT CONSENT FORM C

This study involves individuals from many different regions in the United States. Its objective is to discover and understand the place of foreign languages in the educational landscape in this country, and the impact of foreign language study in the lives and experiences of individuals of different ages and from different walks of life. Quotes from the interview may be used in publications and/or presentations based on the study.

To keep an accurate record of each conversation, we would like your permission to audio tape and videotape the interview. The audio recordings will be transcribed and analyzed by the researcher. The videotapes would be included as part of presentations and discussions of this study at professional conferences.

This is to certify that I, _____, hereby agree to participate
    as a volunteer in this study as an authorized part of the education and research program
    of the University of Michigan.

The study, and my part in it have been defined and fully explained to me by
_____, and I understand his/her explanation.
I have been given an opportunity to ask whatever questions I may have had and all such
    questions and inquiries have been answered to my satisfaction.
I understand that I am free to deny answers to specific items or questions in the interview.
I further understand that I am free to withdraw my consent and terminate my participation
    at any time.

_____　　　　　　　　　_____
Date　　　　　　　　　　　　　　　Signature

　　　　　　　　　　　　　　　　　_____
　　　　　　　　　　　　　　　　　Date of birth

I give my permission to have this interview audio taped; I understand that the audio tapes are intended to ensure accuracy of data gathering and will not be made available to anyone not directly connected with this research study.

_____　　　　　　　　　_____
Date　　　　　　　　　　　　　　　Signature

I give my permission to have this interview videotaped; I understand that the videotape or excerpts from it may be included as part of presentations and discussions of the study at professional conferences.

_____　　　　　　　　　_____
Date　　　　　　　　　　　　　　　Signature

I, the undersigned, have defined and fully explained the investigation to the above subject.

_____　　　　　　　　　_____
Date　　　　　　　　　　　　　　　Investigator's Signature

# Appendix C: Letter Introducing Project

[Northeast Conference Letterhead]

Date

Inside Address

Dear *Potential Interviewee:*

I am writing to invite you to participate in an exciting, national project sponsored by the Northeast Conference on the Teaching of Foreign Languages. The goal of this project is to explore a variety of perspectives on foreign language study. We are interested in looking at the impact that foreign language study has on individuals as well as the role that it plays both within and outside educational contexts. In order to gather information on these questions, I am a member of a team that will conduct interviews with individuals from many different backgrounds, and from different areas of the United States. What we learn from you and others we talk to will form the basis of a chapter in a volume entitled *Voices from the Field,* to be published by the Northeast Conference in 1995. Our team of researchers includes individuals from the faculties of *[list the schools, but **exclude** your own institution: University of Georgia, St. Olaf College, Chicago State University, the Florida State University, University of Michigan, Marquette University, University of Tennessee, the Pennsylvania State University, Georgetown University].*

We believe this project to be of great importance to everyone involved in foreign language education in this country: teachers, researchers, materials developers and publishers, administrators and other decision makers. The voices we hear—and I hope yours will be among them—will give us fresh and valuable insights.

I will be conducting interviews in this area and will be calling you within the next few weeks to arrange a convenient time for an interview. Your involvement is a vital element in insuring the success of this timely and innovative project, and we hope that we can count on your participation.

Sincerely,


*Dr. Your Name*
University Affiliation

# Appendix D: Venerable Voices

**Evelyn Brega**. High School French Teacher and Coordinator of Foreign Language Instruction, Lexington, MA. *Career Highlights*: Palmes Académiques, 1984; MAFLA Outstanding Contribution to the FL Profession. *Years in the profession*: 37.

**Germaine Brée**. Professor of French literature. *Career Highlights*: Author; President, MLA, 1975; French Army, 1943–45; Decorated Bronze Star Medal; Chevalier de la Légion d'Honneur. *Years in the profession*: 54.

**Kenneth Chastain**. Professor of Spanish, University of Virginia; High School Spanish and English teacher. *Career Highlights*: Author of several books on foreign language pedagogy, including *Developing second language skills: Theory to practice* (3rd ed.). *Years in the profession*: 37.

**John Carroll**. Kenan Professor of Psychology, University of North Carolina. *Career Highlights:* Developed Modern Language Aptitude Test, Educational Testing Service. *Years in the profession*: 42.

**Stephen Freeman**. Professor of French and developer of The Language Schools, Middlebury College. *Career Highlights:* Vice-President, Middlebury College, 1943–1963; five honorary degrees. *Years in the profession*: 40.

**Frank Grittner**. High School German and Spanish teacher; Wisconsin Foreign Language Supervisor. *Career Highlights*: Editor, *Foreign Language Annals*; President, ACTFL, AATG; established Central States Conference Proceedings. *Years in the profession*: 31.

**Eleanor Jorden**. Mary Denlon Alger Professor of Linguistics, Bryn Mawr. Professor of Japanese; Linguist, Foreign Service Institute. *Career Highlights:* Anthony Papalia Award for Excellence in Teacher Education, 1994. *Years in the profession*: 51.

**Constance Knop**. Professor of French and Curriculum and Instruction, University of Wisconsin, Madison. *Career Highlights*: author of various French texts; Outstanding Teacher of French Award, Outstanding French Educator in the state of Wisconsin; Florence Steiner Award. *Years in the profession*: 30.

**Wilga Rivers**. Professor of French and Coordinator of Language Instruction, Harvard University. *Career Highlights*: author of numerous teacher training texts; founder, Sine Nomine, a support group for language teachers. *Years in the profession*: 53.

**Eleanor Sandstrom**. High School Spanish Teacher and Department Head, West Philadelphia High School, Philadelphia, PA. *Career Highlights*: Creator, Adult Evening School for Cultural Studies, Philadelphia; Night School for Veterans, 1945, Philadelphia. *Years in the profession*: 43.

**Earl Stevick**. Professor of Linguistics, Foreign Service Institute. *Career Highlights*: author, supervisor, student of Latin, German, Russian, East Armenian, Shona, Portuguese, Spanish, Swahili, Turkish, Hebrew, Greek. *Years in the profession*: 40.

**Mary Thompson**. French and Spanish Teacher, Glastonbury, Fairfield, CT; *Career Highlights*: Developer of French and Spanish FLES programs; Director, ALM project, U.S. Office of Education. *Years in the profession*: 35.

**Albert Valdman**. Professor of Linguistics, Indiana University. *Career Highlights*: Guggenheim Fellow, Fulbright Lecturer and Research Fellow, Officier des Palmes Académiques, author of several books and textbooks. *Years in the profession*: 35.

**Laurence Wylie**. C. Douglas Dillon Professor of French Civilization, Harvard University; *Career Highlights*: Officier de la Légion d'Honneur; Nelson Brooks Award; author, *Village in the Vaucluse, Les Français*. *Years in the profession*: 50.

# Appendix E: Venerable Voices: Interview Questions

1. Please tell me about what influenced your decision to study a foreign language.
2. Do you recall any memorable experiences in teaching or learning another language?
3. What do you think people "get" out of learning a foreign language?
4. Do you think foreign language study is different from studying other disciplines? In what way(s)?
5. Why do you think that Americans are not perceived to be good language learners?
6. Who had the most impact on your life? Why is that?
7. Can you suggest ideas for future directions in foreign language education?
8. If you were beginning your career over again tomorrow, what do you think would make you most apprehensive? What would you be most looking forward to?
9. What advice do you have for prospective language teachers?
10. What do you think of the current state of teacher training in this country? What are the issues that most need to be addressed in training?

Depending on the time, some of these questions were omitted and at other times additional questions were added, such as the following questions asked by Young:

11. Can you comment on the polarization we see in the field between language and literature?
12. What words of wisdom do you have for the plight of junior faculty who direct, coordinate, or supervise language programs in this country?

In addition to these questions, Kimball typically asked interviewees to share . . .

13. . . . stories from their own teaching experiences.
14. . . . their perceptions and interpretations of the place and value of language learning.
15. . . . a description of changes they have perceived over time with respect to language teaching.
16. . . . the value of foreign languages in their own lives.
17. . . . a description of a typical day in one of their classes.

# Northeast Conference Officers and Directors since 1954

Abbott, Martha G., Fairfax County (VA) Public Schools, Director 1994-97.

Anderson, Nancy E., ETS, Director 1990-93, ACTFL Representative 1994.

Andersson, Theodore†, [Yale U]* U of Texas, Director 1954-56.

Andrews, Oliver, Jr., U of Connecticut, Director 1971-74.

Arndt, Richard, Columbia U, Director 1961.

Arsenault, Philip E., Montgomery County (MD) Public S, Local Chair 1967, 1970; Director 1971, 1973-74; Vice Chair 1975; Conference Chair 1976.

Atkins, Jeannette, Staples (Westport, CT) HS, Director 1962-65.

Baird, Janet, U of Maryland, Local Chair 1974.

Baker, Robert M., Middlebury C, Director 1987-90.

Bashour, Dora, [Hunter C], Secretary 1963-1964; Recording Secretary 1965-68.

Baslaw, Annette S., [Teachers C], Hunter C, Local Chair 1973.

Bayerschmidt, Carl F., [Columbia U], Conference Chair 1961.

Bennett, Ruth, Queens C, Local Chair 1975-76.

Bertin, Gerald A., Rutgers U, Local Chair 1960.

Berwald, Jean-Pierre, U of Massachusetts-Amherst, Director 1980-83.

Bird, Thomas E., Queens C, Editor 1967-68; Director 1969.

Bishop, G. Reginald, Jr., Rutgers U, Editor 1960, 1965; Director 1961-62, 1965, 1968; Vice Chair 1966; Conference Chair 1967.

Bishop, Thomas W., New York U, Local Chair 1965.

Born, Warren C., [ACTFL], Editor 1974-79.

Bostroem, Kyra, Westover S, Director 1961.

Bottiglia, William F., MIT, Editor 1957, 1962-63; Director 1964.

Bourque, Jane M., [Stratford (CT) Public S], Mt. Vernon (NY) Public S, Director 1974-75; Vice Chair 1976; Conference Chair 1977.

Brée, Germaine, [New York U, U of Wisconsin], Wake Forest U, Conference Chair 1955; Editor 1955.

Brennan, Judith, Virginia Beach Public S, Director 1995-98

Bressler, Julia T., Nashua (NH) Public S, Director 1991-94; Vice Chair 1995.

Brod, Richard I., MLA, Consultant to the Chair, 1983; Director 1985-88.

Brooks, Nelson†, [Yale U], Director 1954-57, 1960-61; Vice Chair 1959.

Brooks-Brown, Sylvia R., [Baltimore (MD) City S], Baltimore County (MD) Public S, Director 1988-92; Vice Chair 1993, Conference Chair 1994.

Brown, Christine L., [West Hartford (CT) Public S], Glastonbury (CT) Public S, Director 1982-85; Vice Chair 1986; Conference Chair 1987.

Byrnes, Heidi, Georgetown U, Director 1985-88; Vice Chair 1989; Conference Chair 1990; Editor 1992.

Cadoux, Remunda†, [Hunter C], Vice Chair 1969; Conference Chair 1970.

*Where a change of academic affiliation is known, the earlier address appears in brackets.

Campbell, Hugh, [Roxbury Latin S], Rocky Hill Country Day S, Director 1966-67.

Cannon, Adrienne G., Prince George's Co (MD) Public S, Director 1993-96.

Carr, Celestine G., Howard County (MD) Public S, Director 1993-96.

Churchill, J. Frederick, Hofstra U, Director 1966-67; Local Chair 1971-72.

Ciotti, Marianne C., [Vermont State Department of Education, Boston U], Barre (VT) Public S, Director 1967.

Cincinnato, Paul D., Farmingdale (NY) Public S, Director 1974-77; Vice Chair 1978; Conference Chair 1979.

Cintas, Pierre F., [Dalhousie U], Pennsylvania State U-Ogontz, Director 1976-79.

Cipriani, Anita A., Hunter C Elem S, Director 1986-89.

Clark, John L.D., [CAL], DLI, Director 1976-78; Vice Chair 1979; Conference Chair 1980.

Clark, Richard P., Newton (MA) HS, Director 1967.

Clemens, Brenda Frazier, [Rutgers U, U of Connecticut], Howard U, Director 1972-75.

Cobb, Martha, Howard U, Director 1976-77; Recording Secretary 1978.

Covey, Delvin L., [Montclair State C], Spring Arbor C, Director 1964-65.

Crapotta, James, Barnard C, Director 1992-95.

Crawford, Dorothy B., Philadelphia HS for Girls, Conference Chair 1956.

Dahme, Lena F., Hunter C, Local Chair 1958; Director 1959.

Darcey, John M., West Hartford (CT) Public S, Director 1978-81; Vice Chair 1982; Conference Chair 1983; Editor 1987.

Dates, Elaine, Burlington (VT) HS, Recording Secretary 1991.

Del Olmo, Filomena Peloro, [Hackensack (NJ) Public S], Fairleigh Dickinson U, Director 1960-63.

De Napoli, Anthony J., Wantagh (NY) Public S, Local Chair 1980-82, 1987; Director 1982-85.

Di Donato, Robert, MIT, Consultant to the Chair 1986.

Díaz, José M., Hunter C HS, Director 1988-91; Vice Chair 1992; Conference Chair 1993; Consultant to the Chair 1995.

Didsbury, Robert, Weston (CT) JHS, Director 1966-69.

Dodge, James W.†, [Middlebury C], Editor 1971-73; Secretary-Treasurer 1973-89.

Dodge, Ursula Seuss, Northeast Conference Secretariat, Interim Secretary-Treasurer 1990.

Donato, Richard, U of Pittsburgh, Director 1993-96.

Dostert, Leon E., [Georgetown U], Occidental C, Conference Chair 1959.

Dufau, Micheline†, U of Massachusetts, Director 1976-79.

Dvorak, Trisha, U of Michigan, Editor 1995.

Dye, Joan C., Hunter C, Local Chair 1978.

Eaton, Annette, Howard U, Director 1967-70.

Eddy, Frederick D.†, [U of Colorado], Editor 1959; Director 1960.

Eddy, Peter A., [CAL/ERIC], CIA Language S, Director 1977-78.

Edgerton, Mills F., Jr., Bucknell U, Editor 1969; Director 1970; Vice Chair 1971; Conference Chair 1972.

Elkins, Robert, West Virginia U, Director 1991-94.

Elling, Barbara E., SUNY-Stony Brook, Director 1980-83.

Feindler, Joan L., East Williston (NY) Public S, Director 1969-71; Vice Chair 1972; Conference Chair 1973.

Flaxman, Seymour, [New York U], City C of New York, Editor 1961; Director 1962.

Freeman, Stephen A., [Middlebury C], Director 1957-60.

Fulton, Renee J., New York City Board of Education Director 1955.

Gaarder, A. Bruce, [USOE], Director 1971-74.

Galloway, Vicki B., [ACTFL], Georgia Technological U, Consultant to the Chair 1985.

Geary, Edward J., [Harvard U], Bowdoin C, Conference Chair 1962.

Geno, Thomas H., U of Vermont, Director 1975-76; Vice Chair 1977; Conference Chair 1978; Recording Secretary 1979; Editor 1980-81.

Gilman, Margaret†, Bryn Mawr C, Editor 1956.

Glaude, Paul M., New York State Dept of Education, Director 1963-66.

Glisan, Eileen W. Indiana U of Pennsylvania, Director 1992-95.

Golden, Herbert H., Boston U, Director 1962.

Goldfield, Joel, Fairfield U, Director 1995-98.

Grew, James H., [Phillips Acad], Director 1966-69.

Gutiérrez, John R., Pennsylvania State U, Director 1988-91.

Hancock, Charles R., The Ohio State University, Editor 1994

Hartie, Robert W., Queens C, Local Chair 1966.

Harrison, John S., Baltimore County (MD) Public S, Local Chair 1979, 1983; Director 1983-86; Recording Secretary 1988-89.

Harris-Schenz, Beverly, [U of Pittsburgh], U of Massachusetts-Amherst, Director 1988-91.

Hayden, Hilary, OSB, St. Anselm's Abbey S, Vice Chair 1970; Conference Chair 1971.

Hayes, Alfred S. †, CAL, Vice Chair 1963; Conference Chair 1964.

Hernandez, Juana A., Hood C, Director 1978-81.

Holekamp, Elizabeth L., Executive Director 1990-95.

Holzmann, Albert W.†, Rutgers U, Director 1960.

Hurtgen, André, St. Paul's School (NH), Director 1992-95.

Jalbert, Emile H., [Thayer Acad], Berkshire Comm C, Local Chair 1962.

Jarvis, Gilbert A., Ohio State U, Editor 1984.

Jebe, Suzanne, [Guilford (CT) HS], Minnesota Dept of Education, Director 1975-76; Recording Secretary 1977.

Johnston, Marjorie C., [USOE], Local Chair 1964.

Jones, George W., Jr. †, Norfolk (VA) Public S, Director 1977-80.

Kahn, Timothy M., S Burlington (VT) HS, Director 1979-82.

Keesee, Elizabeth, [USOE], Director 1966-70.

Kellenberger, Hunter†, [Brown U], Conference Chair 1954, Editor 1954.

Kennedy, Dora F., Prince George's County (MD) Public S, Director 1985- 88; Recording Secretary 1990; Consultant to the Chair 1991.

Kesler, Robert, Phillips Exeter Acad, Director 1957.

Kibbe, Doris E., Montclair State C, Director 1968-69.

Kline, Rebecca, [Dickinson C], Pennsylvania State U, Director 1990-93, Vice-Chair 1994; Conference Chair 1995.

Koenig, George, State U of New York-Oswego, Recording Secretary, 1993.

Kramsch, Claire J., [MIT], Cornell, Director 1984-87.

La Follette, James E., Georgetown U, Local Chair 1959.

La Fountaine, Hernan, New York City Board of Education, Director 1972.

Lenz, Harold, Queens C, Local Chair 1961.

Lepke, Helen S., [Kent State U], Clarion U of Pennsylvania, Director 1981-84; Vice Chair 1985; Conference Chair 1986; Editor 1989.

Lester, Kenneth A., Connecticut State Dept of Education, Recording Secretary 1982.

Levy, Harry†, [Hunter C], Fordham U, Editor 1958; Director 1959-61; Conference Chair 1963.

Levy, Stephen L., [New York City Board of Education], Roslyn (NY) Public S, Local Chair 1978, 1980-82, 1984-85, 1987-present; Director 1980-83; Vice Chair 1984; Conference Chair 1985; Consultant to the Chair 1994.

Lieberman, Samuel, Queens C, Director 1966-69.

Lipton, Gladys C., [New York City Board of Education, Anne Arundel County (MD) Public S], U of Maryland-Baltimore County, Director 1973-76; Newsletter Editor 1993-94.

Liskin-Gasparro, Judith E., [ETS], Middlebury C, Recording Secretary 1984; Director 1986-89; Vice Chair 1990; Conference Chair 1991.

Lloyd, Paul M., U of Pennsylvania, Local Chair 1963.

Locke, William N.†, MIT, Conference Chair 1957; Director 1958-59.

MacAllister, Archibald T.†, [Princeton U], Director 1955-57, 1959-61.

Magnan, Sally Sieloff, University of Wisconsin-Madison, Editor 1990.

Masciantonio, Rudolph, School District of Philadelphia, Director 1969-71.

Mead, Robert G., Jr., U of Connecticut, Director 1955; Editor 1966; Vice Chair 1967; Conference Chair 1968; Editor 1982-83.

Mesnard, Andre, Barnard C, Director 1954-55.

Micozzi, Arthur L., [Baltimore County (MD) Public S], Local Chair 1977, 1979, 1983, 1986; Director 1970-82.

Mirsky, Jerome G.†, [Jericho (NY) SHS], Shoreham-Wading River (NY) HS, Director 1970-73; Vice Chair 1974; Conference Chair 1975.

Nelson, Robert J., [U of Pennsylvania], U of Illinois, Director 1965-68.

Neumaier, Bert J., Timothy Edwards (S Windsor, CT) MS, Director 1988-92.

Neuse, Werner†, [Middlebury C], Director 1954-56.

Nionakis, John P., Hingham (MA) Public S, Director 1984-87; Vice Chair 1988; Conference Chair 1989.

Obstfeld, Roland, Northport (NY) HS, Recording Secretary 1976.

Omaggio, Alice C., U of Illinois, Editor 1985.

Owens, Doris Barry, West Hartford (CT) Public S, Recording Secretary 1983.

Pane, Remigio U., Rutgers U, Conference Chair 1960.

Paquette, Andre, [Middlebury C], Laconia (NH) Public S, Director 1963-66; Vice Chair 1968; Conference Chair 1969.

Parks, Carolyn, [U of Maryland], French International S, Recording Secretary 1981.

Peel, Emily S., Wethersfield (CT) Public S, Director 1991-94.

Perkins, Jean, Swarthmore C, Treasurer 1963-64; Conference Chair 1966.

Petrosino, Vince J., Baltimore (MD) City S, Local Chair 1986.

Phillips, June K., [Indiana U of Pennsylvania, Tennessee Foreign Language Institute], US Air Force Acad, Director 1979-82; Vice Chair 1983; Conference Chair 1984; Consultant to the Chair 1986, 1989, 1990, 1992; Editor 1991, 1993.

Prochoroff, Marina, [MLA Materials Center], Director 1974.

Reilly, John H., Queens C, Local Chair 1968-69; Director 1970.

Renjilian-Burgy, Joy, Wellesley C, Director 1987-90; Vice Chair 1991; Chair 1992.

Riley, Kerry, U of Maryland, Consultant to the Chair 1986.

Riordan, Kathleen M., Springfield (MA) Public S, Director 1988-91; Recording Secretary 1992.

Rochefort, Frances A., Cranston (RI) Public S, Director 1986-89.

Rosser, Harry L., Boston College, Director 1994-97.

Russo, Gloria M., [U of Virginia], Director 1983-86.

Sandstrom, Eleanor L., [School District of Philadelphia], Director 1975-78.

Selvi, Arthur M., Central Connecticut State C, Director 1954.

Senn, Alfred, U of Pennsylvania, Director 1956.

Serafino, Robert, New Haven (CT) Public S, Director 1969-73.

Sheppard, Douglas C., [SUNY-Buffalo], Arizona State U, Director 1968-71.

Shilaeff, Ariadne, Wheaton C, Director 1978-80.

Shuster, George N.†, [U of Notre Dame], Conference Chair 1958.

Simches, Seymour O., Tufts U, Director 1962-65; Vice Chair 1965.

Sims, Edna N., U of the District of Columbia, Director 1981-84.

Singerman, Alan J., Davidson C, Editor 1988.

Sister Margaret Pauline, [Emmanuel C], Director 1957, 1965-68; Recording Secretary 1969-75.

Sister Margaret Therese, Trinity C, Director 1959-60.

Sister Mary Pierre, Georgian Court C, Director 1961-64.

Sousa-Welch, Helen Candi, West Hartford (CT) Public S, Director 1987-90.

Sparks, Kimberly, Middlebury C, Director 1969-72.

Starr, Wilmarth H., [U of Maine], New York U, Director 1960-63, 1966; Vice Chair 1964, Conference Chair 1965.

Steer, Alfred G., Jr., Columbia U, Director 1961.

Stein, Jack M.†, [Harvard U], Director 1962.

Stracener, Rebecca J., Edison (NJ) Public S, Director 1984-87.

Tamarkin, Toby, Manchester (CT) Comm C, Director 1977-80; Vice Chair 1981; Conference Chair 1982; Recording Secretary 1987.

Thompson, Mary P., [Glastonbury (CT) Public S], Director 1957-62.

Trivelli, Remo J., U of Rhode Island, Director 1981-84.

Tursi, Joseph, [SUNY-Stony Brook], Editor 1970; Director 1971-72; Vice Chair 1973; Conference Chair 1974.

Valette, Rebecca, Boston C, Director 1972-75.

Vasquez-Amaral, Jose, Rutgers U, Director 1960.

Walker, Richard H., Bronxville (NY) HS, Director 1954.

Walsh, Donald D.†, [MLA], Director 1954; Secretary-Treasurer 1965-73.

Walton, A. Ronald, U of Maryland, Director 1990-93.

Warner, Pearl M., New York City Public S, Recording Secretary 1985.

Webb, John, Hunter College HS, Consultant to the Chair, 1993; Director 1995-98.

White, Arlene, Salisbury State U, Recording Secretary 1994.

White, Emile Margaret, [District of Columbia Public S], Director 1955- 58.

Williamson, Richard C., Bates C, Director 1983-86; Vice Chair 1987; Conference Chair 1988.

Wing, Barbara H., U of New Hampshire, Editor 1986; *Newsletter* Editor 1987-93; Recording Secretary 1995.

Woodford, Protase E., ETS, Director 1982-85.

Yakobson, Helen B., George Washington U, Director 1959-60.

Yu, Clara, Middlebury College, Director 1994-97.

Zimmer-Loew, Helene, [NY State Education Dept], AATG, Director 1977-79; Vice Chair 1980; Conference Chair 1981.

# Northeast Conference Reports, 1954–1994

**Building Bridges and Making Connections.** June K. Phillips, ed. Eileen W. Glisan and Thekla F. Fall: "Adapting an Elementary Immersion Approach to Secondary and Postsecondary Teaching: The Methodological Connection." Diane Larsen-Freeman: "ESL and FL: Forging Connections." Karen E. Breiner-Sanders: "Higher-Level Language Abilities: The Skills Connection." Barbara Schnuttgen Jurasek and Richard T. Jurasek: "Building Multiple Proficiencies in New Curricular Contexts." Juliette Avots: "Linking the Foreign Language Classroom to the World." Elana Shohamy: "Connecting Testing and Learning in the Classroom and on the Program Level." 1991.

**The Challenge for Excellence in Foreign Language Education.** Gilbert A. Jarvis, ed. Barbara H. Wing: "For Teachers: A Challenge for Competence." Diane W. Birckbichler: "The Challenge of Proficiency: Student Characteristics." Michael Canale: "Testing in a Communicative Approach." Glyn Holmes: "Of Computers and Other Technologies." Christine L. Brown: "The Challenge for Excellence in Curriculum and Materials Development." 1984.

**Culture in Language Learning.** G. Reginald Bishop, Jr., ed.: "An Anthropological Concept of Culture." William E. Welmers: "Language as Culture." Ira Wade: "Teaching of Western European Cultures." Doris E. Kibbe: "Teaching of Classical Cultures." Leon I. Twarog: "Teaching of Slavic Cultures." 1960.

**Culture, Literature, and Articulation.** Germaine Bree, ed.: "The Place of Culture and Civilization in FL Teaching." A.T. MacAllister: "The Role of Literature in Language Teaching." Mary P. Thompson: "FL Instruction in Elementary Schools." Robert G. Mead, Jr.: "FL Instruction in

Secondary Schools." Barbara P. McCarthy: "Classical and Modern FLs: Common Areas and Problems." Nelson Brooks: "Tests: All Skills, Speaking Test." A.G. Grace: "The Preparation of FL Teachers." J.V. Pleasants: "Teaching Aids and Techniques: Principles, Demonstrations." W.H. Starr: "The Role of FLs in American Life." 1955. Out of print.

**Current Issues in Language Teaching.** William F. Bottiglia, ed.: "Linguistics and Language Teaching." Alfred S. Hayes: "Programmed Learning." Nancy V. Alkonis and Mary A. Brophy: "A Survey of FLES Practices." 1962.

**FL Learning: Research and Development.** Thomas E. Bird, ed.: "Innovative FL Programs." Seymour O. Simches: "The Classroom Revisited." Mills F. Edgerton, Jr.: "Liberated Expression." 1968.

**FL Teachers and Tests.** Hunter Kellenberger, ed: "The Qualifications of FL Teachers." Arthur S. Selvi: "FL Instruction in Elementary Schools." Nelson Brooks: "Tests: Listening Comprehension, Other Skills." Norman L. Torrey: "The Teaching of Literature." Theodore Andersson: "The Role of FLs in American Life." Richard H. Walker: "Linguistic Aids." 1954.

**FL Teaching: Challenges to the Profession.** G. Reginald Bishop, Jr., ed.: "The Case for Latin." Stephen A. Freeman: "Study Abroad." A. Bruce Gaarder: "The Challenge of Bilingualism." Micheline Dufau: "From School to College: The Problem of Continuity." 1965.

**FL Teaching: Ideals and Practices.** George F. Jones, ed.: "FL's in the Elementary School." Milton R. Hahn: "FL's in the Secondary School." Roger L. Hadlich: "FL's in Colleges and Universities." 1964.

**FL Tests and Techniques.** Margaret Gilman, ed.: "Teaching Aids and Techniques: The Secondary School Language Laboratory." Stanley M. Sapon: "Tests: Speaking Tests." Mary P. Thompson: "FL Instruction in Elementary Schools." Ruth P. Kroeger: "FL Instruction in Secondary Schools." Josephine P. Bree: "The Teaching of Classical and Modern FLs: Common Areas and Problems." Robert J. Clements: "The Role of Literature in Language Teaching." John B. Carroll and William C. Sayers: "The Place of Culture and Civilization in FL Teaching." Wilmarth H. Starr: "The Role of FLs in American Life." 1956.

**FLs: Reading, Literature, Requirements.** Thomas E. Bird, ed.: "The Teaching of Reading." F.A. Paquette: "The Times and Places for Literature." John F. Gummere: "Trends in FL Requirements and Placement." 1967.

**FLs and The 'New' Student.** Joseph A. Tursi, ed.: "A Relevant Curriculum: An Instrument for Polling Student Opinion." Robert J. Nelson: "Motivation in FL Learning." Eleanor J. Sandstrom: "FLs for All Students?" 1970.

**Foreign Language and International Studies: Toward Cooperation and Integration.** Thomas H. Geno, ed.: "A Chronicle: Political, Professional, and Public Activities Surrounding the President's Commission on Foreign Language and International Studies." Donald H. Bragaw, Helene Z. Loew, and Judith S. Wooster: "Global Responsibility: The Role of the Foreign Language Teacher." Claudia S. Travers: "Exchanges and Travel Abroad in Secondary Schools." Richard C. Williamson: "Toward an International Dimension in Higher Education." Lucia Pierce: "International Training." "Reactions of the Northeast Conference to the Recommendations of the President's Commission on Foreign Language and International Studies." 1981.

**The Foreign Language Teacher: The Lifelong Learner.** Robert G. Mead, Jr., ed. Marilyn J. Conwell and April Nelson: "American Sign Language." David Gidman: "The Chinese Language." Toshiko Phipps and Jean-Pierre Berwald: "Intensive Japanese." Marie Cleary: "Intensive Latin." Rosemarie Pedro Carvalho: "Intensive Portuguese." Robert L. Baker: "Intensive Russian." Pierre Maubrey: "La France Contemporaine." Barbara Elling and Kurt Elling: "Die Bundesrepublik heute." Remo J. Trivelli: "L'Italia Contemporanea." John M. Darcey: "La Espana de Hoy." Frank Dauster: "La Cultura Contemporanea de Hispanoamerica." Elizabeth G. Joiner and June K. Phillips: "Merging Methods and Texts: A Pragmatic Approach." Judith E. Liskin-Gasparro and Protase E. Woodford: "Proficiency Testing in Second Language Classrooms." Carolyn H. Parks: "Audiovisual Materials and Techniques for Teaching Foreign Languages: Recent Trends and Activities." John S. Harrison: "Applications of Computer Technology in Foreign Language Teaching and Learning." 1982. Out of print.

**The Foreign Language Teacher in Today's Classroom Environment.** Warren C. Born, ed.: "Educational Goals: The Foreign Language Teacher's Response." Carol Hosenfeld: "Cindy: A Language Learner in Today's Foreign Language Classroom." Gilbert A. Jarvis: "The Second Language Teacher: A Problem of Reconciling the Vision with the Reality." 1979.

**Foreign Languages: Key Links in the Chain of Learning.** Robert G. Mead, Jr., ed. Myriam Met, et al.: "Elementary School Foreign Language: Key Link in the Chain of Learning." Alice C. Omaggio, et al.: "Foreign Languages in the Secondary Schools: Reconciling the Dream with the Reality." Claire Gaudiani, et al.: "Nurturing the Ties that Bind: Links between Foreign Language Departments and the Rest of the Post-Secondary Educational Enterprise." Vicki Galloway: "Foreign Languages and the 'Other' Student." H.H. Stern: "Toward a Multidimensional Foreign Language Curriculum." Jane McFarland Bourque: "Thirty Years of the Northeast Conference: A Personal Perspective." 1983.

**Goals Clarification: Curriculum, Teaching, Evaluation.** Warren C. Born, ed.: "Goals Clarification: Background" and "Goals Clarification: Implementation." 1975.

**Language: Acquisition, Application, Appreciation.** Warren C. Born, ed.: "Language Acquisition." Kenneth Lester: "Language Application." Germaine Bree: "Language Appreciation." 1977.

**Language and Culture: Heritage and Horizons.** Warren C. Born, ed.: "The French Speaking." Helene Z. Loew: "The German Speaking." Grace Crawford: "Classics in America." 1976.

**The Language Classroom.** William F. Bottiglia, ed.: Blance A. Price: "Teaching Literature for Admission to College with Advanced Standing." Nelson Brooks: "Spoken Language Tests." James H. Grew: "The Place of Grammar and the Use of English in the Teaching of FLs." Renee J. Fulton: "The Drop-Out of Students after the Second Year." John B. Archer: "The Philosophy of the Language Laboratory." Jeanne V. Pleasants: "Teaching Aids and Techniques." 1957.

**The Language Learner.** F.D. Eddy, ed.: "Modern FL Learning: Assumptions and Implications." G.R. Silber: "A Six-Year Sequence." Filomena C. Peloro: "Elementary and Junior High School Curricula." Nelson Brooks: "Definition of Language Competences Through Testing." 1959.

**Language Learning: The Intermediate Phase.** W. F. Bottiglia, ed.: "The Continuum: Listening and Speaking." George Scherer: "Reading for Meaning." Marina

Prochoroff: "Writing as Expression." 1963.

**The Language Teacher.** Harry L. Levy, ed.: "The Teaching of Writing." James H. Grew: "Single vs. Multiple Languages in Secondary Schools." Margaret E. Eaton: "The FL Program, Grades 3-12." Dorothy Brodin: "Patterns as Grammar." Donald D. Walsh: "The Ghosts in the Language Classroom: College FL Departments, College Board Examinations, the Administration, the Textbook." Carolyn E. Bock: "Means of Meeting the Shortage of Teachers." 1958.

**The Language Teacher: Commitment and Collaboration.** John M. Darcey, ed. Claire L. Gaudiani: "The Importance of Collaboration." Humphrey Tonkin: "Grassroots and Treetops: Collaboration in Post-secondary Language Programs." Gordon M. Ambach: "Incorporating an International Dimension in Education Reform: Strategies for Success." Alice G. Pinderhughes: "Baltimore's Foreign Language Mandate: An Experiment That Works." Richard C. Wallace, Jr., Mary Ellen Kirby, and Thekla F. Fall: "Commitment to Excellence: Community Collaboration in Pittsburgh." Carolyn E. Hodych: "Canadian Parents for French: Parent Action and Second Official Language Learning in Canada." Badi G. Foster: "The Role of the Foreign Language Teacher in American Corporate Education." 1987.

**Language Teaching: Broader Contexts.** Robert G. Mead, Jr., ed.: "Research and Language Learning." Brownlee Sands Corrin: "Wider Uses for FLs." Genevieve S. Blew: "Coordination of FL Teaching." 1966.

**Languages for a Multicultural World in Transition.** Heidi Byrnes, ed.: Ofelia García: "Societal Multilingualism in a Multicultural World in Transition." Guadalupe Valdés: "The Role of the Foreign Language Teaching Profession in Maintaining Non-

English Languages in the United States."
Claire Gaudiani: "Area Studies for a Mul-
ticultural World in Transition." Vicki Gal-
loway: "Toward a Cultural Reading of
Authentic Texts." John M. Grandin, Kan-
dace Einbeck, and Walter von Reinhart:
"The Changing Goals of Language Instruc-
tion." Clara Yu: "Technology at the Cutting
Edge: Implications for Second Language
Learning." 1992.

**Leadership for Continuing Develop-
ment.** James W. Dodge, ed.: "Professional
Responsibilities." Jerome G. Mirsky: "In-
service Involvement in the Process of
Change." Francois Hugot: "Innovative
Trends." 1971.

**Listening, Reading, Writing: Analysis
and Application.** Barbara H. Wing, ed.
Carolyn Gwynn Coakley and Andrew D.
Wolvin: "Listening in the Native Lan-
guage." Elizabeth G. Joiner: "Listening in
the Foreign Language." Michael L. Kamil:
"Reading in the Native Language." Eliza-
beth B. Bernhardt: "Reading in the Foreign
Language." Trisha Dvorak: "Writing in the
Foreign Language." 1986.

**Modern Language Teaching in School
and College.** Seymour L. Flaxman, ed.:
"Foreword: Learning a Modern FL and
Communication." Genevieve S. Blew:
"The Preparation of Secondary School
Teachers." Jack M. Stein: "The Prepara-
tion of College and University Teachers."
Evangeline Galas: "The Transition to the
Classroom." Guillermo del Olmo: "Coor-
dination between Classroom and Labora-
tory." 1961.

**New Contents, New Teachers, New Pub-
lics.** Warren C. Born, ed.: "New Contents." William E. DeLorenzo: "New
Teachers." Joseph A. Tursi: "New Pub-
lics." 1978.

**Our Profession: Present Status and Fu-
ture Directions.** Thomas H. Geno, ed.:
"Current Status of Foreign Language

Teaching: A Northeast Conference Survey." Robert C. Lafayette: "Toward an Articulated Curriculum." Mills F. Edgerton,
Jr.: "Competence in a Foreign Language: A
Valuable Adjunct Skill in the Eighties?"
James W. Dodge: "Educational Technology." Helen L. Jorstad: "New Approaches
to Assessment of Language Learning."
David P. Benseler: "The American Language Association: Toward New Strength,
Visibility, and Effectiveness as a Profession." 1980.

**Other Words, Other Worlds: Language
in Culture.** James W. Dodge, ed.: "On
Teaching Another Language as Part of An-
other Culture." G.R. Tucker and Wallace
E. Lambert: "Sociocultural Aspects of FL
Study." Samuel Lieberman: Greece and
Rome; Gerard J. Brault: France; Marine
Leland: French Canada; Harry F. Young:
Germany; Joseph Tursi: Italy; Walter F.
Odronic: Japan; Irina Kirk: The Soviet Un-
ion; John W. Kronik: Spain; Frank N.
Dauster: Spanish America. 1972.

**Proficiency, Curriculum, Evaluation:
The Ties that Bind.** Alice C. Omaggio, ed.
Frank W. Medley, Jr.: "Designing the Pro-
ficiency-Based Curriculum." Jeannette D.
Bragger: "The Development of Oral Profi-
ciency." Heidi Byrnes: "Teaching toward
Proficiency: The Receptive Skills." Sally
Sieloff Magnan: "Teaching and Testing
Proficiency in Writing: Skills to Transcend
the Second-Language Classroom." Wendy
W. Allen: "Toward Cultural Proficiency." J.
David Edwards and Melinda E. Hanisch:
"A Continuing Chronicle of Professional,
Policy, and Public Activities in Foreign Lan-
guages and International Studies." 1985.

**Reflecting on Proficiency from a Class-
room Perspective.** June K. Phillips, ed.:
"Proficiency-OrientedLanguage Learning:
Origins, Perspectives, and Prospects."
Alice Omaggio Hadley. "Proficiency as a
Change Element in Curriula for World Lan-
guages in Elementary and Secondary
Schools." Robert LaBouve. "Using For-

eign Languages to Learn: Rethinking the College Foreign Language Curriculum. Janet Swaffar. "Proficiency as an Inclusive Orientation: Meeting the Challenge of Diversity." Marie Sheppard. "Perspective on Proficiency: Teachers, Students, and the Materials that They Use." Diane W. Birckbichler and Kathryn A. Corl. "On Becoming a Teacher: Teacher Education for the 21st Century." Anne Nerenz. "Forty Years of the Northeast Conference: A Personal Perspective." Stephen L. Levy.

**Sensitivity in the Foreign-Language Classroom.** James W. Dodge, ed.: "Interaction in the Foreign-Language Class." Hernan LaFontaine: "Teaching Spanish to the Native Spanish Speaker." Ronald L. Gougher: "Individualization of Instruction." 1973.

**Shaping the Future Challenges and Opportunities.** Helen S. Lepke, ed. June K. Phillips: "Teacher Education: Target of Reform." Carol Ann Pesola and Helena Anderson Curtain: "Elementary School Foreign Languages: Obstacles and Opportunities." Helen P. Warriner-Burke: "The Secondary Program, 9-12." Dorothy James: "Re-shaping the 'College-Level' Curriculum: Problems and Possibilities." Galal Walker: "The Less Commonly Taught Languages in the Context of American Pedagogy." Emily L. Spinelli: "Beyond the Traditional Classroom." 1989.

**Shifting the Instructional Focus to the Learner.** Sally Sieloff Magnan, ed. Elaine K. Horwitz: "Attending to the Affective Domain in the Foreign Language Classroom." Rebecca L. Oxford: "Language Learning Strategies and Beyond: A Look at Strategies in the Context of Styles." Nancy Rhodes, Helena Curtain, and Mari Haas: "Child Development and Academic Skills in the Elementary School Foreign Language Classroom." Anne G. Nerenz: "The Exploratory Years: Foreign Languages in the Middle-Level Curriculum." Thomas Cooper, Theodore B. Kalivoda, and Genelle

Morain: "Learning Foreign Language in High School and College: Should It Really Be Different?" Katherine M. Kulick: "Foreign Language Proficiency and the Adult Learner." 1990.

**Sight and Sound: The Sensible and Sensitive Use of Audio-Visual Aids.** Mills F. Edgerton, Jr., ed.: "Non-Projected Visuals." Jermaine Arendt: "Sound Recordings." Hilary Hayden: "Slides and Filmstrips." James J. Wrenn: "The Overhead Projector." Allen W. Grundstrom: "Motion Pictures." Joseph H. Sheehan: "Television." 1969.

**Teaching, Testing, and Assessment: Making the Connection.** Charles Hancock, ed.: Rebecca M. Valette: "Teaching, Testing, and Assessment: Conceptualizing the Relationship." Charles W. Stansfield: "Developments in Foreign Language Testing and Instruction: A National Perspective." Grant Wiggins: "Toward More Authentic Assessment of Language Performances." Peggy Boyles: "Assessing the Speaking Skill in the Classroom: New Solutions to an Ongoing Problem." Donna Reseigh Long and Janice Lynn Macián: "Listening Skills: Acquisition and Assessment." James J. Davis: "Authentic Assessment: Reading and Writing." Zena T. Moore: "The Portfolio and Testing Culture." Pat Barr-Harrison and Elaine K. Horwitz: "Affective Considerations in Developing Language Tests for Secondary Students." Leslie L. Shrier and JoAnn Hammadou: "Assessment in Foreign Language Teacher Education." 1994.

**Toward A New Integration of Language and Culture.** Alan J. Singerman, ed. Peter Patrikis: "Language and Culture at the Crossroads." Angela Moorjani and Thomas T. Field: "Semiotic and Sociolinguistic Paths to Understanding Culture." Robert C. Lafayette: "Integrating the Teaching of Culture into the Foreign Language Classroom." Claire J. Kramsch: "The Cultural Discourse of Foreign Language Textbooks." Jean-Pierre Berwald: "Mass Media and Authentic Documents: Language in Cultural Context." Seiichi Makino: "Integrating Language and Culture Through Video: A Case Study from the Teaching of Japanese." Aleidine J. Moeller: "Linguistic and Cultural Immersion: Study Abroad for the Younger Student." Norman Stokle: "Linguistic and Cultural Immersion: Study Abroad for the College Student." Barbara Lotito and Mireya Pérez-Erdélyi: "Learning Culture through Local Resources: A Hispanic Model." 1988.

**Toward Student-Centered Foreign-Language Programs.** Warren C. Born, ed.: "Training for Student-Centered Language Programs." Anthony Papalia: "Implementing Student-Centered Foreign-Language Programs." Rene L. Lavergneau: "Careers, Community, and Public Awareness." 1974.

Copies of the Reports issued since 1992 may be ordered from National Textbook Co. Reports issued 1954–91 may be obtained from Northeast Conference, 29 Ethan Allen Drive, Colchester, VT 05446. Please write for ordering information.